Curriculum Research in the Context of Curriculum Reform

Lyu Lijie

Translated by Lang Xiaojuan

Revised by Gao Wen and Chen Juan

CHICAGO ACADEMIC PRESS

Curriculum Research in the Context of Curriculum Reform
Edited by Lyu Lijie
Translated by Lang Xiaojuan
Revised by Gao Wen and Chen Juan
Language: English
Word Count (for space of all pages): 294 thousand words
Publisher: Chicago Academic Press
Number of Pages: 356
ISBN: 979-8-901-86003-8

Publishing	Chicago Academic Press
	5923 N Artesian Ave
	Chicago IL 60659
Email	contact@chicagoacademicpress.com
Website	http://chicagoacademicpree.com/
Book Size	6X9 inches
First Edition	December, 2025

Contents

Part 1 Course Design and Decision-Making in Educational Policy

Chapter 1 The Process and Key Elements of National Curriculum Policy Formulation

National curriculum design can be studied from various perspectives. It can be viewed as the initial stage of curriculum development, as a large-scale research process, or as a national public-policy-making endeavor. Since the 1980s, countries such as the United States and the United Kingdom, which previously adopted decentralized curriculum management systems, have shifted towards implementing nationwide, unified curriculum plans and standards. These reforms were designed to guide, regulate and enhance the efficiency and quality of education. In contrast, countries with more centralized curriculum policies, such as China, France, and Russia, have adjusted the roles of national curriculum policies, narrowing their scope to macro-level curriculum planning, value definition, and the selection of disciplinary core content. Evidently, contemporary countries have all gained a renewed understanding and positioning of national curricula. It is precisely because this positioning exhibits global convergence that various countries have adopted reforms in different directions for their national curriculum policies in response to their respective historical contexts. As a specific form of modern public policy, the development of national curriculum policies shares both common and distinctive processes and characteristics with other public policies.

1. Politics, Educational Policy, and Curriculum Policy

What is policy? An American scholar, David Easton (1953), put forward a well-known definition: "Policy is the authoritative allocation of values for a society." This definition suggests that policy is a government-driven process aimed at addressing public issues by reallocating social values in ways that promotes the coordination of interests and support social development. In modern society, policy extends beyond economic concerns to encompass issues of rights, obligations, responsibilities, respect, and order in public affairs. Thus, discussions of policy often focus on public policies, which govern the distribution of these values across society. In effect, the effectiveness of public policy lies in its ability to allocate values in a way that balances the needs of various groups. Inevitably, such a distribution meets the needs of some people while harming the interests of others. Therefore, as an authoritative allocation of public policy, the rationality it pursues lies in achieving a balance among different interest groups that is most conducive to social stability and development, and solving social problems caused by the imbalance of interests and values.

In the 1950s, when policy science was in its infancy, the American founding father Lasswell defined policy science as explaining the processes of policy formulation and policy implementation, focusing on collecting data and providing explanations for policy issues in specific periods. Based on quantitative research, it integrates methods such as operations research, systems analysis, linear programming, and cost-benefit analysis, regarding policy formulation as a rational process and exploring the optimal decision-making model within it. In the 1960s, a paradigm revolution occurred in sociological methodology, and people's skepticism about absolute rationality was also reflected in the interpretation of the policy-making process. Herbert Simon, a key figure of this period, argued that absolute rationality in decision-making is unattainable in practice. He highlighted the challenges of decision-making, including differing values among organizations and their members, limited information available to decision-makers, and the bounded nature of rationality in real-world decisions. Simon's work shifted the focus to the decision-making process itself, rather than just the rationality of the outcomes, just as he put it, "Previous decision theories focused on the rationality of decision outcomes but seldom considered the process itself. In fact, decision-making is not just a final event, but an ongoing process" [1].This process may not always be perfectly organized or logical, but it ultimately shapes the policy outcome. In David Easton's work, this decision-making process is metaphorically referred to as a "black box" — an elusive, hard-to-observe mechanism. In modern policy research, understanding this invisible process is crucial to studying how policies are formed.

British scholar Michael Hill argued that, "The study of the policy process should focus on case studies, using qualitative methods, while quantitative methods are mostly employed to analyze the outcomes of policies." [2]Hill viewed the policy formation process as inherently political, where some political actors hold more legitimate decision-making power than others. This creates a potential conflict between the ideal decision-making methods and the political entities with the authority to implement them. Thus, key questions arise: Who decides the policy? How is it decided? Research into the policy-making process aims to analyze the roles and relationships of the actors involved. This includes examining the policy agenda, bargaining processes, administrative dynamics, and the influence of institutions and culture on decisions. By understanding these elements, we can better assess the legitimacy of policies and how they come to be.

Educational policy, like other forms of public policy, aims to address public issues, but its scope is particularly broad. The primary authorities behind educational policy include national political parties and governments, which set the overall direction for educational development. When the reality of education diverges from the intentions of those in power, problems arise in public education. These problems often lead to the creation of new educational policies. Each new policy seeks to adjust and guide educational

---

① Piao Zhenzi, and Jin Jionglie. Theory of Policy Formation. Shandong People's Publishing House, 2005.
② Hill, Michael. The Policy Process in Modern States. Translated by Zhao Chenggen, China Youth Publishing House, 2004.

development goals, quality standards, and public educational values, which, in turn, often lead to changes in educational practices. This can result in the creation of new educational norms, standards, and behaviors. Some scholars in China argue that educational policy can be understood from four key perspectives: its phenomenological form, ontological form, process characteristics, and its unique nature. The phenomenological form refers to the entire body of policy documents that include political measures within the education sector, implicitly conveying the policy's goals and content. These documents can be interpreted in various ways, depending on the background of the readers.The ontological form concerns the distribution of educational interests. Policies redistribute educational resources among different interest groups, reflecting the state's control over the direction and significance of educational development. The process characteristics describe the dynamic, ongoing process of active choice. From a policy outcome perspective, educational policy is the result of government decisions. However, from a policy-making process perspective, it involves a complex interaction between individual and collective choices. The unique nature of educational policy lies in its public welfare orientation and non-commercial character. Unlike commodities, the services provided by educational policies are not intended for profit. Effective educational policies must be grounded in a respect for the inherent principles of education itself.

Curriculum policy is a specific component of educational policy. While it shares the broader power and significance of general education policy, it also includes specialized content, structure, and operational mechanisms. The purpose of curriculum policy is to address discrepancies between educational goals, content, and methods used in schools. When national authorities manage the formulation of curriculum policy, such policies fall under the broader category of public policy. National curriculum policy can take various forms and levels, including: Macro-level curriculum policy, which establishes the values and norms guiding national curriculum development. It outlines the goals and objectives specified by the state, defining the types of talents that the curriculum is supposed to produce, and the values and institutional requirements necessary to develop the talents. Specific curriculum policies, which are more concrete and detailed. These policies focus on the functional significance of each subject, the selection of knowledge content, and methods of implementation. Complementary curriculum policies, which consist of a series of administrative measures designed to ensure the effective implementation of both macro-level and specific curriculum policies. Together, these three categories form the framework of curriculum policy. Generally speaking, static curriculum policies typically include documents such as curriculum plans, curriculum standards, syllabi, textbooks, and other related administrative or explanatory materials.

2. The Process of Formulating Curriculum Policy

There are two primary interpretations of policy formulation. One view sees policy formulation as encompassing the entire policy process, including execution, evaluation, and revision, treating policy formulation as a dynamic, ongoing process. The other view considers policy formulation to be a distinct stage in the creation and planning of policy, separate from execution, feedback, and improvement. In this context, we integrate both perspectives, treating curriculum policy formulation as a continuous and adaptive process. The formation and planning of curriculum policy represent one stage within this broader process, though it remains relatively independent and consists of a distinct set of steps in the creation of curriculum policy. In policy research, the policy formulation process is typically divided into three stages: setting the policy agenda, planning the proposal, and legitimizing the proposal. [①]

Stage One Setting the Curriculum Policy Agenda.

This stage involves investigating and researching curriculum-related issues to ensure that the curriculum policy addresses real and pressing concerns. Society faces numerous challenges that require government intervention, but only a select few of these issues receive attention and become part of the political agenda and decision-making process. The prioritization of these issues is, in fact, the process of establishing the policy agenda—deciding which problems are most critical to address. When curriculum issues are included in the policy agenda, it signifies a significant misalignment between the current state of the curriculum, the evolving needs of society, and the expectations of political leaders. Political leaders, drawing on their knowledge, authority, expertise, and practical experience, identify and predict key curriculum policy issues, elevating them to the political agenda. Alternatively, education researchers or field-specific experts may identify critical issues and help bring them to the attention of policymakers, through their research and social influence, either directly or through the social media. Regardless of the source, once curriculum issues are brought onto the agenda, they must be validated through empirical research to confirm their legitimacy as problems that deserve attention.

Stage Two Curriculum Scheme Planning and Development. Curriculum scheme planning refers to the process of developing solutions or proposals based on the analysis of curriculum policy issues. This stage is defined by a specific time period during which various tasks are combined and organized. The process can be broken down into distinct phases. The first step is to

---

① Cai Qingtian. Curriculum Policy Decision: Educational Decision-making. Taipei: Wunan Publishing, 2003.

identify the core problems that the curriculum policy aims to address. This involves highlighting the gap between the current and desired states of the curriculum, as well as establishing clear educational goals for the policy. Next, relevant data and information are collected. This phase draws on existing research to inform the development of policy content. Following this, the potential environment for implementing the plan is assessed, and possible outcomes are projected. Finally, among the various proposed plans, the most reasonable and effective solution is selected.

Stage Three: The Legitimization of Curriculum Policy

The legitimization of curriculum policy refers to the process through which a policy gains legal validity. This involves a series of steps, including consultations, discussions, reviews, approvals, signings, and promulgation, all conducted in accordance with established legal procedures and authority. The sources of curriculum policy legitimization are varied. Expert Endorsement: Curriculum policy may be legitimized through discussions that secure the endorsement of education experts, scientists, and sociologists. Stakeholder Consultation: It may also involve consultations with relevant stakeholders. This allows for evaluation and feedback, fostering communication and understanding among those who will be responsible for implementing the curriculum. Approval by Authoritative Institutions: Most importantly, curriculum policy is legitimized when it is approved by relevant authoritative institutions. This approval grants the policy its legal and binding status. This stage is essential for the policy to be enacted and serves as the foundation for completing the policy's legitimization process.

3. The Nature of the Curriculum Policy Formulation Process

House, Corbett, and others argue that curriculum decisions can be examined through three distinct lenses: the technical approach, the political approach, and the cultural approach[①]. The technical approach to curriculum policy reform treats it as a process that can be replicated and transferred. In this approach, specialists in curriculum policy use their expertise, methods, and materials to drive change. The political approach focuses on the various conflicting interests involved in curriculum reform, such as those of governments, teachers, education administrators, and parents. Political decision-makers aim to balance these opposing interests, seeking compromises and fostering mutual acceptance. The cultural approach to curriculum policy highlights the role of differing cultural backgrounds and values among participants in the curriculum reform process. Together, these approaches underscore the complexity of curriculum policy formulation, indicating that it is not simply a technical or technological process, but one deeply intertwined with politics and social culture.

3.1 Curriculum Policy Formulation as a Political Process

Curriculum policies, especially national curriculum policies, are part of public policy and are consequently influenced by political ideologies. This ideological influence stems from the fundamental function that curriculum development serves as a clear example of the intersection of policy and politics. Prior to the 1980s, the UK lacked a unified national curriculum. However, after the 1980s, substantial changes were made to the country's educational guidelines, with explicit political aims and national policy goals in mind. Following World War II, the UK experienced sluggish economic growth, a phenomenon that became known as the "British disease." Contributing factors included an outdated industrial structure, a bloated public sector, and heavy welfare costs. A major issue was the slow rate of increase in labor productivity, which politicians often blamed on the poor quality of education. Former Education Minister Baker once remarked that

① Chen Zhenming. Policy Science. Beijing: Renmin University Press, 1998.

the UK's education system was a "freak" in comparison to those in France and Germany, as it lacked centralization. He argued that curriculum standards in the UK were too low, particularly in terms of consistency for students aged 14 to 16. In 1979, the Thatcher government began implementing a series of economic reforms, abandoning post-war Keynesianism (which had advocated for increased government spending and consumer demand to stimulate economic growth). Instead, Thatcherism prioritized free markets and centralized state authority, seeking to create a society dominated by market forces while simultaneously ensuring greater state intervention. In education, this market-driven approach encouraged school autonomy, viewing parents as consumers of education and responding to their demand for educational choice. The introduction of a unified curriculum and standardized testing not only provided parents with tools to evaluate schools but also made transferring between schools easier. After 1997, influenced by Giddens, the Blair government embraced a "Third Way" that sought a balance between laissez-faire capitalism and the welfare state. While the government began emphasizing equal educational opportunities for all students and schools, it continued to align with the conservative goal of improving educational quality and diversity. As a result, issues such as national curriculum standards and national testing remained central to education policy. Education reform, alongside the restoration of the UK's international standing, became a shared goal for both politicians and the public.

3.2 Balancing Democracy and Authority

Every public policy, whether overtly or implicitly, carries inherent authority, as it is governed by the state's authoritative institutions. Public policy is legitimate and requires enforcement. At the same time, since policy represents the public legitimization of individual interests and values, democracy plays a crucial role in modern policy-making. According to

Lasswell, "Policy science is the study of democracy; it involves individual choices and must be grounded in a democratic system."① Without democracy, a policy cannot be considered public policy; it becomes an "edict," legitimized through the unconditional reverence for human representatives of divine authority. Modern society, however, strives to create an orderly existence free from divine-like authority. The foundation of order lies in rules that reflect the collective will of various interest groups, which are agreed upon and followed voluntarily. In curriculum policy, the goal is to establish common rules for the selection and application of knowledge, hoping that these rules will form the basis of an ordered system. Allowing stakeholders in knowledge—whether holders or users—to express their views during the policy-making process is crucial for ensuring the legitimacy and enforceability of the curriculum policy. As a result, various value-related stakeholders express their opinions in different ways and from different perspectives. The rationality and legitimacy of the policy-making process depend on creating mechanisms that allow for the expression of diverse interests. Curriculum policy is formulated through democratic consultations among different stakeholders, aiming to reduce the authoritarian nature of the policy while granting greater decision-making autonomy to professional bodies. However, while the government asserts its authority in this process, it remains in tension with anti-authoritarian forces. The formulation of curriculum policy attempts to strike a balance between these competing elements.

3.3 The Need for a Procedural Decision-Making Mechanism in Curriculum Policy Formulation

Public policy represents a set of binding rules, and once implemented, it allocates benefits among its recipients. As such, the fairness and rationality

① Chen Zhenming, *Policy Science* [M]. Beijing: Renmin University of China Press, 1998: 5.

of the policy require that the policy-making process itself be legitimate. Modern policy theory emphasizes that the process of policy formulation must be a normative act, following a strict and standardized procedural system. Curriculum policy, at its core, is the authoritative arrangement of educational values. It requires the development of legal and actionable frameworks. Thus, the formulation of curriculum policy must adhere to scientifically and normatively defined decision-making processes. Information collection, data analysis, and adherence to standardized procedures are essential to ensure fairness and rationality in the policy formulation process.

3.4 Curriculum Policy Formulation as a "Limited Rationality" Process of "Value Authority Configuration"

While the process of formulating curriculum policy requires rationality, the outcomes cannot be entirely rational. Policy-makers represent diverse political, professional, and societal values, each influencing the process through different channels. As a result, policy cannot be divorced from the interests, conflicts, autocracy, or justice inherent in it. The value subjects involved in curriculum policy formulation differ from those in other public policies in that they include a significant number of professionals whose values often align with spiritual, ideological, and professional interests. This complexity makes it harder to definitively judge the reasonableness of competing value demands. Even when presented with the same information, policy-making often leads to different interpretations. Policies are products of negotiation and compromise among various interest groups at different stages. The policy-making process is characterized by contingency, flexibility, and bargaining, especially within the government[①]. Consequently, the final curriculum policy may appear unclear, reflecting the compromises and reconciliations of conflicting interests. The goal is to ensure that all

① Stephen J. Ball, *Education Reform: A Critical and Post-structuralist Perspective* [M]. Translated by Hou Dingkai, Shanghai: East China Normal University Press, 2002: 31.

stakeholders can accept, or at least tolerate, the final policy and its associated costs.

3.5 Curriculum Policy Formulation as a Closed, Professional Theoretical Process

Curriculum policy stands out from other public and educational policies due to its distinct professional nature. Not only must it align with national ideology and educational principles, but it also needs to integrate the logical relationships within various subject areas, the developmental characteristics of children, and the changing social and cultural needs. The goal is to translate this broad understanding of subjects, child development, societal life, and national growth into enforceable, authoritative guidelines that can be implemented within the educational system. As such, the process of creating curriculum policy requires years of in-depth, multidimensional theoretical development, making it highly specialized. Unlike other public or educational policies, curriculum policy cannot afford widespread public involvement or mass participation in the planning process. Due to the technical nature of the issues involved, curriculum decision-making "is largely controlled by experts, with little interference from outsiders." Therefore, the formulation of curriculum policy is a highly specialized, closed, and professional process. ①

3.6 Curriculum Policy Formulation as a Text, System, and Ongoing Process

During implementation, policies inevitably encounter "other realities"—such as classroom disruptions, inadequate teaching materials, or multilingual classrooms. Some policies may slightly alter the work environment, but they cannot change all of its aspects. For this reason,

① Brian Holmes, and Martin Mclean. The Curriculum: A Comparative Perspective. Translated by Zhang Wenjun, Beijing: Education Science Publishing House, 2001.

without a strong supporting framework, even the best curriculum policies are merely a stroke of luck.[1]

Curriculum policies must be accompanied by supporting measures, including funding systems, evaluation frameworks, teacher training programs, and management strategies. Curriculum policy is also a part of a broader educational policy system and contributes to the structure of public policy, rather than being an isolated component. It must coordinate with other policies within the broader system, requiring attention to goal alignment, functional compatibility, and timing considerations. Thus, the formulation of curriculum policy is not limited to the publication of policy documents; the true conclusion of curriculum policy formulation occurs when curriculum issues are fully resolved, with no further contradictions between needs and reality. Consequently, after a policy is implemented, it is essential to collect feedback, make adjustments, and update the policy. These are key components of the ongoing curriculum policy formulation process.

[Original text from *The Process of National Curriculum Design: A Case Study on Now Curriculum Design of Chinese Basic Education*, 2008 (by Lyu Lijie)]

① Stephen J. Ball. Educational Reform: A Critical and Post-Structural Approach. Translated by Hou Dingkai, Shanghai: East China Normal University Press, 2002.

Chapter 2 The Processes and Characteristics of Large-scale Curriculum Design

— A Comparative Analysis of Chinese and Western Models

I

The reform of basic education in China, which began in 1996, spanned five years and concluded in 2001 with the publication of the *Outline for Basic Education Curriculum Reform (Trial)* and curriculum standards for various subjects in compulsory education. This five-year period marked a significant milestone in the evolution of curriculum research and design in China.

In 1996, the State Education Commission's Department of Basic Education signed a cooperation agreement with UNICEF to study the development of compulsory education in developing countries. With funding from this international project, the Department conducted a large-scale survey on the implementation of the "Nine-Year Compulsory Education Curriculum Plan." In July 1996, a team of experts and scholars from six national normal universities and the Central Institute of Educational Sciences was organized by the Department to conduct a nationwide investigation into the status of curriculum implementation in compulsory education. This survey, launched in May 1997, involved students, teachers, principals, parents, and other stakeholders, primarily members of the National Committee of the Chinese People's Political Consultative Conference, across nine provinces and cities. Samples were drawn from 72 regions at the prefecture level. The survey questions focused on various aspects, including the implementation of curriculum goals, the current educational process, the state and impact of exams, and students' academic burdens and school experiences. Feedback from principals, teachers, students, and parents provided valuable insights into these issues. After completing the survey, the project team analyzed the results and drafted a report, which outlined the initial direction for China's upcoming curriculum reform. Based on this report, in 1998, the relevant authorities began drafting the guiding documents for the new round of curriculum reform. Following nearly two years of revisions, the *Outline for Basic Education Curriculum Reform (Trial)* was finalized, serving as the guiding principle and foundation for the new curriculum design.

In 1999, the Ministry of Education officially prioritized the curriculum reform as part of the national educational reform agenda. This year also marked the beginning of preparations for the detailed implementation of the new curriculum. A critical aspect of this phase was the "anonymous project bidding," aimed at selecting research teams and experts to develop curriculum standards for various subjects. To ensure fairness, the project applications were anonymized, allowing reviewers to assess only the project justifications without knowledge of the applicants' identities. Following this evaluation process, 18 curriculum standard development groups, comprising hundreds of experts, were established in May and June 2000.

In October 1999, based on the preliminary studies, the drafting of the curriculum standards entered its next phase. This phase involved "preliminary research," which formed the foundation of the development process. "Preliminary research" referred to the five special studies that each curriculum standard project team had to carry out. Taking the preliminary research of the mathematics curriculum team as an example, it included the following five topics: A. An analysis of international trends in the latest mathematics curriculum reform, B. An assessment of the current state of mathematics curriculum implementation in China, C. A study of the psychological development of primary and secondary school students and its relation to the mathematics curriculum, D. A forecast of societal needs for mathematics, and E. An examination of the development of modern mathematics and its impact on primary and secondary school curricula.

Based on the findings from these preliminary studies, the curriculum standards for each subject were subsequently drafted.

Each curriculum standard group and project team included members from across the country. As a result, the development teams convened once a month for about a week. During each week-long session, more than 200 experts from the teams involved in developing the new curriculum would first receive unified directives and feedback from the Ministry of Education regarding the drafting process. Most of the time was dedicated to internal communication and discussion within the project teams, while also providing progress reports to the Ministry of Education. The development teams were composed of members with diverse professional backgrounds. Curriculum design personnel from universities were divided into subject experts and curriculum experts. Curriculum experts typically came from normal universities and educational research institutes, with backgrounds in education, psychology, or curriculum theory. Subject experts generally came from normal or general universities as academic researchers. The team also included experienced teachers, teaching researchers, and prominent educators, some of whom were nationally recognized master teachers. Additionally, researchers from publishing houses participated due to their familiarity with both past and current curriculum and textbook materials in China. Consequently, many curriculums standard groups included members from publishing houses.

Once the drafts of the curriculum standards for each subject were developed, a large-scale public consultation was conducted, engaging three primary groups of participants. The first group included educational professionals and individuals from various sectors of society, such as senior executives from 67 major state-owned enterprises, Sino-foreign joint ventures, foreign-owned enterprises, and private tech companies. This group featured individuals in roles like chairpersons, general managers, chief engineers, and chief economists. The second group comprised front-line teachers. For example, after the draft of the mathematics curriculum was finalized, feedback was sought from several provinces and cities, with 138 front-line teachers contributing to the discussions. The third group included academicians from the Chinese Academy of Sciences and the Chinese Academy of Engineering, as well as historians, artists, and education experts, who provided input on the curriculum standards for each subject. The experimental drafts of the full-time compulsory education curriculum standards and the general senior high school curriculum standards were officially published in 2001 and 2003, respectively.

The primary goal of the new curriculum design was to establish an ideal curriculum system that would influence and guide the development of China's basic education and the broader educational landscape. The curriculum design process involved a careful selection, arrangement, and optimization of relevant elements, all aimed at achieving the established ideal. These elements included object-related factors such as curriculum philosophy, objectives, content, implementation methods, evaluation methods, curriculum resources, and textbooks; instrumental factors like designers, time, space, and funding; and procedural factors such as text creation, curriculum promotion and implementation, public outreach, text revision, and teacher training.

Throughout the design process, coordinating these elements was an ongoing task, all directed toward realizing the intended ideal. As such, the design process was action-oriented, focused on achieving specific goals. However, it was also generative, not mechanical or dehumanized, filled with uncertainties. Changes in personnel, conflicting viewpoints, and fluctuations in time and budget often arose, requiring continuous adjustments to the "engineering" design components. This process was illustrated in the creation of a research process diagram.

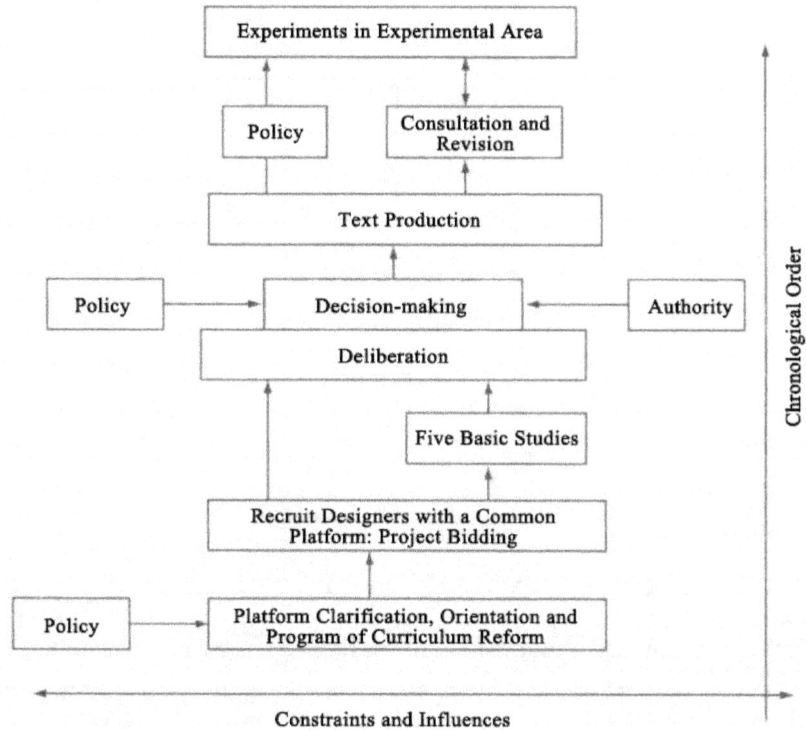

Figure 1-1 Diagram of the New Curriculum Design Process

II

In the 1960s and 1970s, American curriculum scholar Decker F. Walker gained valuable insights into the nature of curriculum design by tracking and documenting large-scale curriculum development processes.

In the late 1960s, Walker took part in the supervision and evaluation of the Kettering Art Project. Over the course of three years, he meticulously recorded the actions, debates, and decisions made by the curriculum design team. By analyzing meeting transcripts and collecting various materials, Walker was able to identify key elements of the curriculum design process. When comparing major national curriculum design projects in the U.S. during the 1960s and 1970s, he outlined a natural progression for the curriculum design process:

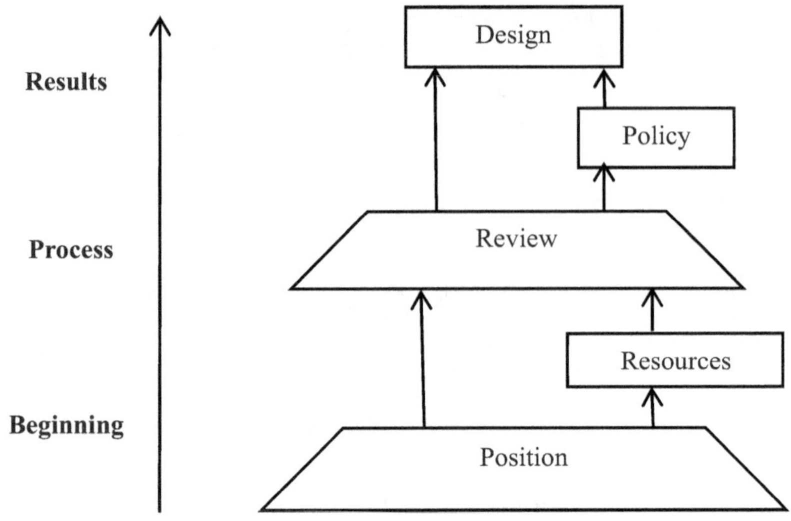

Figure 1-2: Walker's Curriculum Design Model

Walker provided explanations for several key concepts, including the term "position," which refers to beliefs, theories, objectives, and intended processes. He argued that every member of the design team approached the curriculum development process with certain beliefs and values. As a result, the first essential step is to involve all members, encouraging them to express, discuss, and even debate the fundamental goals of the program. Walker's use of "position" serves as a foundation for further discussion. The team would then engage in debates over key issues, presenting various possible solutions and carefully weighing the advantages and disadvantages of each. This process of making a selection is referred to as "deliberation." While this stage can be chaotic and time-consuming, its value becomes evident if it leads to the clarification of issues. Deliberation is not spontaneous; it is rooted in shared beliefs, theories, goals, and procedures. When decisions cannot be made based solely on these positions, empirical "data" is used to justify one's views. The term "design" refers to the decision-making process that guides the final actions after deliberation.

III

A comparison of Walker's curriculum design model with the process of new curriculum development in China reveals several parallels in both elements and stages:

1. Shared Vision and Philosophy. Curriculum designers must share a fundamental vision and philosophy, which refers to a common philosophy of curriculum and an orientation toward reform. In the case of the new curriculum in China, this shared "position" is established through the promotion of guiding principles for curriculum reform and the project bidding process. Before developing curriculum standards, designers must already hold a particular philosophical view of the curriculum, and their progressive perspectives drive the reform. As a controlled social activity, curriculum reform is naturally shaped by the philosophy of its initiators and organizers. Curriculum design, which involves the selection of learning content, is also about guiding societal values. Therefore, all participants in the reform process should either hold or at least understand this shared position. The establishment of this guiding orientation is not only a response to the goals of the reform but also an essential prerequisite for the curriculum design process. It represents both a temporal and a logical starting point.

2. Empirical Research Accumulation. There must be an accumulation of empirical research. Each research group involved in the new curriculum must have a background in empirical research. Moreover, the curriculum design process itself includes empirical research, as all curriculum standard designers were required to participate in the "five basic research projects." These studies provide a deep understanding of the curriculum's direction and perspective. More specifically, they intentionally guide designers to reflect on the course of curriculum reform within each subject matter, fostering a shared consensus. Additionally, the empirical findings from these

foundational studies serve as the most reliable basis for designers when disagreements arise. As Walker noted, "When decisions cannot be made based on position alone, empirical 'data' should be used to clarify one's viewpoint." In this context, "position" and "concept" represent theoretical understanding and judgment, while curriculum design involves making decisions on the scale and depth of real curriculum contexts. Empirical research, therefore, offers valuable insight by analyzing the structure and characteristics of the subject matter, providing the foundation for value-based judgments in specific curriculum decisions.

In fact, the diagram below reflects the overall thinking process rather than a strict, step-by-step logical sequence. The five research projects, as an interconnected and holistic foundation of information, are embedded in the designers' knowledge backgrounds. When expressing their disciplinary positions, designers may do so either implicitly or explicitly.

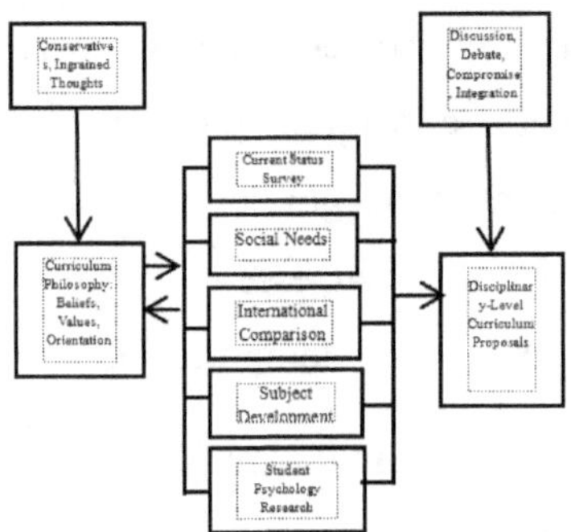

Figure 1-3: Five Fundamental Research Areas in the Development of the New Curriculum

3. The Deliberative Discussion Method. Curriculum design requires a multidimensional approach, considering issues such as the knowledge system, societal needs, student characteristics, and the varying curriculum conditions across different regions. Curriculum designers are confronted with a heterogeneous and complex object. In attempting to understand such an

object, each perspective and viewpoint is inherently relative and limited, though each viewpoint holds its own distinct validity. The concepts of limitation and validity are mutually interdependent and exist dialectically within human cognitive capabilities. That is, during communication and discourse, each participant not only contributes their own direction and uniqueness of understanding but also imparts their biases and limitations to the subject under study. Therefore, it is crucial for designers to engage in dialogue grounded in diversity, to listen with tolerance to differing viewpoints, and to not only accept but also actively welcome heterogeneous perspectives and evaluation criteria. Furthermore, maintaining a positive, complementary, and dialogical relationship between these differing viewpoints is essential.

4. Influence of External Factors on Decisions. The outcomes of curriculum decisions must be shaped by factors such as "policy" and others. Curriculum decisions, particularly in large-scale design projects, are influenced by multiple factors. The differences of opinion arising from deliberation are ultimately influenced by the decisions of policymakers. Walker also noted, "When a deliberation group lacks the power to make and implement decisions, the perspectives gained through deliberation can only influence curriculum implementers to a certain degree. However, if deliberation disregards the preferences of decision-makers, it also results in a waste of time." In the case of China's new curriculum, a large-scale national initiative, the national education authorities serve as the primary organizers of the design process. As a result, the regulation of the curriculum design process is much more pronounced.

There are many factors that influence curriculum design, as Clark summarized in ten key categories: the public, political leaders, textbook publishers, exam intermediaries, the media, university faculty, educational professional organizations, central government departments, teacher associations, and individual teachers. Beyond the personnel factors identified by Clark, other forces such as social ideologies, societal changes (particularly educational reforms), international relations, national politics, and the general level of social and economic development also play a direct or indirect role in shaping curriculum decisions. While some of these forces may not be consciously recognized, the curriculum is undoubtedly a product of the interaction of these various influences. These competing forces often counterbalance one another. As Clark observed, "Each influence must be constrained by others; decision-makers influence each other, and as a result, the final decision deviates from each individual's original intention. Therefore, the curriculum is a political issue, not a technical one."

IV

In his work, Western scholar Marsh analyzed and evaluated the characteristics of large-scale curriculum design, highlighting both its advantages and disadvantages. The advantages include: **Unified System**: Large-scale curriculum design provides a unified system for delivering curriculum standards, which enhances the uniformity of educational requirements, promotes curriculum standards, and improves fairness in resource allocation; **Efficiency**: It saves time by eliminating the need for detailed analysis of each individual school's needs, thereby reducing management costs, energy, and financial expenses; **Continuity**: It ensures continuity, as policies can remain in effect for many years, allowing students and parents to benefit from the same policies even when students transfer schools; **Consolidation of Expertise**: It consolidates professional expertise by leveraging expert teams and effectively allocating funds to produce valuable outcomes; **System Integration**: It fosters a strong connection between schools and the education system, enabling the education department to manage schools and ensure they meet specific goals. Whereas, the disadvantages include: **Limited Teacher Initiative**: It often fails to enhance teachers' initiative, treating them as passive participants with little flexibility or creative input in the curriculum design process; **Lack of Implementation Strategies**: There is a lack of clear implementation strategies, with minimal focus on providing school-level strategies, and staff from the education center are rarely involved in monitoring implementation; **Narrowed Curriculum Goals**: There is a tendency to narrow curriculum goals, assuming that all schools are the same, which can lead to inflexible curriculum standards; **Rational Model Assumptions**: It relies on a rational model that assumes all school personnel will eagerly implement centrally developed policies, without considering potential resistance or challenges.

National curriculum design typically benefits from the resources and funding to organize large-scale professional teams of curriculum designers. Marsh's analysis of the advantages and disadvantages of expert-driven curriculum design is insightful. His observations underscore the importance of enriching the roles and perspectives within the design team and adopting a deliberative process. These challenges highlight the need to improve teachers' initiative, offer school-level implementation strategies, and ensure genuine support from all personnel for the reforms.

[Original Article Published in *New Curriculum Research* (Educational Research and Experiment), 2005, Issue 4 (Lyu Lijie)]

Chapter 3 Promoting 'Human-Centered Research' and Its Implications for High School Curriculum Reform in China

In 2004, China's high school curriculum reform entered the experimental stage, and as of today, 15 provinces and cities have implemented the reform. This reform has received significant attention from national and local governments, schools, teachers, and parents. A major issue that needs to be addressed is how to ensure that the high school curriculum reform progresses effectively, avoiding superficial implementation. This paper compares and analyzes the "Human Studies" curriculum model in the U.S., its promotion in the U.K., and the promotion of China's new high school curriculum, with the goal of drawing lessons and insights to improve the implementation and advancement of the reform in China.

1. The "Human Studies" Curriculum Model

In 1957, following the successful launch of the Soviet satellite, the U.S. shifted its focus to education, attributing its technological lag to deficiencies in its educational system. In 1958, the National Defense Education Act was enacted, emphasizing the importance of school education. It was in this context of striving for excellence that the "Human Studies" curriculum emerged. Developed in the 1960s under the guidance of prominent scholars such as Jerome Bruner and Ballix at the Cambridge Educational Development Center in Massachusetts, "Human Studies" was initially a reform initiative for primary school social studies.

The promotion of "Human Studies" in the U.K. began in 1970, with Steinhoff and Darroch discussing the program with Francis Lincoln, the leader of its U.S. promotion efforts. At that time, "Human Studies" aligned well with the U.K.'s educational values and principles. Steinhoff and others traveled to the U.S. for training, and from 1970 to 1987, they worked to promote the "Human Studies" model in the U.K., making it a significant case study in curriculum implementation. This case offers valuable lessons and insights that can inform China's ongoing reform efforts.

1.1 The Purpose of the "Human Studies" Curriculum

"Human Studies" transformed Jerome Bruner's educational philosophy into a curricular framework. The curriculum emphasized education as a process, using subject structure as a tool to help students explore important issues. It advocated inquiry-based learning, encouraged student discussions, and redefined the teacher's role as a resource facilitator, guiding students through their learning journey.

1.2 The Content of the "Human Studies" Curriculum Reform

The "Human Studies" curriculum posed a challenge to traditional knowledge content, bringing about significant changes in textbooks, subject matter, learning methods, and teaching strategies.

Textbooks and Support Materials: The curriculum introduced new textbooks and a variety of supplementary materials, including film-based units of study. These resources, organized by subject, were based on Bruner's cognitive theory and aimed to enrich the learning experience.

Learning Methods: "Human Studies" focused on the structure and transfer of knowledge, guided by Bruner's cognitive development theory. The curriculum emphasized the learning process, presenting materials in an ordered and sequential manner while highlighting the critical role of prior experience in promoting cognitive development. Learning was seen as an ongoing process rather than a mere outcome, with strong emphasis on making connections between students' prior experiences and new information. It advocated for discovery-based learning, positioning students as active participants.

Teacher Expectations: The curriculum set higher expectations for teachers, requiring them to guide students in posing new questions, provide relevant learning resources, and adapt their teaching strategies to match students' cognitive stages. Teachers were also encouraged to act as researchers in the classroom, reflecting on and refining their teaching practices[①].

2. The Promotion Strategy and Reflection on the "Human Studies" Curriculum

The promotion of the "Human Studies" curriculum in the U.K. was managed by the Educational Application Research Center at the University of East Anglia. Steinhoff and Darroch, who had been involved in promoting the "Humanities Curriculum" drew on their hands-on experience to promote "Human Studies" in the U.K. from 1970 to 1987, establishing a 17-year-long promotional effort.

2.1 Key Concepts in Promoting the "Human Studies" Curriculum

A. Teachers Play a Central Role. Teachers were the driving force behind the promotion of the "Human Studies" curriculum, as they were expected to actively engage with the new ideas and strategies.

B. Inquiry-Based Training. The new curriculum concepts were introduced through inquiry-based training, which was non-didactic. This approach allowed teachers to develop their understanding of the curriculum through hands-on experience and reflection, fostering deeper engagement with the material.

C. Adopting a Critical Stance. Unlike the U.S., where the program was adopted without question, the U.K. treated "Human Studies" as a "hypothesis to be tested." This allowed for adaptation based on the professional culture

---

① Cai Qingtian. Curriculum Innovation[M]. Taipei: Wu Nan Book Company, 2006.

of teachers, ensuring the curriculum was flexible and responsive to local needs.

D. Controlled Distribution of Materials. The curriculum materials were only sold to schools and institutions that participated in the training, ensuring the integrity and consistency of the curriculum's implementation.

2.2 Promotion Strategy of "The Study of Man" — Teacher-Centered, Phased Downward Promotion Strategy

In the U.K., the promotion of "The Study of Man" followed a teacher-centered research and diffusion model, using a phased downward approach. Initially, "seed teachers" were trained to serve as leaders who would help promote the curriculum to other schools, effectively spreading the reform ideas throughout the country[①].

1. The Role of Seed Teachers.

The training process began with the cultivation of seed teachers, who were responsible for helping other teachers understand the principles and strategies of the curriculum reform. These teachers facilitated demonstrations and training sessions, which created an environment for inquiry-based learning. This method allowed participants to form their own understanding of the curriculum, integrating these insights into their teaching practices.

2. Addressing Practical Issues Faced by Teachers.

Throughout the training and promotion process, attention was paid to addressing the practical challenges teachers faced in implementing the new curriculum. This ensured that teachers were not only equipped with theoretical knowledge but also with concrete strategies for overcoming obstacles in real classroom settings. The UK promotion of "The Study of

① Fullan Michael. Change Forces. Translated by Central Institute of Educational Sciences, Beijing: Education Science Publishing House, 2004.

Man" took into account lessons learned from the American implementation, placing greater emphasis on curriculum acceptability among teachers. It also focused on enhancing teachers' professional development. The training program was divided into two main components: the curriculum concept framework and the course resources. Mornings were dedicated to discussing the underlying philosophy and framework of the curriculum, while afternoons focused on examining the course materials, exploring the relationship between the resources, teaching methods, and principles, and discussing their practical application.

3. Ongoing Teacher Training. The teacher training program was primarily delivered through workshops, which included both national and regional sessions. National workshops were held once or twice a year in various locations, aiming to cultivate a culture of research and reflection among teachers. Local workshops were led by teachers from different schools and colleges across the UK, who volunteered their time to discuss teaching improvements and assist new teachers interested in participating in the program.

4. Turning Course Promotion into a Dialogue. Teachers involved in "The Study of Man" in the UK formed a network for professional development, which enabled direct interaction between teachers and course promoters. This created effective communication channels among teachers, promoters, and the program itself. The network structure ensured that the curriculum could be adjusted in response to real-world needs, facilitating more effective and widespread promotion.

2.3 Reflection on the Promotion Strategy of "The Study of Man"

Based on insights gained from promoting the "Humanistic Curriculum Program," the implementation of "The Study of Man" in the UK enhanced interaction between course implementers and promoters. When issues arose, implementers could seek advice from promoters or peers, and teachers had the opportunity to exchange teaching strategies. However, the promotion of this program faced several challenges, including:

1. External Training Fails to Address Specific Classroom Challenges. Although "The Study of Man" employed a range of teacher training strategies, many teachers felt they had not received sufficient practical teaching experience. They were uncertain about how to apply the theoretical concepts from the training sessions to their actual teaching contexts and students. Classroom issues could not be addressed in real time, which underscored the difficulty of resolving such problems solely through external training. As a result, the focus shifted toward enhancing teachers' professional skills, enabling them to reflect independently and take action to drive change.

2. Neglecting Internal Communication Among Teachers Within Schools. The phased downward promotion strategy of "The Study of Man" included both national and local in-service teacher training, contributing to the establishment of a professional development network for continuing education. While this was beneficial for teachers' professional growth, the external networks created for the program's promotion were artificially constructed and lacked long-term stability. In contrast, communication and collaboration among teachers within schools are crucial for shaping teaching behaviors and supporting the long-term implementation of curriculum reforms.

3. Underestimating Cultural Resistance Within School Organizations. If a new curriculum reform is not met with some level of cultural resistance, it suggests that the reform is not truly transformative. This was the case with *"The Study of Man,"* which brought about changes in teaching methods, content knowledge, and teacher roles. These shifts inevitably created conflicts with the traditional school culture. Despite establishing communication channels between promoters and teachers, the promotion strategy did not adequately address the internal support needed within schools. The assumption that changing classroom teaching alone would suffice for the successful implementation of the curriculum overlooked the importance of support from school administrators and the broader organizational structure. This lack of internal coordination led to teachers feeling isolated during the implementation process.

4. Insufficient Ongoing Financial Support. Between 1972 and 1973, only 4 local education authorities, 19 schools, and 50 teachers participated in the promotion of *"The Study of Man."* By 1983, only around 100 schools in the UK had formally adopted the curriculum. Several factors contributed to the program's limited expansion, including political changes and insufficient financial investment. While in-service training and materials were funded by educational authorities, government investment fell short of addressing the ongoing needs of teachers. This lack of financial support made it difficult to sustain the reform over the long term.

3. Promotion Strategies for High School Curriculum Reform in China

China's high school curriculum reform entered its experimental phase in September 2004. To date, 15 provinces and municipalities have implemented the new curriculum, with several provinces making valuable attempts to refine their promotion strategies.

3.1 A Three-Tier Decentralized Curriculum Management System

On one hand, schools and local educational authorities are granted greater autonomy and responsibility for curriculum implementation, which encourages their active participation in the reform and fosters the creation of innovative teaching practices. On the other hand, the establishment of a provincial joint conference system for the experimental high school curriculum enables implementers to collaborate with the Ministry of Education to address challenges encountered during the implementation of the new curriculum. This system fosters a shared commitment to the reform, strengthens local responsibilities, and ensures the Ministry's guiding role is effectively utilized.

3.2 Teacher-Centered, Comprehensive Training

Before the new curriculum is implemented in experimental regions, extensive training sessions are organized for local educational administrators, teaching researchers, and school leaders. The training covers the background of the high school curriculum reform, its guiding principles, and the specifics of the new curriculum, including practical topics such as course scheduling and selection. To minimize discrepancies in training effectiveness across different levels, many provinces gather all relevant high school teachers in provincial capitals for centralized training. Some provinces also adopt a "train-the-trainers" model, where expert teams from universities travel to experimental areas to conduct on-site training. This approach allows curriculum promoters to engage directly with frontline teachers, fostering greater communication between teachers and curriculum designers. As a result, the training becomes more relevant, addressing the real concerns of teachers in the field. Naturally, the process of moving from understanding to internalization takes time, as implementers deepen their understanding through practical experience.

3.3 Focus on Research into Issues Relating to the High School Curriculum

The high school curriculum reform is a complex and multi-faceted project, and various challenges inevitably arise during its implementation. These challenges include how to promote research-based learning, how to implement a credit system, and how to design and manage elective courses.

One of the most pressing issues is the college entrance examination (Gaokao), which profoundly influences school curricula, teaching methods, and even teacher evaluation and personnel management. To address Gaokao-related issues, the Ministry of Education set up a research team focused on Gaokao policies before the new curriculum was implemented. Once the curriculum entered experimental regions, each province established dedicated institutions to research Gaokao-related issues. By consulting widely with local schools, each province developed its own Gaokao policy, ensuring that it was aligned with the new curriculum while also reflecting local conditions.

3.4 Using Modern Information Technology to Promote the New Curriculum

The rapid development of information technology has played a crucial role in promoting the new high school curriculum. Information technology has provided an efficient means of delivering teacher training and disseminating the new curriculum philosophy. For example, online training programs have been created, enabling teachers in different regions and schools to access the same information. Additionally, a specialized website for the new curriculum has been established to promote the new curriculum philosophy and to facilitate communication between administrators, curriculum designers, educators, and implementers.

4. Insights from "Human Studies" for China's High School Curriculum Reform Promotion Strategies

Both "Human Studies" and China's new curriculum reform represent large-scale educational changes. Analyzing the successes and challenges of promoting the *"Human Studies"* curriculum offers valuable insights for improving and refining the strategies for promoting China's high school curriculum reform.

4.1 Increasing Financial Investment in High School Curriculum Reform

In addition to increasing national funding, local governments should actively support national policies and explore multiple avenues for raising funds. Special attention should be given to increasing financial support for the promotion of the new curriculum in urban high schools through preferential policies and targeted funding allocations. Adequate financial resources must also be allocated to teacher training, ensuring the quality and effectiveness of training programs that support the new curriculum. However, simply increasing funding is insufficient; it is equally important to improve financial management practices to ensure that limited resources are used efficiently and effectively. Many experimental regions involved in curriculum reform have accumulated valuable experience in this area. Local governments should organize staff to share, distill, and disseminate this experience, ultimately developing a set of best practices that can be broadly applied.

4.2 School Systems as a Crucial Factor in Curriculum Promotion

The school system plays a vital role in bridging national curriculum policies with changes in classroom teaching, making it a critical factor in the success of curriculum promotion. The promotion of *"Human Studies"* failed to adequately account for the role of school organizations and systems, which led to significant barriers. A genuinely innovative curriculum will inevitably face resistance from entrenched school cultures. In many schools, a conservative and passive acceptance of change reflects the inertia of traditional cultural norms. As Fuller aptly stated, "it is unrealistic to expect success through a series of reforms, or even major initiatives, in an institution with a structure that is hard to change. These efforts can discredit the reform."[①] The promotion of a new curriculum requires the creation of an internal organizational structure within schools that supports the curriculum's success, transforming the school into a learning organization. To achieve this, the first step is to change the attitude of school principals, helping them develop a sense of ownership over the new curriculum and encouraging them to act as advocates and leaders in the reform process. Principals should provide teachers with both material and emotional support, particularly when teachers face challenges, offering affirmation and encouragement during difficult times.

4.3 Continuing Focus on Curriculum Implementers—Teachers

Teachers are the ultimate implementers of the curriculum. Their beliefs, values, and attitudes significantly influence both the curriculum reform process and the transformation of curriculum policies into practical classroom applications[②]. In addition to establishing multi-level and diverse training networks, promoting the high school curriculum in China should also focus on the role of teacher culture in the reform process. Teacher culture refers to the shared values, beliefs, attitudes, habits, assumptions, and behaviors within a specific group of teachers. This culture plays a critical role in shaping teaching behaviors[③]. Classroom teaching is the cornerstone of whether substantial reforms take place, and fostering a collaborative teacher culture is essential for the deeper integration of the new curriculum. Developing such a cooperative culture within traditional teaching environments requires a long-term effort and the active cooperation of school organizations. Teacher development should be supported by mechanisms that

---

① Fullan Michael. Change Forces. Translated by Central Institute of Educational Sciences, Beijing: Education Science Publishing House, 2004.
② Xu Jicun. The Curriculum Policy and Teaching Culture in the UK[J]. Foreign Education Research, 1999(5): 1-5.
③ Andy Hargreaves, Michael, G. Fullan. Understanding teacher development [M]. New York: Teachers College Press,1992.

encourage collaborative research and innovation. School principals' attitudes toward leadership and reform are also crucial to this process.

4.4 Gaining Support from Parents and Society Outside the School

High school education is particularly sensitive to societal issues, and the Gaokao directly affects the interests of many families. For the new high school curriculum to be successfully promoted, it must gain understanding, recognition, and support from society, parents, and other key stakeholders. This requires schools to continuously listen to the opinions of curriculum experts, school leaders, and teachers, while also considering the perspectives of parents and the wider community regarding the curriculum reform. Establishing a democratic mechanism that actively involves parents and community members in the reform process is crucial for the smooth and sustained promotion of the new curriculum.

[Originally published in the *Journal of Hebei Normal University* (Education Science Edition), 2008, Issue 10 (Lyu Lijie and Du Caihong)]

Chapter 4 Curriculum Review in Basic Education Design: A Methodological Approach to Practical Decision-Making

The concept of curriculum deliberation, introduced by Schwab in 1969, has become a widely adopted method for research and decision-making in curriculum design since the 1970s. In the context of China's basic education curriculum reform, the design of the new curriculum represents the largest and most participatory process in the history of national curriculum design. It also marks a significant application of curriculum deliberation as a method of curriculum research. To better understand this process, the author conducted interviews with over 20 individuals directly involved in the formulation of curriculum standards. These individuals included curriculum managers from the Ministry of Education, senior curriculum theorists, subject experts, and other key stakeholders. With the assistance of relevant departments, the study also gathered meeting records from the curriculum standards development process. Drawing from these materials, the author provides a reflection on the practical aspects of this process, with the aim of contributing to ongoing and future curriculum research in China.

1. Curriculum Deliberation in the New Curriculum Design

1.1 Heterogeneity in the Search for Consensus: The Structure of Deliberation Participants

The participants in the new curriculum design process came from a wide range of backgrounds. These included individuals from universities, educational research departments within the basic education system, frontline teachers from primary and secondary schools, and personnel from publishing houses. The university-based curriculum designers were classified into subject experts and curriculum experts. Curriculum experts typically hailed from normal universities or educational research institutes, with backgrounds in pedagogy, psychology, or curriculum theory. Subject experts, on the other hand, were generally academic researchers from normal or regular universities specializing in specific disciplines.

The expert group also included educational researchers and senior teachers, some of whom were nationally recognized model teachers. Personnel from publishing houses were familiar with the history and current state of China's curricula and textbooks, which is why many curriculum design teams included representatives from these institutions. In fact, many of the curriculum designers had multifaceted professional and career backgrounds, making it difficult to strictly classify them into one category. For example, in the development group for the mathematics curriculum standards at the compulsory education stage, there were 31 members from 14 provinces (autonomous regions and municipalities directly under the central government). Of these, 29 identified their specialization as "mathematics education," 1 in "basic mathematics," and 1 in "pedagogy." However, many of those who identified as specializing in "mathematics education" had diverse academic and professional experiences, such as studying mathematics at the undergraduate level and pedagogy or teaching theory at the graduate level, or having worked in both primary and secondary education as well as university research centers. These varied backgrounds facilitated the introduction of multiple perspectives during the curriculum design process.

In addition to the core researchers, other participants in the curriculum deliberation process included scientists, sociologists, members of the National People's Congress (NPC) and the Chinese People's Political Consultative Conference (CPPCC), as well as representatives from media organizations, educational testing agencies, and relevant educational management departments from the Ministry of Education and local governments.

The differing knowledge structures and social statuses of these participants determined the distinct roles they played in the curriculum design process. According to a Chinese curriculum expert, the core members of the curriculum design group typically include curriculum experts, subject experts, and teachers, while school administrators, educational policymakers, media experts, students, parents, and representatives from relevant institutions or industries can be consulted during the deliberation process[①]. This structure largely aligns with the conclusions drawn by the expert regarding the composition of the new curriculum design team.

1.2 Seeking Common Ground Amidst Differences: Negotiation Among Deliberators

The deliberation group was composed of individuals from diverse research fields, professional backgrounds, roles, and regions. The rationale behind this structure is that the integration of these diverse perspectives allows for complementary viewpoints, which is both the significance and the ideal outcome of curriculum deliberation. However, the process of forming these complementary perspectives has been marked by conflicts and communication challenges among the deliberators. Clarifying the issues involved is often a complex and challenging process. As such, disputes, negotiations, compromises, persistence, and even "bargaining" have fostered a distinct deliberative culture.

1. Conflicts and Communication Among Designers.

The underlying philosophy of the new curriculum is to promote "the rejuvenation of the Chinese nation and the development of every student,"

① Huang Zhengjie. Curriculum Design [M]. Taipei: Donghua Book Company, 1991: 97.

with a focus on cultivating students' "innovative spirit, practical abilities, and both scientific and humanistic literacy." Behind these broad ideals, however, each designer's deep and fundamental understanding of the curriculum, their views on the subject, their habitual ways of thinking, academic affiliations, and even emotional attachments to the disciplines they worked on emerged during debates and negotiations. Moreover, conflicts of values and interests between designers from different regions and professions permeated the entire curriculum design process. These confrontations stemmed from a variety of sources, including differences between educational researchers and university faculty, disagreements between researchers with varying professional orientations within the same subject, and tensions between subject experts, curriculum experts, and government officials. For example, consider the interaction between subject experts and curriculum experts. Both groups possess a strong theoretical foundation, meaning they are well-versed in the technical language used for communication and have a certain level of professional confidence. However, the structures of their respective theories differ significantly, which makes the integration of their perspectives a challenging task. In interviews, participants shared their views on each other's roles in curriculum design. One subject expert commented:

"I believe many issues in curriculum theory are overly idealized, and much of what is suggested in theory is impractical when put into actual practice. The ideas proposed by curriculum experts need to be carefully considered by those of us involved in the subject. We cannot blindly follow the approach of curriculum experts because each subject has its own inherent logic and structure."

A curriculum expert responded:

"One Chinese language expert once said, 'If you don't master Chinese, what else can you do?' I find this viewpoint too extreme. According to the curriculum standards for compulsory education, mastering Chinese is

essential, but how many students will ultimately work in the field of Chinese language? We shouldn't always assume that because I am a Chinese expert, Chinese should be the top priority. A geography expert might argue: 'From the moment you're born, you're connected to the Earth, and when you die, you return to it. Your entire life is about interacting with the Earth. Wouldn't you say geography is important?' A foreign language expert might add: 'I don't need to emphasize how important foreign languages are—after all, the national leadership has stressed that foreign languages must be taught from a young age.'"

The first interviewee is a subject expert from the curriculum standards team. He believes the curriculum expert's approach is "idealistic," while subject experts tend to rely on the "logic and regularities of their specific disciplines." However, curriculum experts argue that this reliance on the logic of individual subjects leads to a narrow perspective. The two groups differ significantly in how they arrange, select, and present curriculum content. While curriculum experts may be ahead of subject experts, both in terms of logical structure and even timing, this has created a sense of constraint for subject experts during the design process.

At the heart of the debate between curriculum experts and subject experts is the question of how to view the role of curriculum experts. This disagreement is rooted in differing ideals about what constitutes an ideal curriculum. Since the establishment of curriculum studies in the early 20th century, curriculum experts have played a crucial role in curriculum design, particularly in the context of progressive educational practices. However, after the 1960s, subject experts largely supplanted curriculum experts. Experts from various disciplines became the primary decision-makers and reformers, and neither private foundations nor government bodies regarded curriculum scholars as leaders in curriculum reform[①], leading to the near demise of the curriculum studies field. Nevertheless, the curriculum reforms in the United States during the 1960s were seen as unsatisfactory. Subject experts had sought to approach curriculum design scientifically, but their efforts led to a decline in students' academic performance. In the 1970s, Schwab, a former subject expert, reflecting deeply on the situation, proposed a new curriculum research paradigm centered around deliberation. This restored the prominence of curriculum experts in the design process. Since then, various new theoretical frameworks—such as phenomenology and critical theory—have emerged within the field of curriculum research, leading to a vibrant and diverse discourse. China's curriculum system is distinct from that of the U.S., and its history of curriculum research differs as well. In the context of China's national curriculum design history, this marks the first time a large number of curriculum experts have been involved, or more precisely, the first time a deliberation method has been adopted. Additionally, the collaboration between subject and curriculum experts is unprecedented. So, how do curriculum experts view their role in the curriculum design process?

One curriculum expert remarked:

"When creating standards, the role of curriculum experts is twofold: one aspect is conceptual, and the other is technical. First, curriculum standards must respect the internal logic of the curriculum system. Subject experts typically begin by focusing on the subject content, while curriculum experts tend to approach the issues from the students' perspective. Hence, dialogue is essential. It is not acceptable to fully align with one side; both parties must find a middle ground. Subject experts emphasize completing the teaching content and focusing on 'basic knowledge and skills.' In this

① Zhou Peiyi. From Social Critique to Postmodernism: A Study of Ji Hu's Curriculum Theory [M]. Taipei: Shida Book Garden Co., Ltd., 2000: 56.

dialogue, curriculum experts must assert their position and fulfill their role. Secondly, curriculum development requires technical support. Curriculum development, design, and planning are all technical tasks, and curriculum experts can support subject experts in these areas, such as by determining which action verbs to use in the curriculum standards. We provide these verbs to subject experts, who then organize the content accordingly."

This curriculum expert has thoughtfully reflected on his role in the design process, dividing it into two main aspects: conceptual and technical. These aspects align closely with the nature of curriculum design itself. He believes that curriculum experts should be involved throughout the entire process, providing a framework for ideas and guiding thought. From a logical standpoint, their role is foundational, as it is integral to the nature of the curriculum. Given the clear divergence of views that arise from different professional perspectives, collaboration between both sides is essential throughout the design process. The boundaries between the disciplines are distinct, with each participant's cognitive structure influencing the information they prioritize and the criteria they use when making decisions about students and subjects. These cognitive structures represent what is known as a "legitimate prejudice" in hermeneutics, as understanding is impossible without some form of bias. This "prejudice" is the necessary foundation for people to make sense of the world, and intellectuals are tasked with shaping culture because they possess this legitimate "prejudice." However, this 'prejudice' should not hinder the development of a shared culture. The key lies in participants' willingness to listen, empathize, and appreciate the validity of differing perspectives.

A subject expert reflected on this process:

"When we were working on the compulsory education curriculum standards, I initially found it awkward to engage with the ideas of those who specialized in pedagogy and psychology. I thought their suggestions were

sometimes irrelevant. But later, I realized that their ideas made sense. The combination of both perspectives and their mutual promotion has proven quite valuable. For instance, their ideas on the three-dimensional educational goals were things we had already recognized, but they systematized them, which was a significant advancement."

This subject expert's shift in perspective—from initially dismissing the curriculum experts' ideas as irrelevant to recognizing them as valuable and contributing to a "good promotion"—was a result of his increasing understanding of the concepts advocated by curriculum experts and their approach to curriculum issues. Over time, he began to accept and even adopt the thinking of those trained in pedagogy and psychology. Ultimately, he concluded that "combining both perspectives and promoting each other is highly beneficial."

2. The Emergence of Decision-Making

In every curriculum standards group, discussion is a continuous and evolving process. After conflicts and communication, how are decisions ultimately made? Different developers provided varying responses.

An expert from the standards group shared:

"Everyone is eager to voice their opinions, but in the end, a core group gradually emerges. Eventually, someone has to make the final decision. This role is usually taken by someone from a university. For example, during the debate about the curriculum structure and whether to include a basic component, one teacher was especially insistent. He argued, 'Because we conducted the early research, we understand China's situation the best, so we suggest having a required basic component.' This opinion was rejected in the third and fourth meetings. Later, he stopped speaking out, but when he did, he simply restated his reasoning. By the fourth or fifth meeting, the group

had reached a consensus. Ultimately, the person who had studied the issue most deeply had the greatest chance of seeing their opinion adopted."

Another expert in the group explained:

"There's no single decision-maker. It's a collective debate, and the majority opinion becomes the standard. It's not about the project leader having the final say—it's a scientific decision-making process. For example, when we make content choices, it's not about one person making the decision—it's the result of repeated discussions. You present your view, I present mine, and through the debates, ideas gradually become clearer. In the end, we reach a consensus. I think this process is very reasonable, and there's no one person making the final call. That's how it is in our standards group—it's a scientific and democratic process."

The first account clearly identifies the emergence of a decision-making center, an authority that naturally evolves within the discussion, though this authority is not necessarily the convener. The individual who assumes this role and ultimately drives the decision-making process possesses two key traits. First, thorough research. Their preliminary research is the most extensive, which makes their views the most rational and convincing. Second, persistence and patience. They continuously present their reasoning, allowing the group's understanding to gradually coalesce into a unified perspective. Consensus does not emerge spontaneously but is built upon shared beliefs, theories, goals, procedures, and other common positions. When a shared stance is insufficient to make a choice, empirical data from foundational research becomes the most persuasive tool. The individual in question, who presents this reasoning, has conducted thorough "preliminary research" and thus has a deep understanding of "China's current situation." As Dewey famously said, "Children and the curriculum are the two poles of the educational process," and "The current level or starting point of children, along with the facts and truths within the subject, can determine teaching methods." [1] In other words, decisions based on preliminary research concerning students (children) can guide the inclusion of "core compulsory content" in the curriculum. Because this decision-making authority is separate from the convener (the administrative leader), opposing voices are free to continue expressing dissent without fear of retribution. However, over time, as the group absorbs the existing research, consensus naturally develops.

The second account does not identify a clear decision-making center. Respondents frequently refer to "everyone" and "consensus," with different issues being decided through the contributions of various individuals. After removing the authority of the administrative leader, the group gradually arrives at conclusions through the discussion process. The reason the curriculum standards group has a convener, rather than a designated group leader, is to minimize the idea of a sole decision-maker, ensuring democratic participation and scientific decision-making. In this relatively free and flexible administrative structure, decision-making power rests with those who are confident and bold enough to express their opinions, even stubbornly. As sociologists argue, "Autonomy is a crucial characteristic of leadership authority. Only when a person believes in and values their own particular tendencies can they produce something valuable." [2] Of course, this stubbornness and confidence are not blind; they are grounded in a well-considered understanding of the issues at hand and are supported by solid reasoning.

One expert from the curriculum standards group shared:

"Before working on the curriculum standards, we had written several high school textbooks and conducted empirical research for three years. As a result, we felt we had special authority when speaking. Subconsciously, we

---

① Dewey, John. The Child and the Curriculum. Translated by Lin Baoshan and Kang Chunzhi, Taipei: Wunan Publishing, 1990.
② Charles Norton Cooley. Human Nature and Social Order. Translated by Bao Fanyi and Wang Yuan, Beijing: Huaxia Publishing House, 1999.

believed that our experience in writing textbooks and our empirical research gave us a unique credibility in the process."

Another expert from the curriculum standards group added:

"Once, during a presentation on curriculum design, a speaker made a remark: 'Who should curriculum reform listen to? Whoever's voice is louder, that's whose opinion will prevail.' I believe the 'louder voice' refers to the recognition of one's professional expertise within the group. This makes sense. In the curriculum standards group, there are often many unresolved issues, and when this happens, the opinion of the person that everyone agrees with tends to become the leading opinion."

Some curriculum designers, after reflecting on their experience in the curriculum design deliberation process, have emphasized the importance of rational decision-making. Whether through the accumulation of research or professional competence, their views converge on one point: an informal decision-making center naturally forms within the design team. This center is not based on a hierarchical administrative structure, but rather on the persuasive power of the participants' viewpoints. When all team members understand that presenting their views is both a right and a responsibility, and when they respect knowledge, science, and reason, this decision-making center is seen as legitimate by the designers.

2. Understanding Curriculum Deliberation

The development of the new curriculum can be understood as a process of localizing the deliberative approach in China. Curriculum deliberation, as a research method, plays a distinct role in the design of the new curriculum. By examining how deliberation functions within the context of Chinese cultural settings, we can observe the unique characteristics that arise from its application in new curriculum design.

2.1 Curriculum Design Based on Deliberation: A Pursuit of Practical Rationality

The purpose of deliberation is not to address theoretical questions, but to assess the feasibility of practical solutions. Cognitive rationality seeks consistency in thought and aims for an absolute answer, which works well for theoretical problems that often have a single correct solution. However, practical challenges are more complex. A curriculum plan that works effectively in urban areas may not be suitable for rural settings; a plan that fits large schools may not be feasible in small schools; a program designed for gifted children might not work for average students. As Schwab argues, "In deliberation, there is no one right answer, but there is the best possible solution." [①] Curriculum development, therefore, must be context-dependent, considering the realities of the situation. This judgment and decision-making process relies on a thorough understanding of practical issues. The more specific and realistic the understanding of the context, the more rational the decision-making becomes.

The resolution of practical challenges differs significantly from solving theoretical problems. While theoretical issues can often be addressed using established theories and logical reasoning, practical challenges can only be fully understood and resolved through action and the observation of its outcomes. Schwab's reference to curriculum deliberation primarily concerns curriculum design at the school level, as it is more directly linked to specific contexts and holds more immediate practical significance. However, in the case of China's new curriculum design, this research method is applied at the national level. Despite differences in the nature of the information used when

---

① Joseph. J.Schwab. The practical: a language for curriculum [M]. School Review, University of Chicago Press,1969:1-23.

compared to school-level curriculum deliberation, the theoretical foundation and essential attributes of deliberation remain consistent.

2.2 Basic Research as the Foundation of Curriculum Deliberation

In the design of the new curriculum, each curriculum standards group conducted a variety of investigations around their respective subjects, including surveys of current practices, comparative research, social demand studies, research on subject development, and studies on student psychological development. These research efforts represent both a review of existing theoretical studies and an understanding of the relevant real-world conditions within the curriculum. This research phase forms the foundation of curriculum deliberation, as the knowledge and data collected serve as the basis for judgment.

In the deliberative process, researchers need a shared platform of understanding. American curriculum scholar Walker referred to this platform as the "position," arguing that every curriculum designer approaches the curriculum development process with certain beliefs and values. These beliefs shape their perspective on the work, influence their identification of key issues, guide the type of solutions they propose, and define their commitment to particular outcomes[①]. While the stance becomes clearer through deliberation, and while basic research does not always lead to unanimous consensus, it does help build a relative agreement. Moreover, the discovery of theoretical dilemmas and the limited understanding of real-world curriculum issues during deliberation spark a deeper and more sustained desire for further curriculum research. It can be argued that curriculum research and deliberation in curriculum design have a co-constructive relationship.

① Colin J. Marsh. Key concepts for understanding curriculum [M]. The Falmer Press, 1992:123.

2.3 The Deliberation Process Should Be Decentered: Rejecting Authority but Relying on Expertise

The "center" here refers to the traditional administrative power center within a hierarchical system. Toffler discussed how, in such systems, due to their durability, hierarchy, and division of labor, individuals often entrust their futures to the future of the organization. Over time, this leads to a sense of loyalty to the organization, making individuals passive and subservient. However, after the era of hierarchical systems, human society is expected to evolve into what Toffler calls a "temporary system" (or "special organizations"). These are organizations formed to address a specific problem and disband once the problem is resolved. In this system, administrative personnel and managers act as coordinators among professional teams. They are familiar with the terminology of various expert groups and facilitate communication between familiar with the terminology of various expert groups and facilitate communication between them, translating technical language into more accessible forms[①]. In such a system, the old sense of loyalty to the organization fades, replaced by loyalty to the profession itself. This shift encourages more rule-breaking, innovation, and risk-taking, as professionals are rewarded for their contributions beyond their immediate circles. Toffler believed that early forms of such individuals already exist in contemporary organizations. The "temporary system" he envisioned bears a strong resemblance to expert teams in curriculum design. In a "temporary system," the thinking and discourse of design experts are not subordinated to administrative control. Instead, the deliberative process relies on the autonomy and flexibility of each expert to generate meaning and drive progress.

Deliberation rejects hierarchical authority because its very foundation is a relaxed, open public space with a democratic, egalitarian atmosphere where every designer has the right and responsibility to express their views.

---

① Alvin Toffler. Future Shock [M]. Translated by Meng Guangjun, Beijing: Xinhua Publishing House, 1996.

Therefore, in a deliberative team, there can be no absolute command center. However, despite the decentralized nature of deliberation, competing opinions often arise. Since the effectiveness and rationality of a plan can only be assessed once it is implemented, the "recognized" theory—the one that is well-grounded in expertise and a comprehensive understanding of the curriculum's practical realities—ultimately influences and guides the opinions of the team.

2.4 The Fusion of Perspectives is a Difficult Process; It Requires Tolerance, Patience, and Even a "Bargaining" Strategy

Merging different viewpoints in curriculum deliberation is no easy task. Beneath seemingly shared curriculum values, each designer brings deep-rooted differences in experience, thought processes, and judgment principles. These differences surface in the exploration, judgment, and decision-making processes regarding specific issues. The value of design in this context lies in expressing the unique characteristics of each discipline. Disagreement itself, far from being a roadblock, becomes a form of communication and mutual training that gradually diminishes the distinctiveness of individual subjects, leading to a unified understanding. There are two paths to resolve disputes: one is the reflective introspection on premises that suddenly flashes in the argument—a kind of transcendent cognition. Thus, multiple subjects who are opposed and contradictory at the same level are elevated, they abandon their inherent recalcitrance， and everyone's thinking enters a new level. The second is that "the success of the deliberation process requires all participants to have certain standards or expectations in the process. These standards or expectations include listening attentively to others' viewpoints and arguments, accepting or rejecting them cautiously rather than agreeing or rejecting them without thinking, compromising between the rupture of one's own position and the value of others' positions, and committing to the standards finally accepted in the deliberation, etc. This is not something that dogmatists and uncooperative people can do."①

2.5 Deliberation Requires Designers to Have Multicultural Literacy and a Positive Cultural Psychological Reconstruction

The quality of a curriculum product is decided on how well the design integrates reality with ideals. Curriculum designers must have a strong cultural foundation in curriculum theory, as it forms a key background for their thinking. At the same time, they must be familiar with the real-world curriculum environment and be able to anticipate potential changes. This dual focus requires long-term, regular, and latent curriculum research, along with the diversity needed in the cultural backgrounds of the designers. Curriculum activities exist within a broader context, and no theory is without its limitations. Effective curriculum judgment and action require complex research methods, drawing on diverse sources of knowledge, theory, and principles.②

During the deliberation process, cultural differences between designers often lead to dilemmas in mutual recognition. This is partly due to the paradox between the relativity of social situations and the transcendence of universal truths, as well as the challenge of achieving "convergence" between different knowledge structures. These cultural divides can even manifest as contradictions within an individual's own self-identity. This stems from the "duality" inherent in the education intellectuals have received, or the divergence between their formal education and local experience.③ To navigate this, deliberators must undergo a psychological reconstruction

① Short. E. C. Shift paradigms: implications for curriculum research and practice/ paradigms debate in curriculum and supervision: modern and postmodern perspectives [M]. Jeffery Gland, Linda S, Behar Hohenstein,2000.
② Ilene Harris. Deliberative inquiry: the arts of planning [M]. E. C. Short, Forms of Curriculum Inquiry, State University of New York Press,1990:285-303.
③ Tao Dongfeng. Social Transformation and Contemporary Intellectuals [M]. Shanghai: Shanghai Sanlian Bookstore, 1999: 39.

through continuous, interactive curriculum research, where theory and practice complement each other.

2.6 Deliberation Necessarily Unites the Pre-determined and the Emergent in Curriculum Design

Predeterminedness refers to the shaping influence of established curriculum culture on the design process. However, curriculum deliberation groups often face constraints in their understanding of both theoretical and practical knowledge, compounded by limited resources—particularly time and funding. Additionally, deliberative capacity, or the authority to implement the results of deliberation, is crucial. Without decision-making and implementation power, the viewpoints developed during deliberation can only exert limited influence on curriculum implementers. On the other hand, if deliberation ignores the desires of curriculum decision-makers, it risks wasting valuable time and resources[①].

Emergence, in contrast, reflects the creative potential of designers in reconstructing the new curriculum. The decision-making process in deliberation is not linear or unidirectional; instead, it is bidirectional and multi-dimensional, characterized by constant interaction. No individual can predetermine the outcomes, and creativity plays a central role in weighing various alternatives. This interactive, dynamic process is the essence and significance of curriculum deliberation.

[Original text published in *Education Research*, Issue 2, 2005 (by Lyu Lijie and Ma Yunpeng)]

① Decker F. Walker. Fundamentals of curriculum passion and professionalism [M]. Mahwah, New Jersey: Lawrence Erlbaum Associates,2003:217-239.

Chapter 5 The Organizational Structure of Curriculum in School-Based Curriculum Development

1. Understanding School-Based Curriculum Organization

1.1 Definition of School-Based Curriculum Organization

Curriculum organization is often defined in terms of its function. In 1949, Tyler, the father of modern curriculum theory, identified four fundamental issues in curriculum development: setting objectives, selecting experiences, organizing experiences, and evaluating the curriculum. Curriculum organization is considered a critical step in this development process. Tyler emphasized, *"In order for educational experiences to have an accumulative effect, they must be organized so that they reinforce each other... Curriculum organization is the process of organizing learning experiences into units, sequences, and teaching plans."*①

A well-designed curriculum has clear objectives and a rich array of elements that must be carefully "woven" together. How these elements are interwoven determines how the curriculum is presented and the developmental outcomes it achieves. This approach aligns with modern systems theory, where the whole is made up of interconnected parts, yet the whole is more than the sum of its parts②. If the structure of the elements is well-designed, the system's function will be greater than just the individual components. Thus, curriculum organization is the framework that ensures the various parts of the curriculum are connected, forming a coherent and effective whole.

① Ralph Tyler. Basic Principles of Curriculum and Teaching. Beijing: China Light Industry Press, 2008.
② Li Jinsong. Systems Theory, Information Theory, and Cybernetics in Educational Reform [M]. Wuhan: Hubei Education Press, 1989: 21.

Curriculum organization is also a multi-level concept. Researchers like Skilbeck [①]and Goodlad[②] have categorized it from different levels of analysis. Posner highlights two primary levels: the macro level, which refers to relationships between curricula across different educational stages (such as elementary vs. secondary education) and across educational types (such as vocational vs. general education); and the micro level, which pertains to the relationships between specific elements like concepts, facts, and skills within a single lesson. Between these two levels, there are several intermediary levels of organization[③]. At the school level, curriculum organization involves three main aspects: a) The organization of the entire curriculum system; b) The organization of a specific subject; c) The organization of curriculum elements within a particular lesson. School-based curriculum development needs to address curriculum organization at all three levels. This article focuses on the third aspect: how to organize themes, concepts, knowledge, principles, skills, and values within a specific subject.

1.2 Principles and Methods of Curriculum Organization

There is broad consensus among curriculum researchers on the principles and methods of curriculum organization. Tyler first proposed three fundamental standards for effective organization: continuity, sequence, and integration. Over time, these principles have been further developed. Chinese scholar Professor Lin Zhizhong summarized these principles into categories, sequence, continuity, integration, balance, coherence, and learning trajectories[④].

In general, curriculum organization must consider:

---

① Skibeck M. Curriculum organization in A. Lewy. international encyclopedia of curriculum [M]. Oxford: Pergamon Press,1991:342-346.
② Lin Zhizhong, et al. Curriculum Organization [M]. Beijing: Educational Science Press, 2006: 2.
③ Posner, G. J. The Curriculum Analyzing. Xi'an: Shaanxi Normal University Press, 2005.
④ Lin Zhizhong, et al. Curriculum Organization [M]. Beijing: Educational Science Press, 2006: 2.

a) The internal logic of the discipline

b) The cognitive characteristics, interests, and needs of learners

c) The available resources in the learning environment

In terms of methods, curriculum organization can be divided into vertical and horizontal approaches. Vertical organization involves structuring content in ways that reflect logical relationships, such as segmentation, layering, linear progression, or a spiral approach. Researchers like Hermo, Posner, and Lin Zhizhong have outlined these methods to guide curriculum development[①] (See Figure 1-4).

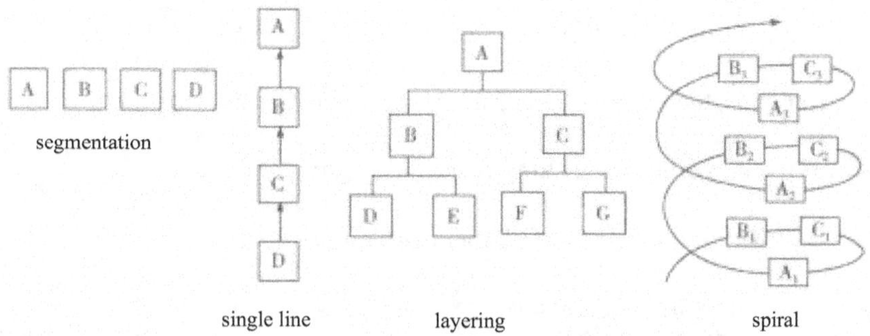

Figure 1-4: Vertical Curriculum Organization

Horizontal organization refers to the integration of courses to varying degrees. Within integrated curriculum organization, the forms of integration are diverse. Drawing from their research experience, Drake and Burns identified three main methods of integrated curriculum: multidisciplinary, interdisciplinary, and transdisciplinary[②]. These approaches to curriculum integration highlight different levels and strategies for organizing content across subjects.

① Posner, G. J. The Curriculum Analyzing. Xi'an: Shaanxi Normal University Press, 2005.
② Drake S. Meeting Standards Through Integrated Curriculum. Translated by Liao Shan, Huang Jinghui, and Pan Wen, Beijing: China Light Industry Press, 2007: 9.

Scholars like Jacobs[①], Marva[②], Erickson[③], and Drake [④]have further developed the concept of integration, arranging various methods of curriculum integration in a logical sequence. This progression reflects a continuous process, with the level of integration becoming progressively deeper. For instance, Fogarty used different lenses as metaphors to illustrate these varying levels of integration. Each lens represents a method of curriculum organization with increasing depth [⑤]. Specifically, these metaphors include:

a) Isolated and fragmented subject organization

b) Parallel themes within subjects

c) Attention to multiple aspects of knowledge and skills within a subject

d) Consistent conceptual arrangements across subjects

e) Co-constructed teaching plans across subjects

f) Broad organization of elements around a theme

g) Connecting elements to larger concepts

h) Interdisciplinary integration forming new models

i) Filtering subject content through learners' experiences and interests

j) Establishing internal connections between experiences and subjects based on learners' academic perspectives

---

① Lin Zhizhong, et al. Curriculum Organization [M]. Beijing: Educational Science Press, 2006: 106-107.
② Lin Zhizhong, et al. Curriculum Organization [M]. Beijing: Educational Science Press, 2006: 108.
③ Drake S. Meeting Standards Through Integrated Curriculum. Translated by Liao Shan, Huang Jinghui, and Pan Wen, Beijing: China Light Industry Press, 2007: 27.
④ Drake S. Meeting Standards Through Integrated Curriculum. Translated by Liao Shan, Huang Jinghui, and Pan Wen, Beijing: China Light Industry Press, 2007: 27.
⑤ Fogarty R. Ten ways to integrate curriculum [J] Educational Leadership,1991(2).

Each of these levels represents a different approach to curriculum integration, progressing from simple thematic connections to deeper interdisciplinary and transdisciplinary approaches. (See Figure 1-5)

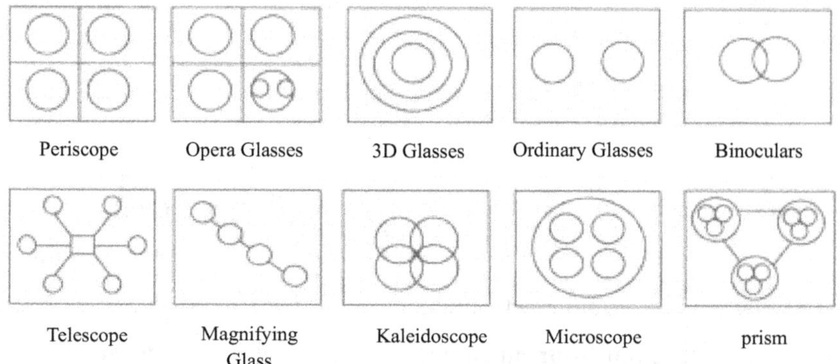

Figure 1-5: Fogarty's Ten Gradually Integrating Curriculum Organization Methods

2. "Organization" Practice in the Development of Two School-Based Curricula

U-S collaboration refers to the partnership between universities and primary/secondary schools aimed at jointly improving school education. University researchers, leveraging their theoretical expertise and professional backgrounds, assist schools in refining their educational philosophy, improving curricula and teaching, and promoting teacher professional development. As a university researcher, the author participated in two comprehensive school-based curriculum development projects with N Primary School and F Primary School. Through co-constructing and developing school-based curricula with the school principals and teachers, it became evident that, during the course organization phase, both university researchers and teachers must play their unique roles and contribute their value. The primary goal of developing school-based curricula at both N Primary and F Primary Schools was to realize their educational philosophy and unique cultural characteristics. Although the curriculum organization methods at the two schools were different, they both demonstrated the importance of effectively organizing and integrating curriculum content to achieve course goals, ensure feasibility in implementation, and make optimal use of available resources.

2.1 Concentric Circle Model — Organization of the "Chinese Symbols" School-Based Curriculum at N Primary School

N Primary School is an ordinary primary school in Changchun City. After the new curriculum reform, the school independently introduced several interest-based and elective school-based courses, such as *Go*, roller skating, and musical instrument courses. In 2005, the school began offering a traditional Chinese culture course, with the goal of establishing it as a signature course. In 2008, with the financial support from the local education bureau, the school constructed a new campus. Building on this new educational environment, the school further refined its educational direction, making "cultivating students' Chinese cultural awareness" the core of its educational philosophy and unique cultural feature. To highlight this feature in the school culture, beautiful woodblock prints were displayed in the corridors of the new teaching building, featuring themes centered on "Chinese symbols," such as the Four Treasures of the Study, the abacus, the compass, and the Terracotta Army.

How could the "Chinese symbols" in the physical space of the school be transformed into qualities that students identify with and internalize? The principal hoped that each class would research the "Chinese symbols" displayed outside their classrooms. During discussions with the teachers, we proposed transforming the fragmented activities of observing and exploring "Chinese symbols" into a systematic, research-based school course. In the first round of discussions, the school required each class to submit a research theme based on a "Chinese symbol," chosen collaboratively by both the teachers and students, which helped form the initial curriculum content structure. (See Table 1-1)

Table 1-1: Curriculum Content Structure Designed by Teachers in the First Round at N Primary School

1.1	Drum	2.1	Lantern	3.1	Chinese Calligraphy	4.1	Four Treasures of the Study	5.1	Square Hole Coins	6.1	Bronze Vessels
1.2	Abacus	2.2	Fan	3.2	Cloisonné (Jingtai Blue)	4.2	Stone Lion	5.2	Jade	6.2	Terracotta Warriors
1.3	Chinese Knot	2.3	Lion Dance	3.3	Erhu (Chinese Two-Stringed Fiddle)	4.3	Cloisonné (Jingtai Blue)	5.3	Silk	6.3	Ancient Locks
1.4	Paper Cutting	2.4	Peking Opera	3.4	Peking Opera	4.4	Jade Pendant	5.4	Jade Pendant	6.4	Tripod Cauldron

We discussed this plan with the N Primary School curriculum development team and concluded that, while the content accounted for the teachers' and students' preferences and was aligned with the school's physical space, the 24 symbols used as course content lacked sequence and logical structure. The repeated content also made it difficult to implement the course in a way that ensured continuity. Therefore, we restructured the content based on the teachers' and students' preferences. Vertically, the content follows a hierarchical structure: under the main theme of Chinese symbols, there are six research topics suitable for each grade, and within each research topic, there are subtopics for each class to explore. In terms of horizontal organization, we adopted an interdisciplinary approach to integrate the content, emphasizing the design and development of material based on children's life experiences. From the perspective of Fogarty's "magnifying glass," we used larger thematic concepts to connect relevant elements. The final design consists of six major themes and 24 Chinese symbol elements. (See Table 1-2)

Table 1-2: Second Round Design of Course Content Structure

Traditional Cuisine	Traditional Customs	Chinese Calligraphy	National Essence: Peking Opera	Silk Road	Ancient Civilizations
1.1 Dumplings	2.1 Lantern	3.1 Four Treasures of the Study	4.1 Erhu	5.1 Tea	6.1 Bronze Ware
1.2 Mooncakes	2.2 Chinese Knot	3.2 Famous Calligraphers	4.2 Drum	5.2 Jade	6.2 Terracotta Warriors
1.3 Yuanxiao (Sweet Rice Dumplings)	2.3 Lion Dance	3.3 Calligraphy Styles	4.3 Face Masks	5.3 Silk	6.3 Ancient Coins (Round Coins with Square Hole)
1.4 Zongzi (Sticky Rice Dumplings)	2.4 Paper Cutting	3.4 Famous Calligraphy Works	4.4 Peking Opera Roles	5.4 Porcelain	6.4 Tripod Cauldrons (Ding)

The planning of the "Chinese Symbols" course organization is primarily based on the following considerations:

1. The Premise of Course Organization: Consideration of Course Goals and Content

The goals and content selection for this course are clearly defined and straightforward to implement. The course content directly supports the school's distinctive educational goal of "cultivating students with a Chinese cultural sentiment." With this focus, the overall course objectives are established, and the content themes are primarily centered around highly representative Chinese elements. The selection process also takes into account the relevance of these elements to real-life situations, allowing students to connect both the past and the future of Chinese culture with their present-day lives. In fact, the range of content options is quite broad.

2. Consideration of Children's Cognitive Levels to Form a Sequential Cognitive Path

The course content cannot cover every aspect of Chinese traditional culture but must focus on the most representative elements. This "representative" content is organized according to children's cognitive levels, forming six thematic units for six grades: Traditional Cuisine, Traditional Customs, Chinese Calligraphy, Peking Opera, The Silk Road, and Ancient Civilizations. These six themes correspond to the cognitive development of students at each grade level. As students' themes expand, they will encounter representative "symbols" of Chinese culture. Beginning with younger students' experiences in family life and holiday activities, such as food and traditional games, middle-grade students will learn about Chinese calligraphy and national arts (Peking Opera) through school lessons and public media, and finally, upper-grade students will explore ancient civilizations through history. The course content gradually unfolds, from the near to the distant, following a stable gradient. Throughout the course, Chinese representative elements are emphasized. (See Figure 1-6)

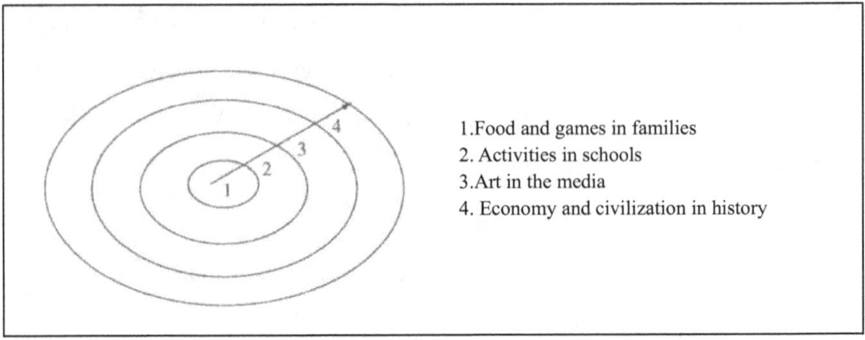

Figure 1-6 The Arrangement Sequence of Concentric Circles School-Based Curriculum

3. Cognition, Experience, and Emotions as Interdependent Purposes and Means, Forming the Structure of Children's Development

The course gradient incorporates diverse implementation methods. For example, in the first grade, the research theme is Chinese cuisine, which is closely related to children's family food and life. It is an activity that children are "willing" to engage in and can easily share with others. The course implementation focuses on experience, with activities such as inviting parents to make dumplings together, sharing mooncakes after the Mid-Autumn Festival, and storytelling in small groups as possible options. In the second grade, the research theme shifts to Chinese traditional customs—such as lanterns, Chinese knots, lion dances, and paper cutting. Students can engage in activities like drawing and cutting to appreciate and begin to understand these cultural traditions. In the third and fourth grades, students are expected to use resources like the internet to search for texts, photos, and other materials, organize information, and present their findings in class. For the fifth and sixth grades, students experience the full research process, including identifying questions, selecting topics, creating research plans, gathering and organizing materials, and presenting findings—all while researching Chinese elements. Throughout this process, children's understanding of Chinese culture, their hands-on experiences, and the emotional enrichment they gain through cognition and experience are key. Cognition, experience, and emotional engagement are both the goals of the course and the means to achieve them. These three aspects serve as interdependent purposes and methods, working together to foster changes in children's literacy.

4. The Themes for Each Grade Align with National Curriculum, Forming a "Relevant Curriculum"

In the national compulsory education curriculum, there are no designated hours for comprehensive practice activities (including research-based learning) in the first and second grades. Therefore, the first-grade theme of traditional Chinese food can be integrated into the Moral and Life Education curriculum. The second grade can incorporate this topic into the art class, adapting the content to fit the art curriculum. Starting in the third grade, the "Chinese Symbols" course can directly rely on the comprehensive practice activity class, aligning with the calligraphy course offered by the school. In the fourth grade, the music class can also include an appreciation of and learning to sing Peking opera. For the fifth and sixth grades, the themes of the Silk Road and Ancient Civilizations can correspond with topics in the Moral and Society and Chinese Language classes.

After two rounds of implementing the "Chinese Symbols" school-based curriculum, we held discussions with teachers. They shared that students enjoyed the course, and teachers were enthusiastic about it. However, since each class had different research themes, teachers in the same grade could not share resources, which increased their workload and hindered collaboration and exchange of results within the grade. Additionally, teachers found that while students displayed high enthusiasm for certain topics, they were indifferent to others. Based on this feedback, the school's curriculum development team decided to redesign the content structure of the "Chinese

Symbols" curriculum. The new structure consists of one research theme and two specific research topics for each grade. (See Table 1-3)

Table 1-3 Third Round Design of the Course Content Structure

Grade Level	Theme	Content	Main Subjects	Supporting Subjects
Grade 1	Chinese Cuisine	Dumplings, Mooncakes	Ethics and Life	Chinese Language
Grade 2	Traditional Customs	Lanterns, Paper Cutting	Art	Chinese Language
Grade 3	Calligraphy Art	Poems, Calligraphy	Comprehensive Practical Activities	Calligraphy, Art
Grade 4	Peking Opera Culture	Famous Peking Opera Artists, Face Masks	Comprehensive Practical Activities	Music, Art
Grade 5	Silk Road	Tea, Jade	Comprehensive Practical Activities	Chinese Language, Ethics and Society
Grade 6	Ancient Civilizations	Bronze Ware, Terracotta Warriors	Comprehensive Practical Activities	Chinese Language, Ethics and Society

Currently, N Primary School's "Chinese Symbols" school-based curriculum has undergone multiple rounds of implementation, and the teachers have explored various methods for course delivery at each grade level, as well as different research approaches for students and guidance strategies for teachers at each stage of the same theme. Clearly, after standardizing and structuring the course design, the teaching team has begun to think systematically about course-related issues, and the professional quality of the course itself has improved.

2.2 Spiral Ascending Model — F Primary School "Chess Culture" School-Based Curriculum Organization

F Primary School is an ordinary primary school in Anshan City. The school began offering "Chess Education" as a special activity in 2002. Over more than a decade, the school's chess activities have gained significant influence in the city, with competitive achievements among the best in the region. The school has always provided chess lessons (technical skills) to students. In grades one and two, a general chess education course is offered to all students, while from grade three onwards, elective courses are available for students who excel in chess or have a strong interest in it.

In our discussions, we collaborated with the school to refine its educational philosophy of "a happy life, a wise life" for children. This philosophy reflects, on one hand, the aim to integrate chess education into students' lives: grades one and two focus on providing basic chess knowledge (covering three main types of chess: Chinese Chess, Go, and International Chess), with the goal of cultivating an interest in chess and fostering it as a lifelong hobby—a "happy life." From grade three onwards, for children who enjoy chess and have a natural aptitude for it, the goal shifts to enhancing their skills and deepening their understanding of chess strategies—a "wise life." On the other hand, all of the school's courses and activities are aligned with the goal of offering students a "happy life and wise life." Reflecting on this philosophy, the school principal and teachers were always wondering whether children are truly on the path to happiness and wisdom through their chess experiences. It appears that there are some deficiencies. For example, students are overly focused on rankings, are unwilling to confront defeat, and often argue during games. Even parents sometimes become involved in disputes, contesting their children's rankings during competitions. It seems that simply mastering the techniques of chess does not necessarily lead to "happiness" or "wisdom." Therefore, the principal decided, together with the teachers, to develop a "Chess Culture" school-based curriculum. This new curriculum aims to help students understand the history of Chinese chess culture and the wisdom embedded in it, using chess culture to foster character development.

What content should the "Chess Culture" school-based curriculum include? After several brainstorming sessions with the principal and teachers, it was agreed that the curriculum should encompass three main categories: first, the profound Chinese characters and literature embedded in chess, such as poems, proverbs, couplets, and idioms related to chess; The etiquette and moral cultivation in chess culture, including principles like "no regrets in moves" and adherence to the rules; The psychological qualities necessary for children, such as resilience, handling failure, and maintaining calmness—traits that are especially important for children today. These three categories form the basic framework for the "Chess Culture" curriculum (See Table 1-4)

Table 1-4: Outline of the "Chess Culture" Curriculum Content Structure

Primary Concept	Secondary Concept	Executor
A. Chess-related Language and Literature	Poems, Proverbs, Couplets, Idioms, Famous Quotes, Stories	Chinese Language Teacher
B. Chess-related Etiquette and Moral Cultivation	Regret-free Moves, Truth-seeking, Following the Rules, Watching without Commenting	Moral Education Teacher
C. Psychological Qualities in Chess	Resilience, Coping with Setbacks, Adaptability, Unfazed by Success or Failure, Patience, Avoiding Indecision	Psychology Teacher

From a horizontal integration perspective, the course adopts a "telescope" approach to integrating content. This means it focuses on the theme of chess culture while connecting relevant elements from subjects such as Chinese Language, Ethics, and Psychology. These content elements should be arranged in a logical sequence along the vertical axis. Our recommendation is to present the content in a spiral ascending order, introducing literature, ethics, and psychological qualities at appropriate levels for lower, middle, and upper grades. The depth and breadth of the content should gradually expand as students progress by grade. (See Figure 1-7)

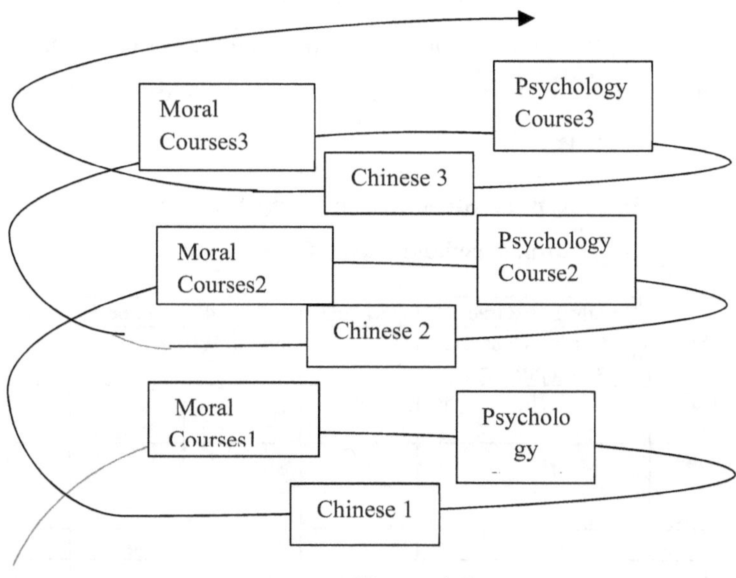

Figure 1-7

In this structural approach, teachers at F Primary School began selecting and organizing the course content. However, a new challenge emerged: After gathering a large amount of material, how should the content be arranged to ensure a spiral progression? How can the content be divided among the teachers and then integrated cohesively?

After discussing with the principal and teachers, we developed a structure diagram that unified both the content structure and the class schedule. We expanded the primary concepts into seven areas: historical stories, etiquette and moral cultivation, writing, literature, and so on. Additionally, we decided that the "Chess Culture" course would be mandatory for grades 1 and 2, with six lessons per semester, while for grades 3 through 6, the course would be elective, with eight lessons per semester.

This content and scheduling structure was then combined into a two-dimensional matrix. The teachers in the curriculum development group were assigned specific content areas based on their expertise and grade level. Two to three teachers were responsible for each content area, tasked with organizing, revising, and editing the course content according to the outlined structure, which matched the amount of content and the corresponding grade levels. Finally, the work from each teacher was consolidated into the final curriculum. (See Table 1-5)

Table 1-5: Conceptual Structure and Time Structure of the "Chess Culture" School-Based Curriculum

Content Area	Grade 1	Grade 2	Grade 3	Grade 4	Grade 5	Grade 6
	Nurturing Character (Compulsory)		Enhancing Wisdom (Elective)			
Historical Stories	+	+	+			
Etiquette and Moral Cultivation	+	+	++	+	+	+
Character	+++	++				
Literature		+	++	+	+	+
Strategy and Tactics			+	++	++	++
Biographies and Anecdotes			+	++	++	++
Mental Growth	+	+	+	++	++	++
Total Hours	6	6	8	8	8	8

The design of the "Chess Culture" course is relatively difficult because it does not rely on any specific, established subject area. The content cannot directly adopt the logical frameworks of a particular discipline. Instead, it requires creative selection and organization based on the course objectives. Many of the knowledge elements related to chess necessitate designers to consider the appropriate age stage for learners and, at times, to rewrite the content accordingly. Additionally, the designer also has to consider the implementation methods and available resources. These considerations collectively present significant challenges for the curriculum development team.

3. Reflections on Organizational Issues in School-Based Curriculum Design

3.1 Teachers Are Still the Main Agents of School-Based Curriculum "Organization"

Teachers remain the primary agents in the development of school-based curricula. Even within collaborative frameworks involving universities and primary or secondary schools, where university researchers contribute theoretical perspectives, the primary responsibility for curriculum organization rests with teachers. School-based curricula are designed for students in schools and emerge from the school environment, making teachers uniquely qualified to address the complexities of curriculum design.

During the school-based curriculum design process, the "organization" phase is often a technical step overlooked by teachers, making the involvement of university-based theoretical researchers particularly valuable. However, their role is to provide a conceptual framework, rather than replace teachers in the design process. Teachers must refine, reorganize, and perfect the curriculum content within the framework of curriculum structure. In doing so, they gain theoretical expertise in curriculum development. This process requires the practical wisdom of both educators and researchers. On one hand, university researchers must understand the demands of school curricula and identify the points they can contribute to. On the other hand, teachers must assess the applicability of these theories, seeking practical and feasible ways to bridge theoretical frameworks with real-world educational resources.

3.2 Curriculum Awareness Determines the Extent to Which Teachers Focus on Curriculum Organization

One primary reason for the neglect of the "organization" stage in school-based curriculum development is a lack of curriculum awareness among teachers. As curriculum designers, teachers often start with the selection of content, choosing what they perceive to be valuable contents for students. While the content may indeed benefit students, it can also result in fragmented or limited learning outcomes if not properly organized.

To avoid this, teachers need to approach curriculum design with an awareness of its broader functions in supporting children's development. They must consider not only the value of specific content but also how the curriculum as a whole contributes to students' learning and development. Teachers should consider how a specific school-based course fits within the overall curriculum structure and how to best achieve its educational objectives. Only with this framework in mind, can teachers synthesize various factors—such as content logic, the students' context, implementation methods, and available resources—into a coherent curriculum design.

3.3 The Fundamental Prerequisite for Curriculum Organization—Curriculum Goals

Tyler's principles clearly outline a goal-based approach to curriculum design, which is equally applicable to the organization of school-based curricula. A school-based curriculum must be rooted in clear curriculum goals and potential curriculum elements. These goals should align with the school's philosophy and distinctive educational characteristics, while also considering students' interests, needs, and the developmental demands of the time.

While students' interests are an important starting point for curriculum development, they should be viewed as a baseline condition—necessary, but not sufficient. Children's interests are diverse and often fluid, influenced by situational and methodological factors that can either spark or diminish interest. Therefore, when determining school-based curriculum goals and content, it is equally important to prioritize children's needs as a central factor.

Tyler defines "needs" as "the discrepancy between the learner's current status and recognized norms," meaning that children's needs reflect the gaps in their current knowledge or abilities. This understanding requires curriculum designers to make informed judgments about

what children are lacking in their education. Of course, identifying children's needs and interests is an ongoing process. After the curriculum is implemented, teachers must assess whether it meets the students' interests and needs, which allows for continuous refinement and improvement of the curriculum's content and structure.

3.4 Organizing School-Based Curricula Requires Balancing Within a Multi-Organizational Community

When organizing a single school-based curriculum, arranging content elements such as knowledge, information, and activities into a coherent, sequential system requires more than just following the logical order of the content itself. It is also essential to consider several related structures that influence the curriculum's design and implementation (see Figure 1-8). These structures include the broader educational goals, the cultural context of the school, the needs of the students, the available resources, and the roles of various stakeholders within the school community. Balancing these elements effectively is crucial to ensuring that the curriculum is not only logical and cohesive but also responsive to the dynamic nature of the school environment.

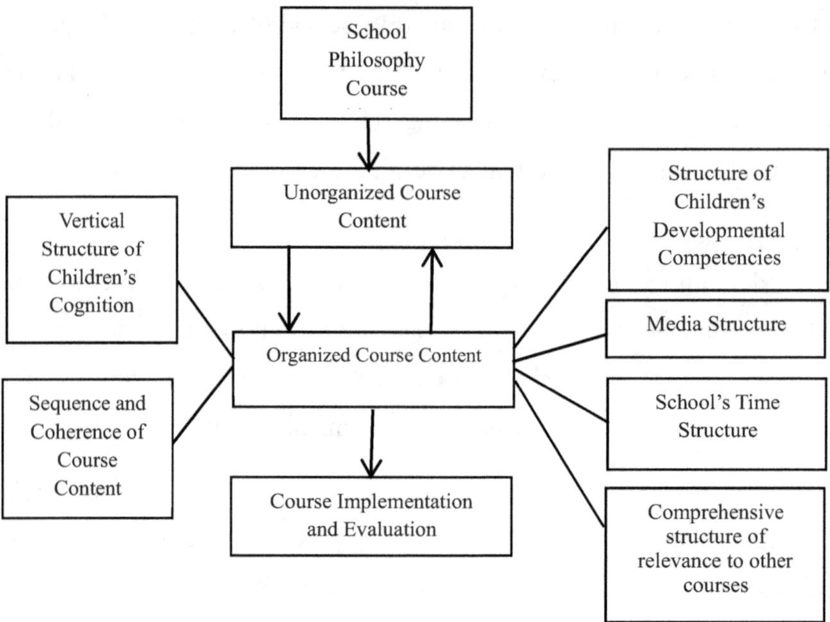

Figure 1-8: The Diverse Organizational Structure of School-Based Curriculum Content

Part 2 Transforming Curriculum to Achieve Competency Targets

Chapter 6 Exploring Pathways for Translating Talent Development Objectives into Curriculum Design

Education today must rise to meet the challenges posed by the evolving talent demands of future societal development and the challenges of talent cultivation in the new era. This challenge is central to educational reforms worldwide, both in developed countries and international organizations. The goals for talent development must be seamlessly integrated into the curriculum in a coherent and continuous way, as this integration is the strategic approach for realizing the vision of talent cultivation. In essence, the implementation of these talent cultivation goals across the curriculum represents a process of transformation. Curriculum transformation refers to the changes in form, transmission cues, and the degree of implementation of educational reform ideals at various curriculum levels. The process of translating national talent cultivation goals into curriculum standards, textbooks, and classroom instruction is a key part of this transformation[①].

Curriculum standards and textbooks are vital vehicles for the curriculum. The design of curriculum standards and textbooks is a crucial step in translating educational goals into curriculum practice. These goals must be realized through curriculum standards and textbooks, and then implemented within schools through teaching activities.

As intermediaries between talent development goals and educational practices, curriculum standards and textbooks play a critical role. The effectiveness of these tools in reflecting the direction of talent cultivation goals is fundamental to guiding educational practices and ensuring the quality

① Lyu, Lijie, & Li Gang. "A Hierarchical Analysis of the Transformation of Core Literacy in School Curricula." Curriculum, Textbook, and Pedagogy, 2016(11): 50-56.

and relevance of future talent. Therefore, it is essential that curriculum standards and textbooks align with the fundamental task of "building moral character" and actively explore how talent cultivation goals are transformed in the curriculum in the new era.

1. The New-Era Challenge of Talent Cultivation Goals

Education today must not only respond to the present needs but also be forward-thinking, preparing students to meet the challenges of an ever-evolving society. As General Secretary Xi Jinping emphasized at the National Education Conference, "Efforts must focus on improving students' overall quality and cultivating innovative, interdisciplinary, and application-oriented talents who can adapt to the needs of the new era." This statement highlights the basic qualities needed for socialist builders and successors, advocating for all-round development in moral, intellectual, physical, aesthetic, and labor dimensions. Xi further emphasized that to fully implement the Party's educational principles, significant efforts must be directed toward several key areas: strengthening students' ideals and beliefs, nurturing patriotism, improving moral character, expanding knowledge, cultivating perseverance, enhancing comprehensive qualities, prioritizing a "health-first" educational philosophy, advancing aesthetic education in schools, and promoting the spirit of labor.

After analyzing talent development goals across China and other countries or organizations, we can categorize these goals into four main areas: values education, basic literacy, key competencies, and the 21st-century framework.

1.1 Values Education

In an increasingly multicultural world, the global order is no longer defined by independent regional developments. Instead, cultures are co-existing and integrating. However, this "global village" has also led to a crisis of national identity and value systems. The erosion of cultural identity and national cohesion is compounded by global concepts like citizenship, universal values, and supranational identities, which can undermine local cultural values. Countries such as Japan, South Korea, France, and Denmark have responded by placing significant emphasis on civic values education within their talent cultivation systems.

In China, the report of the 19th National Congress of the Communist Party of China (CPC) proposed to fully implement the Party's educational policies, upholding the fundamental task of fostering moral character, and promoting quality education. At the same time, the national curriculum stresses the importance of socialist core values education, with a further emphasis on teaching the outstanding traditional culture of the Chinese nation, revolutionary tradition, rule of law education, national security education, ethnic unity education, and ecological civilization education, among others.

1.2 Basic Literacy

The purpose of education extends beyond preparing individuals to face and overcome contemporary challenges; it also aims to equip people for their future roles in society. Education should help individuals attain happiness and fulfillment, whereas fostering responsible and active citizenship. While the frameworks for literacy differ across various societal roles and traditions, they must first address the fundamental literacy needed to navigate modern life. For example, the ongoing transmission of social civilization, the blending of multiple cultures, and the enrichment of the human spiritual world have led to more frequent interactions, reflections, and understanding between individuals and texts, between people and the world, and between individuals and themselves. Essential skills such as reading comprehension and arithmetic are foundational for social integration and continued societal development.

Moreover, the rapid advancement of communication technologies has propelled humanity into the information age, where the digital "flood" created by technologies like "Internet+" has transformed daily life. Every individual has become a "digital citizen," and using digital tools has become a basic life skill. This digital literacy is now critical for personal and professional development, as well as for social participation. While modern society has alleviated many basic survival challenges, it has also led to new issues, such as the physical degeneration caused by excessive reliance on technology and the rise of health-related problems. In response, society has placed greater emphasis on public health and physical activity, making health literacy an increasingly important aspect of overall well-being.

1.3 Key Competencies

In the era of information explosion, the total volume of knowledge is growing exponentially, making it impossible for individuals to stay abreast of developments across all fields. As a result, the focus of education has shifted from cultivating specialized abilities to enhancing general competencies—particularly those key skills needed for lifelong success. In 2017, the General Office of the CPC Central Committee and the State Council issued the "Opinions on Deepening the Reform of the Educational System and Mechanism," which clearly proposed strengthening the cultivation of key competencies—namely, cognitive ability, professional skills, cooperation skills, and innovative ability—while students acquire basic knowledge and skills.

The "21st Century Skills Framework" from the United States highlights competencies that go beyond basic literacy, including learning and innovation skills, information, media, and technology literacy, as well as life and career skills[①]. Similarly, the 2018 OECD report *Education 2030: The*

① Zhang Hua. On the Connotation of Core Literacy [J]. Global Education Outlook, 2016(4): 10-24.

Future of Education and Skills identified critical competencies, including cognitive and metacognitive skills (critical thinking, creative thinking, learning to learn, and self-regulation), social and emotional skills (empathy, self-efficacy, and collaboration), practical and physical skills (using new information and communication technology), and the ability to create new value, resolve challenges, and take responsibility[①]. These key competencies are crucial for adapting to the ever-changing landscape of the information age and the knowledge economy, fostering innovation, and preparing students to tackle the challenges of the future.

1.4 21st Century Concepts

Emerging concepts such as artificial intelligence, big data, the knowledge economy, and the information society are becoming central to the challenges and opportunities of the 21st century. These concepts are difficult to fully address within traditional subject-based curricula and represent new areas for talent cultivation in the modern era. For instance, since the late 20th century, people's living standards have dramatically improved, household incomes have steadily risen, and modes of production have changed fundamentally. The rapid growth of the material resources to the ongoing creation of value. At the same time, global crises, such as the 2008 financial collapse, have demonstrated the volatility of wealth and economic systems.

Given the vast wealth accumulated throughout history, simply maintaining wealth is no longer a viable strategy for addressing the challenges of the 21st century. Instead, the focus must shift to wealth creation. Citizens in the 21st century must develop a clear understanding of economics and recognize that sustained economic growth hinges not on the primitive accumulation of capital, but on continuous innovation and the creation of new value.

① Meng Hongwei. OECD Learning Framework 2030 [J]. Open Learning Research, 2018(6): 9-12.

The "21st Century Skills Framework" emphasizes the need for financial literacy, while the OECD's *Learning Framework 2030* includes entrepreneurship as a key component of education. Finland's "Core Curriculum for Basic Education" similarly highlights the importance of fostering students' professional and entrepreneurial literacy, preparing them to thrive in a rapidly evolving global economy[①].

2. The Metaphorical Characteristics of Talent Cultivation Objectives

A deeper exploration of the metaphorical characteristics embedded in talent cultivation objectives is essential for understanding the direction of curriculum transformation. These metaphors help clarify the multi-dimensional nature of talent development and the goals of education in the new era.

2.1 The Iceberg Metaphor — The Holistic Nature of Talent Cultivation Objectives

The iceberg metaphor offers a vivid illustration of the dual nature of human abilities and qualities. Above the waterline, we find the visible components—knowledge and skills—while beneath the surface lie the invisible elements, such as attitudes, values, and cognition. Similarly, talent cultivation objectives encompass both the visible aspects (knowledge and skills) and the hidden elements (attitudes, cognitive frameworks, and worldview). Both aspects are essential to the holistic development of students and must be cultivated together.

In the context of the new era, in response to the ever-changing world, talent cultivation goals aim for a comprehensive approach that addresses multiple dimensions of human growth: moral, intellectual, physical, aesthetic,

① Finnish National Board of Education. National core curriculum for basic education 2014 [M]. Porvoon Kirjakeskus, Helsinki,2016:32-44.

and labor skills. These objectives emphasize the establishment of a comprehensive framework for goal-setting that includes the depth of knowledge, breadth of abilities, and scope of cognitive and emotional development. This holistic framework underscores the importance of not only mastering knowledge and acquiring skills but also developing a sound worldview and methodology. By doing so, students are better equipped to understand and transform the world around them.

2.2 The Driving Metaphor — The Contextual Nature of Talent Cultivation Objectives

The driving metaphor emphasizes the dynamic, experiential nature of talent cultivation. Just as learning to drive requires practical experience in real-world scenarios—beyond theoretical knowledge and technical skills—talent cultivation in education also depends on creating specific contexts where students can develop their abilities through hands-on experiences, inquiry, and application.

In the same way that driving a car involves more than passing a written exam and practical driving tests, students must be equipped not only with foundational knowledge but also with the ability to navigate complex environments. This includes developing critical thinking, judgment, and character traits, such as respect for others and an awareness of the broader impact of their actions. The metaphor highlights the importance of experiential learning and situational adaptability in nurturing well-rounded individuals[①].

Many of the previously discussed talent cultivation objectives involve higher-order concepts, abilities, and qualities that are built upon foundational knowledge and skills. To achieve these objectives, students must engage in

① Cui Yunhong. On the Curriculum Significance of Core Literacy [J]. Global Education Outlook, 2017(10):24-33.

contexts where they can actively experience, reflect on, and refine their understanding, using their knowledge and skills in a holistic manner. Rather than merely accumulating facts, students should be encouraged to comprehend, innovate, and engage in meaningful dialogue. The goal is not just to load students with knowledge but to equip them with transferable skills that enable them to adapt to real-world challenges and respond effectively to changing circumstances.

2.3 The Ripple Metaphor — The Call of Talent Cultivation Objectives

In nature, ripples occur when an object, such as a stone, is dropped into water, creating waves that spread outward, expanding in area and intensity. Similarly, the talent cultivation objectives of the new era act as the stone dropped into the water, creating ripples that extend far beyond the immediate area. These ripples represent the broader life skills students develop as they continue to grow and evolve, skills that go beyond the initial objectives of talent cultivation[①].

Talent cultivation objectives are not a one-size-fits-all key to success; rather, they act as a starting point that generates the tools needed to unlock diverse opportunities. These objectives define the essential abilities and qualities students should acquire, but their true significance lies in how they shape students' growth. Based on their unique combinations of skills, knowledge, and experiences, students will progressively build their own knowledge, abilities, and emotional intelligence, gradually forming a flexible and adaptive framework for life. This enables them to solve problems, navigate challenges, and create a fulfilling and meaningful life.

---

① Cheng Shangrong, The Chinese Expression of Core Literacy [N]. China Education Daily, 2016-09-19.

3. The Transformation of Talent Cultivation Objectives in the Curriculum

3.1 The Transformation of Talent Cultivation Objectives in Curriculum Standards

Curriculum standards serve as the policy documents that address the challenges of talent cultivation in the modern era. They reflect national priorities, distill disciplinary concepts, and provide a structured framework for education. These standards are not merely technical guides but embody the overarching goals of the education system, representing the disciplinary expression of national educational objectives.

Unlike subject-specific systems, curriculum systems consider both the internal logic of disciplines and the broader needs of societal development, as well as the developmental patterns of children. The goal of a subject curriculum is not simply to transmit knowledge, but to cultivate individuals. To achieve this, it is essential to design curricula that foster key qualities, skills, and ideas, ensuring a harmonious synergy across subjects and educational stages. The core value of curriculum standards is as follow.

First, curriculum standards break down the broad goals of talent cultivation into specific disciplinary components. Textbooks and teaching methods are aligned with the principles and content outlined in these standards, which helps to implement the broader educational objectives of talent development. This process enables both teachers and students to internalize national values, social norms, and key competencies as they learn subject-specific knowledge. Through this, “moral education” can be embedded within each subject area.

Second, curriculum standards provide a blueprint for the development of subject curricula over the course of 9 to 12 years. Textbooks are created based on the disciplinary principles of the standards, ensuring that, while they may vary in style and approach, the core objectives remain consistent. Textbooks across different educational stages are logically connected, following the trajectory of subject literacy as outlined in the curriculum standards, even though each version of textbooks may differ in style. This ensures that learning is progressive and coherent, allowing students to build upon their knowledge and skills over time.

1. Structured Decomposition and Integration

Talent cultivation goals must be integrated into curriculum standards in a scientifically rational manner. The key principles for transforming these goals into curriculum standards include continuity, sequencing, and integration. These principles have their roots in the curriculum design theories of Tyler's "Eight-Year Study" [①] in the U.S., which have influenced curriculum development and textbook design for over half a century.

The talent cultivation objectives within curriculum standards should not be viewed as isolated elements. Instead, they must be systematically and organically organized, with clear interrelationships among them. On one hand, the sequential nature of learning, along with developmental stages, necessitates that cultivation goals be reflected progressively in course content across different learning periods. In other words, each goal and skill should be introduced and gradually developed in curriculum standards, starting with basic concepts and advancing to more complex ones at each educational stage, thereby guiding students' learning. On the other hand, this linear progression should not be construed as a simplistic, one-dimensional approach. The complexity of human development requires that these goals transcend the boundaries of individual subjects, forming a networked structure across disciplines. Different subjects, with their distinct characteristics, should cooperate and complement one another to provide a cohesive and integrated

① Ralph Tyler. Basic Principles of Curriculum and Teaching. Beijing: China Light Industry Press, 2008.

impact on students' growth. Thus, curriculum standards must decompose talent cultivation goals into specific objectives suited for different stages of education—primary, secondary, and high school. These objectives should align across disciplines, creating an interconnected web of learning goals.

2. Content Load

Curriculum standards are the foundation for teachers' instructional design, academic assessments, and textbook compilation. The transformation of talent cultivation goals into curriculum standards is evident not only in the goal system but also in the content system. However, the content within these standards should not merely be a collection of knowledge points; it must also serve as a means to cultivate students' abilities, ideas, and qualities.

Also, curriculum standards should specify which abilities, ideas, and qualities each content area is designed to cultivate in students. For teachers, textbook authors, and evaluators, content is a central element in the curriculum process. Without guiding documents that directly align content with cultivation goals, it becomes crucial for users of curriculum standards to consciously define the goal functions of the content they work with. Failure to do so may lead to misalignment, which could ultimately hinder the effectiveness of course implementation.

Without a systematic approach to reflecting educational goals, talent cultivation objectives risk becoming superficial. Consequently, teaching and assessment processes may degenerate into mere knowledge transmission and rote memorization. Therefore, curriculum standards must systematically embed talent cultivation goals within the content, ensuring that these objectives are actively and effectively implemented in teaching and evaluation.

3.2 The Transformation of Talent Cultivation Objectives in Textbooks

Textbooks are the primary tools for teachers to design and organize classroom instruction. Therefore, textbook design must offer appropriate support for teachers' teaching. First, the concepts, propositions, and principles presented in textbooks serve as the medium for interaction between teachers and students in the classroom. The exercises, experiments, and scenarios provided in textbooks act as materials for teachers to design classroom activities, such as exercises, experiments, discussions, and inquiry-based projects. Second, to assist teachers in effectively organizing classroom activities, textbooks should provide guidance on the teaching process. In other words, textbook designers should break down and present the thinking, activity, and inquiry processes in a way that helps teachers implement effective teaching strategies. Finally, as a medium for cultivation, textbooks should possess inherent educational potential, helping teachers uncover and impart the ideological values embedded within disciplinary knowledge. Moreover, textbooks should provide materials that promote the cultivation of cross-disciplinary skills.

Textbook design must also reflect the staged nature of the learning process, offering scaffolding for both foundational learning and deeper exploration. First, the core logic of textbook design should align with the cognitive development stages of students, with content arranged in a progressive or spiral fashion to match the developmental characteristics of students' cognition. Their cognitive traits, reading habits, and aesthetic needs dictate that textbooks at different educational stages adopt distinct presentation styles and characteristics. Then, textbooks should take into account the contextual framework in which learning takes place. Learning occurs within contexts that involve extending, expanding, and internalizing new knowledge. The scenarios presented in textbooks should connect with students' prior knowledge, activate their preconceptions, and allow them to confront any misconceptions about new knowledge in relation to their previous experiences. Lastly, textbooks should encourage and guide students' inquiry-based activities. Regarding new knowledge, textbook designers should create opportunities for both deep and broad inquiry. Textbooks should provide the necessary materials for these activities, outline key steps involved, and leave ample room for students to explore and act. This interactive approach to textbook design fosters profound and guided learning exploration.

In conclusion, textbooks must undergo a systematic transformation to effectively embody the talent cultivation objectives.

1. The Mediating Transformation of Talent Cultivation Goals in Textbooks

Textbooks are the foundational tools for teachers' instructional designs and act as guides for students' exploration. They must reflect and support the achievement of talent cultivation goals, even though these goals are not always explicitly stated. Talent cultivation goals are often abstract and must be realized through the integration of various content elements, which in turn guide both classroom activities and student learning. For example, the cultivation of critical thinking and the formation of values result from a combined effect of conceptual understanding, emotional engagement, and reflective thinking. In this context, textbooks play a key role by presenting materials that facilitate cognition, emotional engagement, and reflection, acting as intermediaries in this process. Stories, for instance, can serve as effective intermediaries. By being familiar and relatable to students, these stories can be structured to provoke reflection on specific values or moral beliefs, often involving moral dilemmas. The creation of textbooks is not about directly stating moral objectives; rather, it involves selecting and crafting stories that carry these ideas effectively. Through engagement with these materials, students—guided by their teacher—analyze familiar life situations, compare the values of different stakeholders, clarify their own values, and learn the process of value formation.

Similarly, the development of cooperative skills cannot be achieved simply by stating the need for cooperation. True cooperation requires purposeful group activities, clear division of labor, and inquiry-based tasks that act as intermediaries in developing cooperative abilities. Inquiry activities should be carefully designed around unit content, with textbook authors anticipating a full inquiry process. These activities should address key cognitive points while the textbook's structure and presentation guide students' engagement, fostering cooperation and collaborative decision-making. Through these activities, students not only learn inquiry methods but also develop cooperative skills and cultivate habitual thinking patterns.

2. The Multiple Forms of Talent Cultivation Goals in Textbooks

While different subjects may share similar cultivation goals, the unique characteristics of each discipline lead to varied expressions of these skills and values. Talent cultivation goals can be presented as the context for learning content, woven throughout the textbook in a scattered manner, presented as a coherent system, or as a blend of knowledge and experiential learning. Each form impacts students' cognition, emotions, and behavior in distinct ways. For example, the goal of promoting Chinese traditional culture can manifest in different ways within textbooks. It might appear in mathematical problems—such as the traditional Chinese "chickens and rabbits in the same cage" problem or the "measuring depth with a rope" problem—where cultural elements provide the backdrop for learning. Similarly, cultural references can be integrated across subjects like Chinese language or geography, mentioning historical figures or inventions. Alternatively, the achievements of different historical periods in Chinese literature—such as Tang poetry, Song lyrics, Yuan drama, and Ming-Qing novels—could be integrated into the main content, presenting a linear view of cultural elements throughout the textbook. Moreover, geography exercises might ask students to gather and share photographs, stories, or experiences from visits to famous Chinese landmarks, fostering a three-dimensional interaction between geography and cultural learning.

3. The Focused Transformation of Talent Cultivation Goals in Textbooks

In recent years, the concept of "big ideas" in science education has emerged as an approach to focusing talent cultivation goals within textbooks. This approach involves using overarching scientific concepts to organize and integrate knowledge, skills, and information related to those concepts. "Big ideas" serve as a bridge between talent cultivation goals and textbooks, highlighting key abilities within specific content areas.

First, "big ideas" are grounded in facts and knowledge but also incorporate higher-order cognitive elements such as attitudes, values, and ways of thinking[①]. Second, big ideas feature a clear system of knowledge and skills, which can be selected, edited, and organized according to the logical progression of relevant disciplines. This organization simplifies the learning process. By incorporating big ideas into textbook design, students can more easily grasp key concepts, while the content becomes more accessible, addressing common curriculum challenges such as complexity, bias, and outdated material. For example, in science education, the concept of the life cycle could be taught through the stages of butterfly development. However, without the broader context of the life cycle—which encompasses birth, growth, reproduction, and death for all living organisms—this knowledge would remain fragmented. Big ideas help focus the curriculum, creating a more cohesive learning path for students.

---

① Wiggins G, Mctighe J, Alexander V. Understanding by design [M]. Association for Supervision & amp: Curriculum Development,2005:66-78.

4. The Multi-Level Transformation of Talent Cultivation Goals in Textbooks

Students' real-world lives are complex and multifaceted, and similarly, talent cultivation goals span a wide range of areas, including knowledge, skills, and values. Textbooks must offer opportunities for students to engage with content on multiple levels. A single unit can have multiple levels of goals designed to produce different outcomes.

First, textbooks must clearly present foundational knowledge and skills, as these are the starting points for any talent cultivation goal. These are instrumental levels of learning that can be practiced and acquired through exercises. Second, the same content can be used to design reading materials, inquiry-based activities, and group discussions, promoting disciplinary thinking and interdisciplinary skills. Furthermore, post-reading or post-activity reflections can lead to deeper considerations of personal, social, and historical values. These reflections should be intentionally integrated into the textbook as part of the "hidden curriculum." For instance, in a German elementary school math textbook, a section on statistics begins with a pizza-related scenario to review fractions and basic calculations. This is followed by group activities where students conduct surveys, identify mathematical problems in real life, collect and organize data, and apply statistical techniques to analyze the information. Students then apply these skills to broader contexts such as geography, economics, and astronomy, culminating in tiered assessments. This multi-level approach to teaching statistics integrates problem-solving, cooperation, and financial literacy, helping students understand the value of mathematics in both science and daily life while developing their mathematical knowledge and skills.

Ensuring textbook quality involves ensuring their directionality, scientific validity, and appropriateness. During the development process, it is essential to incorporate the latest requirements and structures for talent cultivation goals in the new era, and to explore effective ways to systematically implement these goals within textbooks. Textbook developers should take a strategic approach to ensure that textbooks for each educational stage and discipline systematically reflect these goals in an integrated manner. Textbook writers must not only have a clear ideological direction and a deep understanding of the subject but should also study the principles of textbook writing. Specifically, textbooks for children and adolescents should respect the developmental growth patterns of each age group. This is the fundamental professional guarantee for improving textbook quality and achieving the cultivation goals.

[Original article published in *Education Research*, 2018, Issue 12 (Lyu Lijie, Li Gang)]

Chapter 7 Cultivating Core Competencies in Academic Disciplines: The Value-driven Requirements of Curriculum Implementation

In 2014, the "Opinions of the Ministry of Education on Deepening Curriculum Reform and Implementing the Fundamental Task of Moral Education" highlighted, "Core competencies should be integrated into subject teaching to foster students' holistic and individualized development."(No page number in original book) Since then, core competencies have become a central topic in educational reform, particularly in curriculum design, with subject-specific core competencies becoming a central objective of curriculum implementation. Therefore, this article seeks to address the following key questions within the context of actual curriculum application: What does a teaching model for cultivating subject-specific core competencies look like? What are the theoretical foundations behind this model?

1. Subject-Specific Core Competencies: A Link Between Educational Goals and Curriculum Implementation

1.1 Subject-Specific Core Competencies: Decomposition of Educational Objectives

Core competencies serve as overarching educational goals within basic education. The "Core Competencies for Chinese Students," officially released by the Ministry of Education in September 2016, has become the guiding framework for talent development across various educational levels in China. As a goal focused on the comprehensive development of individuals, core competencies emphasize universal, interdisciplinary principles and are viewed as higher-level, abstract concepts.

To bridge the gap between these broad educational goals and their practical implementation within the curriculum, the concept of subject-specific core competencies was introduced. These competencies are unique to each academic discipline and are designed to help students develop the essential thinking abilities, concepts, and skills needed to engage meaningfully with themselves, others, and the world. For instance, in mathematics, core competencies may include mathematical abstraction, logical reasoning, data analysis, and problem-solving. In physics, core competencies might involve scientific thinking, experimental inquiry, and the development of a scientific attitude and responsibility.

Subject-specific core competencies represent a concrete manifestation of broader core competencies within the practical context of teaching. They help students acquire disciplinary knowledge, methods, values, and emotional responses, fostering the development of crucial skills. Some scholars argue that the relationship between core competencies and subject-specific core competencies is one of global versus specific, general versus individual, and abstract versus concrete[①]. Unlike general core competencies, which are broader and more abstract, subject-specific core competencies are grounded in the unique characteristics of each discipline, forming a bridge between abstract educational goals and their application in the classroom.

1.2 Subject-Specific Core Competencies: Guiding Curriculum Implementation

Subject-specific core competencies are detailed breakdowns of educational goals and act as a bridge between overarching educational objectives and their application within curriculum implementation. If core competencies require realization in broader educational settings, subject-

① Zhong Qiquan. The Development of Curriculum Based on Core Literacy: Challenges and Issues [J]. Global Education Outlook, 2016(12): 3-25.

specific competencies must be realized within the curriculum implementation process (specifically in classroom instruction).

Then, what does curriculum implementation aimed at developing subject-specific core competencies look like in practice? The "21st Century Learning Framework" from the United States declares that "21st-century education should be based on core knowledge, but this knowledge is not about memorizing facts, rather it refers to disciplinary concepts and ways of thinking, with the goal of enabling students to think like experts in their fields."① This perspective aligns closely with the concept of subject-specific core competencies, which similarly advocates for teaching that transcends rote knowledge acquisition. Its objective is to help students, through their learning of disciplinary content, develop a deep understanding of the subject's essence and principles, which in turn will enable them to apply what they have learned in real-life situations and approach problems from a disciplinary perspective.

This approach encourages students to view and analyze problems from the perspective of their respective disciplines, ultimately developing the specialized thinking patterns necessary for that discipline. Therefore, curriculum implementation aimed at subject-specific core competencies not only involves teaching subject knowledge but also emphasizes understanding the fundamental principles of the discipline. The goal is for students to apply what they learn in real-world situations and approach problems from a disciplinary standpoint.

In practical terms, how does this look in the classroom? How can educators guide students to think like experts in their respective fields? What theoretical principles underpin this teaching model? To answer these questions, this study will analyze a case where three teachers teach the same

---

① Zhang Hua. On the Connotation of Core Literacy [J]. Global Education Outlook, 2016(4): 10-14.

lesson using different approaches. This comparison will shed light on how the teaching of subject-specific core competencies can be effectively implemented in the classroom.

2. Distinguishing False from True: What Kind of Teaching Practices Achieve the "Implementation" of Subject-Specific Core Competencies?

What does the teaching aimed at developing subject-specific core competencies actually look like? This study examines a case of "same lesson, different approach" in an 8th-grade mathematics class to analyze which teaching practices align with the cultivation of subject-specific core competencies and which do not. In this case, the system of two linear equations was taught using the "chickens and rabbits in the same cage" problem, a traditional example from the textbook. Despite using the same content, the three teachers—referred to as Teacher A, Teacher B, and Teacher C—employed different teaching strategies, starting points, and emphasis areas. These differences illustrate three distinct levels of understanding regarding the purpose and significance of teaching. From the perspective of teaching aimed at fostering subject-specific core competencies, the way these lessons were conducted offers valuable insights into what constitutes effective teaching practices. By examining these three different approaches, this study will highlight the practices that truly align with the cultivation of subject-specific competencies and those that fall short.

2.1 Teaching Focused on Problem-Solving Skills

Teacher A begins the lesson by emphasizing the conditions and questions within the problem, following a logical sequence to solve it. Students are taught fixed calculation methods and mathematical skills, with the primary goal being to "solve" the problem. In Teacher A's model, the process involves quickly identifying known quantities, memorizing formulas, setting up equations, and applying algorithms to find the solution. Here, the content is simplified to basic theorems and problem-solving algorithms. Students learn one solution method at a time, practicing with exercises to master additional techniques. However, this approach lacks deep engagement and critical thinking. The teaching goal remains focused on learning problem-solving techniques, with students acquiring methods primarily to pass exams.

2.2 Teaching Focused on Knowledge Application

Teacher B's approach can be analyzed from three key aspects. First, Teacher B designs the lesson to engage student interest, introducing a fun television program at the beginning to energize the class. However, upon closer analysis, it becomes clear that the video only serves as a superficial introduction to the topic, lacking a meaningful connection to the subsequent content. While it creates a lively atmosphere, it does not promote genuine reflection from the students. Second, Teacher B incorporates a more modern method by having students solve the problem using two different techniques. They then discuss and compare these methods to explore their respective characteristics. This student-centered approach is commendable as it provides a more comprehensive understanding of the system of equations and its functions. Lastly, while Teacher B encourages independent thinking, the focus remains on applying techniques to solve systems of equations. The students do not fully understand the origin of the equations, their purpose, or how they relate to real-world situations.

2.3 Teaching Focused on Subject-Specific Core Competencies

Teacher C adopts a more holistic approach, guiding students to understand the mathematical significance of the problem by identifying relationships between quantities. Students are encouraged to express these relationships using natural language, graphical representations, and methods such as arithmetic and one-variable equations. These approaches are then compared to emphasize the value of the system of two linear equations. Teacher C extends the solution to a mathematical model, showcasing how different approaches can solve the same problem.

Teacher C's teaching begins by focusing on the mathematical elements and relationships within the story, encouraging students to recognize the problem's mathematical nature and think about potential solutions. Students express these relationships using natural or semi-symbolic language, helping them understand that equations represent relationships between known and unknown quantities. Through this process, they connect abstract concepts with the study of equations, recognizing that the difference between a system of two linear equations and a single-variable equation is not fundamental but rather a matter of algorithmic complexity. As students reflect on the methods they have used, Teacher C emphasizes that these methods reflect the role of mathematics in solving real-world problems. This understanding extends to a more general concept: that equations can solve a wide range of problems. This abstract understanding deepens the students' conceptualization of the subject. Finally, Teacher C helps students develop a subject-specific mindset by connecting real-world problems with various systematic methods and models for solving them. The teaching process establishes a link between the starting point and the final objective, guiding students through experiences of mathematical abstraction, classification, and modeling. This process also highlights the relevance of mathematical development to real-life problems. Over time, this kind of learning experience will further shape students' understanding of mathematics and encourage them to view and analyze the world through a mathematical lens.

What constitutes teaching that develops subject-specific core competencies? As demonstrated by the analysis, subject-specific core competencies involve recognizing the essence, characteristics, laws, and value of a subject, shaped through the accumulation of subject-specific knowledge and experience. Teaching aimed at cultivating these core competencies does not narrow its goals to simply solving example problems or memorizing techniques. It goes beyond superficial engagement or simplifying difficult material to make it more palatable. Rather, teaching for subject-specific core competencies focuses on the process of discovering knowledge and understanding its significance. This approach connects new and existing knowledge, encourages independent thinking and exploration, and synthesizes learning to form a broader understanding of the subject's value, natural laws, and its relevance to social issues.

3. Deep Focus: What Theoretical Foundations Support Teaching That Cultivates Subject-Specific Core Competencies?

3.1 The Starting Point of Teaching: The Inherent Connection with Experience

At the heart of teaching is the need to spark students' interest. "If personal initiative, enthusiasm, participation, and questioning are not integrated into learning, their interest and motivation will be extinguished in monotonous classroom settings. Their critical thinking and spirit of inquiry will be washed away by the beliefs they adhere to."①. However, the key to fostering true engagement lies not just in sparking interest but also in connecting it to new knowledge. Every child possesses a unique worldview, and all learning and development should be seen as extensions, expansions, and transformations of this worldview.

The starting point of teaching must therefore be grounded in the child's lived or cognitive experience. While this idea is frequently emphasized, its true meaning for learning can sometimes be overlooked. Contemporary

① Paul Ernest. *Philosophy of Mathematics Education*. Translated by Qi Jianhua and Zhang Songzhi, Shanghai: Shanghai Educational Publishing House, 1998, pp. 203-217.

learning theorists suggest that "when learning new concepts and methods, new information rarely integrates seamlessly into existing knowledge structures. Instead, existing knowledge often rejects ideas that do not resonate with it... When new information disrupts their perception of the world, learners are likely to reject it, storing it without ever putting it to use."① Thus, the starting point of teaching should not only evoke students' interest but also trigger their cognitive associations, helping them link prior experiences with new knowledge. These connections are vital for meaningful learning. Effective teaching doesn't simply establish these connections; it ensures students can feel and understand them. The relationship between old and new problem-solving methods, as well as between new concepts and familiar phenomena, must be carefully constructed. Only then can students engage critically with their current understanding, breaking down previous knowledge and fostering the growth of new concepts.②

In the example from Teacher C's class, students begin by articulating equivalence relationships in the problem, then abstract these relationships into a graphical representation. This process activates students' cognitive structures, linking their existing knowledge with the new content. This step is crucial for deeper learning of new concepts. Therefore, teaching must not only set the appropriate context to evoke students' experiences but also activate the knowledge systems within these experiences, enabling a deeper and more integrated form of learning.

3.2 The Foundation of Teaching: Deep Interaction with Texts

The way teachers engage with textbooks reveals their deeper understanding of the material. A teacher's comprehension of course content directly influences their approach to teaching. Some teachers rely heavily on

---

① André Giordan. *Apprendre!*. Translated by Hang Ling, Shanghai: East China Normal University Press, 2015.

② John Dewey. *The School and Society · The Child and the Curriculum*. Taipei: Wunan Publishing, 1989.

the textbook, merely transcribing its content into the lesson, leading to students understanding the material only at their current cognitive level. Others may adjust the content by adding, removing, or rearranging material, making the textbook content come alive and transforming static text into dynamic student experiences. However, some teachers go beyond superficial interactions with the text and engage in "deep interaction," considering the material from the perspective of subject matter experts. These teachers guide students to uncover the deeper meanings within the text, connecting it to their experiences and helping them discover the concepts behind the material. This process fosters reflective insight and promotes the integration of principles, enabling students to move from observing phenomena to identifying general rules.

In the case study presented, the teacher's approach to using the textbook reflects various levels of engagement. In one scenario, reading the example problem leads students to focus solely on solving that specific problem. In another, expanding the example to cover a category of similar problems helps students learn techniques for solving other related problems. However, when the teacher uses the example to stimulate continuous thinking—such as by exploring equivalence relationships—students are guided to understand the core concepts of equations. This deeper interaction with the material helps students connect abstract mathematical principles to broader contexts. Through this approach, students begin to engage with the essence of the subject, which in turn allows them to transfer their learning to new and varied contexts. This type of interaction has profound implications for developing students' subject-specific core competencies, helping them see the value of their learning beyond isolated examples.

3.3 The Teaching Approach: An Active Exploration of the World

Dewey compared the content of textbooks to maps, stating that "a map is a summary, an organized arrangement of prior experiences, and can serve as a guide for future experiences."[①]

While maps aid in memory and observation, they detach from the context present at the time of discovery. True learning, however, involves using the map as a guide for active exploration. Teachers, therefore, should intentionally guide students in using the "map" to explore the unknown world.

In the case study, Teacher A merely follows the textbook format. Students identify the logical relationships in the example problem, memorize key concepts, and repeat these limited logical relationships in exercises, reinforcing their memorization. However, this approach makes it difficult for students to transfer their knowledge to new problems. Teacher A addresses this challenge by having students complete numerous exercises, which helps them construct a knowledge framework to prepare for different types of exam questions.

Teacher B, in contrast, emphasizes the characteristics of the example problem, explaining the methods and strategies for solving it. This approach is akin to providing students with a complete "map," guiding them through the entire process. However, students' thinking remains confined to the map, engaging only with abstract solutions. Essentially, this constitutes surface-level learning.

Teacher C, however, encourages students to explore all possible methods for solving the problem and reflects on the continuity and transitions within those methods, exploring the inherent tension and space in problem-solving. Additionally, Teacher C emphasizes the core concept of finding

---

① John Dewey. *The School and Society · The Child and the Curriculum*. Taipei: Wunan Publishing, 1989

equivalence relationships, enabling students to move beyond abstract solutions and experience the adventure of creating their own "map" of equations. This process of map-making is at the heart of developing core competencies in the subject. Developing these competencies requires not only understanding the ideas themselves but also an awareness of these ideas and their application.

3.4 The End Goal of Teaching: Confronting the Essence and Meaning of Knowledge

The core competencies of a subject represent the ultimate objectives of its teaching. Moving beyond simple knowledge delivery and skill training, the focus of current curriculum reforms is on cultivating subject-specific concepts and ways of thinking. When disciplinary knowledge is elevated to core competencies, it means helping students integrate knowledge into a broader context—one that spans history, the present, and the future. Through interconnected and developmental thinking, students can understand, grasp, experience, and apply knowledge, ultimately encountering the essence and meaning of what they are learning. Moreover, they should be able to use systematic knowledge to interpret the world, thereby shaping attitudes toward nature, society, and others. Therefore, the development of disciplinary core competencies involves not only mastering the knowledge itself but also understanding the logic of knowledge and its deeper meaning.

First, teachers must design instruction that links students' existing knowledge with new information. They should anticipate how learners will absorb new knowledge based on their prior understanding, recognizing that new knowledge expands students' worldview and informs their self-identity, as well as their understanding of nature, society, and others. This approach engages students by showing them how new knowledge is relevant to their lives, motivating them to explore it further. As Whitehead noted, "Learners are motivated not by the correctness of new knowledge, but by its value."①

Second, teaching should guide students to comprehend the origins, essence, principles, and significance of knowledge, helping them link it to past, present, and future contexts. Teachers should show students how to apply knowledge to solve real-world problems. As Whitehead emphasized, "Knowledge that cannot be applied is harmful... Knowledge should be interrelated and used holistically, and various propositions can be applied in multiple sequences... Children should understand when they are proving knowledge and when they are using it."②For instance, in Teacher B's class, students learned how to solve equations, but their understanding was limited to answering problems others had designed. Teacher C, however, connected graphical methods, arithmetic methods, and equations with one or two variables. This allowed students to appreciate the differences between these methods, particularly how changes in methods influence their thinking. As a result, students not only began to understand the value and application of solving equations but also saw how mathematical thinking itself can evolve. The new knowledge was integrated into a broader, connected framework of ideas, allowing students to view it from a higher perspective—almost like experts—and even prepare for future learning. This deeper understanding helped them apply new knowledge to current problems and shaped their broader view of the world.

3.5 The Challenge of Teaching: The "Balanced Interaction" of Elements

Whitehead likened the selection of teaching methods to the "rhythm" of teaching, a rhythm that encompasses the timing, order, and frequency of different methods and activities. This rhythm involves choosing the right

① Alfred North Whitehead. *The Aims of Education*. Translated by Zhuang Lianping and Wang Lizhong, Shanghai: Wenhui Publishing House, 2012, pp. 6-7.
② Alfred North Whitehead. *The Aims of Education*. Translated by Zhuang Lianping and Wang Lizhong, Shanghai: Wenhui Publishing House, 2012, pp. 43.

moments for these strategies, aligning them with the content, the teacher's style, and the students' needs.

4. Knowledge vs. Thinking Skills

The debate over the relative importance of knowledge and thinking skills has long been central in education. The relationship between the two, and their mutual reinforcement, dictates that both should be integral to teaching and learning. Whitehead emphasized that students' minds are not passive vessels into which knowledge is simply poured; rather, knowledge serves as "food" for developing minds. While acquiring knowledge is essential, students are not mere "containers" for storing information. Whitehead argued that the ultimate goal of education is not only to convey knowledge but also to develop wisdom—an understanding of how to process, select, and apply knowledge. He compared the acquisition of wisdom and knowledge to freedom and training: "The only way to wisdom is to have absolute freedom in the face of knowledge; however, the only way to knowledge is through systematic training in facts." For Whitehead, the rhythm of education lies in balancing freedom and training. These two principles should not conflict but rather be adjusted to suit the natural development of each child's personality. [①]

In this way, both freedom (which nurtures thinking) and training (which consolidates knowledge) are essential. In an ideal educational system, training should naturally lead to free choice, and freedom should be enhanced through training. Without exploring the essence of a problem, knowledge cannot be solidified, nor can thinking be trained. This is reflected in an integrated approach to teaching goals, which includes knowledge, skills, processes, and attitudes.

① John Dewey. *The Child and the Curriculum*. Translated by Lin Baoshan and Kang Chunzhi, Taipei: Wunan Publishing, 1990, p. 112.

5. Subject Essence and Learner-Centeredness

Current educational reforms emphasize a shift from "teaching-centered" to "learning-centered" classrooms, a logical and progressive approach. Broadly speaking, teaching is part of a larger, orderly learning process in which students actively engage under the teacher's guidance. Teachers must align the curriculum with students' cognitive development, using methods appropriate for their learning stage. However, in response to these reforms, many schools emphasize autonomous and collaborative learning, often minimizing direct teacher instruction. While these changes help combat the entrenched lecture-style teaching, one must question whether this represents the ideal classroom dynamic.

The goal of teaching is to help students construct their own knowledge framework. A teacher's flawless delivery does not automatically guarantee effective student learning, nor does the abandonment of complete teacher explanations necessarily ensure better learning outcomes. In the classroom, while students should have time for independent and collaborative learning, teachers must remain clear on what students are learning—especially whether they are addressing the core concepts of the subject and using its specific modes of thinking.

Both the essence of the subject and learner-centeredness must be considered when designing teaching strategies. As Dewey put it, the relationship between these two elements is like the two ends of an educational process connected by a straight line: the child's current level of understanding and the truths of the subject determine the teaching method. The shift in classrooms is not a move from a subject-centered to a student-centered focus, but rather a transition towards enhancing student learning, which remains deeply tied to the discipline's core content and methods.

The original article was published in *Curriculum, Teaching Materials, and Methodology*, 2017, Issue 9 (Lyu Lijie, Han Jiwei, Zhang Xiaojuan).

Chapter 8 A Hierarchical Analysis of Core Competencies in the Transformation of School Curricula

The promotion of curriculum reform based on students' core competencies has become a global trend, attracting significant attention from international organizations such as the European Union, as well as from many countries and regions around the world. In 2014, China issued the *"Opinions on Deepening Curriculum Reform to Implement the Fundamental Task of Moral Education"* by the Ministry of Education, which defined core competencies as "the essential qualities and key abilities that students need to adapt to lifelong development and societal progress." The establishment of a core competency system for student development is crucial in determining the direction of school education and the development of national and school curricula. Core competencies must be integrated into national curricula, school educational philosophies, and teachers' instructional practices, eventually guiding personalized student development plans.

1. Core Competencies and School Educational Philosophy

1.1 Characteristics of Core Competencies

1. Key Importance

Core competencies are fundamental—they represent the most essential qualities among the many competencies needed for an individual's lifelong development. These competencies are not comprehensive but rather indispensable in specific life contexts. Their significance lies in their foundational nature and their universality. Core competencies are the shared qualities that every individual must possess, laying the foundation for future development. The importance of core competencies is not determined by the individual but by the collective, reflecting societal requirements at a specific time and place. Although the concept of core competencies is relatively new, it is timeless. Its key characteristics change with different eras. For example, physical health was a core competency in the agricultural era, as it was crucial for survival and reproduction. However, in the information era, physical health is considered a basic competency rather than a core one.

2. Comprehensiveness

The comprehensiveness of core competencies manifests in two dimensions: static and dynamic. Static comprehensiveness refers to the integration of students' knowledge, skills, emotions, attitudes, and values within core competencies. These competencies do not refer to isolated knowledge, skills, or thoughts; rather, they synthesize these elements. Core competencies address not only cognitive aspects but also emotional and attitudinal dimensions, thus correcting the previous educational bias toward knowledge at the expense of abilities, attitudes, and values. This approach emphasizes continuous, integrated cultivation. Dynamic comprehensiveness refers to how these competencies are applied in specific actions and contexts. No single core competency can independently solve a problem. Instead, core competencies intersect and integrate, forming strategies and solutions to achieve a goal.

3. Relevance

Core competencies connect individual development with societal progress, linking personal values with societal values. From the individual's perspective, the development of core competencies enables a person to better realize their own value and adapt to future societal changes. From a societal perspective, core competencies are both a product of and a foundation for societal development. Societal progress is deeply tied to the enhancement of individual qualities. Core competencies thus reflect both personal self-requirements and societal expectations, making them highly significant. This dual relevance has positive implications for both the individual and society.

4. Generativity

Core competencies exhibit generativity, meaning they evolve over time. Initially, core competencies are stable, but they later demonstrate generative qualities. Generativity in core competencies encompasses two aspects: cumulative and transformative. Cumulative generativity refers to the gradual formation of a core competency, indicating that it is not achieved all at once but requires continual development and refinement. At different stages, individuals demonstrate different levels of core competencies. Transformative generativity refers to the emergence of new competencies in response to societal demands. These competencies, once recognized, are incorporated into the developmental framework for students.

1.2 Student Competencies in the School Educational Philosophy Framework

Every school should have its own educational philosophy, which reflects the values of its educational stakeholders, including the principal and teachers. This educational philosophy is unique to each institution and reflects a personalized understanding of common educational principles, as well as an individualized expectations of education significance. The philosophy manifests through the school's distinctive cultural values, which develop within a social structure where people have long interacted. In this context, social interactions naturally form standards, customs, and value orientations, resulting in schools with unique cultural and educational philosophies. These philosophies deeply influence the actions of the school's educators and may lead to clear aspirations about the meaning of education.

In recent years, many schools in China have consciously reflected on and clearly articulated their educational philosophies. This study examined the websites of 20 exemplary high schools across the country and analyzed their development plans. The analysis revealed that schools typically present two levels of articulation when defining their development direction: macro educational goals and specific expected student outcomes. At the macro level, the educational philosophy is expressed as an ideal description of the type of person the school aims to cultivate. These descriptions often include terms such as "comprehensive development," "individualized development," "harmonious development," or "multidimensional development." These philosophies reflect the school's values regarding the uniqueness of student development and guide curriculum planning and the creation of school-based courses.

At the second level, the macro educational goals are broken down to describe the characteristics and abilities that the school seeks to cultivate through its educational process, which are viewed as the desired educational outcomes. From the development plans of the 20 exemplary high schools, it is clear that some schools explicitly state their intention to develop student competencies, while others implicitly embed these goals within their overall curriculum or educational objectives. The competencies emphasized include qualities such as "learning to care," "learning to create," "leadership qualities," "sound character," "national sentiment," "international standards," and "innovation abilities." Some schools focus on the nature of the competencies, such as "excellence," "potential," and "the full development of individuality."

1.3 The School's Pursuit of Personalized Core Competencies for Students

A school's educational philosophy reflects both national educational guidelines and developmental goals, while also embodying the school's unique needs and characteristics. The articulation of student competencies within a school should break down this educational philosophy and represent a personalized and distinctive expression of core competencies. This means that many schools, even before the introduction of a national framework for core competencies, were already consciously exploring issues related to students' shared competencies, core competencies, and related concepts. The introduction of national core competencies should not be viewed as a shift in educational objectives but rather as a further clarification. The competencies expressed by schools should be seen as personalized interpretations, based on national educational goals, that consider developmental stages, school characteristics, and student needs.

2. The Role of Student Literacy in the Transformation of School Curriculum

The educational philosophy of a school must be translated into its curriculum system, content, and teaching practices. American scholar John Goodlad, in response to the hierarchical nature of curricula, divides it into five levels: philosophical curriculum, formal curriculum, perceived curriculum, operational curriculum, and experiential curriculum.[①] Other scholars, such as Glatthorn, Brophy J.E., and Posner, have also proposed their own interpretations of curriculum hierarchy. If we regard the school's educational philosophy as the philosophical curriculum, the issue arises of how this philosophy is transformed across the different curriculum levels. In this transformation process, student core literacy serves both as the goal and the intermediary.

2.1 On Curriculum Transformation

What is curriculum transformation? Taiwanese scholar Huang Zhengjie defines it as "the process of gradually transforming abstract and valuable concepts into specific, feasible curricula, based on the principles of teacher

---

① Goodlanji. Curriculum inquiry: the study of curriculum practice [M]. New York: McGraw-Hill,1979:58-64.

instruction and student learning, in order to facilitate effective teaching by teachers and effective learning by students." ① Currently, two major focuses dominate the discussion of curriculum transformation: one is the transformation of the curriculum based on multiculturalism or multicultural education theory, and the other is transformation at different hierarchical levels of the curriculum. The transformation of a multicultural curriculum involves introducing previously underexplored issues—such as ethnicity, race, gender, and religion—into the existing curriculum. This can be achieved through three main methods: infusion, integration, and specialization.② Infusion involves embedding new concepts and content into the existing curriculum, thereby influencing student learning. Integration connects new concepts with the current curriculum, although it may not penetrate deeply. Specialization involves developing specific topics around certain concepts, allowing students to delve deeply into these issues. In essence, multicultural curriculum transformation involves integrating multicultural elements into the existing curriculum. The transformation across hierarchical levels refers to changing the form of the curriculum while maintaining internal consistency between elements at each level. This process of transforming abstract concepts into concrete plans is the transformation from policy-based curriculum to one understood by teachers, and from a designed curriculum to an experiential curriculum for students. In practice, curriculum elements may become diluted, distorted, misinterpreted, or expanded as they move between these levels.

① Cai Qingtian, Chen Yanxing. The Curriculum Transformation of National Core Literacy [J]. Curriculum and Teaching, 2013(3): 65.
② Huang Zhengjie. Curriculum Design [M]. Taipei: Donghua Book Company, 1991: 11.

2.2 The Role of Student Literacy in the Transformation Between Curriculum Levels

Curriculum variation across different levels occurs due to the disconnect between abstract concepts and concrete plans, between macro and micro levels, and between textual and practical aspects. Core literacy serves as the intermediary, bridging these gaps. It makes the educational goals tangible, explicit, and systematic. By using core literacy, the process of curriculum transformation can be transcribed and translated across hierarchical levels, based on a metaphor borrowed from the intergenerational transmission of genes in biology.

If we view the school's educational philosophy as the *DNA* of the curriculum, then core literacy functions as the *messenger RNA* that transmits this *DNA*. The function of messenger RNA is to precisely convey genetic information encoded in the DNA. This process involves two steps: the first is Transcription, where messenger RNA transcribes genetic information from the DNA into a single-stranded sequence, creating a template. The second is Translation, where the template, carrying genetic information, guides the synthesis of proteins, serving as a model for the production of new proteins. Transcription and translation are essential steps in the transmission of genetic information. Using this biological process as a metaphor, we can understand the role of core literacy in the transformation of curriculum. Just as messenger RNA transmits genetic information, core literacy can guide the connection and transformation between different curriculum levels through transcription and translation.

At the school level, the demand for student literacy functions as the *messenger RNA* of the school's educational philosophy, transmitting the school's educational goals. The demand for student literacy makes the educational objectives inherent in the philosophy explicit, clearly defining the expected outcomes—essentially *transcribing* them—thereby making the philosophy visible and sequenced. This explicit sequence carries the school's understanding of education, guiding and framing the educational process, including curriculum design and teaching, thus *translating* it. The literacy system, with its structure, integrates curriculum elements, selecting those that are valuable and aligning them with the literacy system to ensure consistency. This translation process guides the development of school curriculum planning and systems, as well as helps teachers interpret the current curriculum's meanings and formulate personalized guidance for student development.

The process of curriculum transformation between hierarchical levels, mediated by core literacy, is illustrated in Figure 2-1.

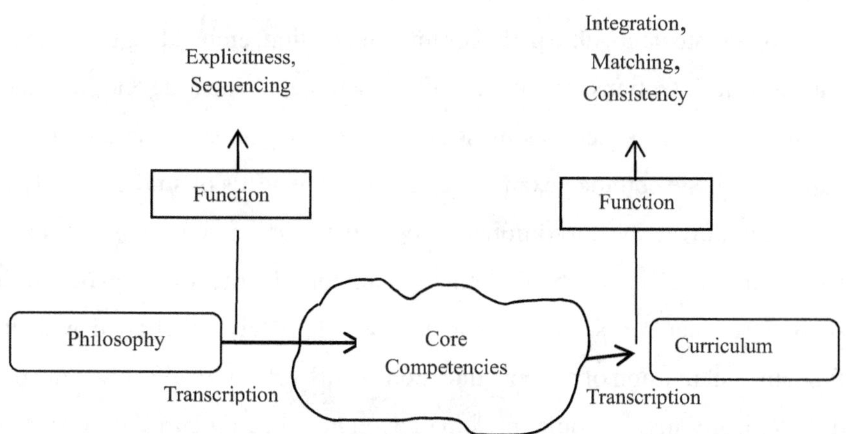

Figure 2-1: The Process of Curriculum Level Transformation Mediated by Core Competencies

3. Three Levels of Curriculum Transformation at the School Level

3.1 Transformation from Intent to Plan: School Curriculum Structure Based on Student Competencies

The first level of transformation involves the shift from educational philosophy to a concrete school curriculum plan. This transition takes educational ideas and intentions and translates them into a systematic, structured curriculum. The outcome of this transformation is the planned curriculum structure, which can be seen as the school's curriculum map. Starting with the development of student competencies and focusing on the structure of these competencies, the school designs its curriculum around these core areas. This logical approach breaks down the educational philosophy into actionable paths for implementation, embedding the school's educational intentions in its teaching methods. When developing their curriculum systems, schools must balance various considerations—such as national college entrance exam requirements, the needs of students applying to foreign universities, traditional school rituals, and activity-based courses. However, these factors should be integrated into the main framework of the school's curriculum structure, which must ultimately be aligned with the fundamental mission of school education and its value pursuits. Over the past decade, many high schools in China have embarked on curriculum reform, introducing a range of school-based courses and developing comprehensive curriculum plans. Yet, some schools encounter challenges when planning their curricula.

1. Curriculum Based on Practical Functions

In some schools, the curriculum is organized according to its practical functions or course origins. For instance, one school may categorize its curriculum into: a) Basic courses (mandatory national courses); b) Extension courses (elective subjects related to the college entrance exam); c) Moral education courses (including traditional ritual education and newer subjects such as career planning and labor education); d) Specialized development courses (catering to students' arts, sports, and extracurricular activities); e) University preparatory courses (offering credits for students applying to universities abroad). While this approach offers a rich variety of content that can foster well-rounded student development, it often lacks a consistent connection to the school's educational philosophy. This system fails to clearly demonstrate how the educational philosophy is being implemented and how the school's competency goals are being addressed through its courses.

2. Curriculum Based on Management Hierarchy

Other schools divide their curriculum into national, regional, and school-based categories. While this division reflects an effort to tailor the curriculum to local needs, it does not clearly show the structured thought behind the curriculum planning or its intended outcomes. For example, the school may not specify which knowledge and skills each course aims to develop in students, nor identify which courses are meant for specific student groups.

3. Curriculum Based on Work Division

Some schools design their curriculum based on internal management structures. For example, the curriculum might be divided into national courses, moral education courses, club courses, and teacher development courses (focused on professional development for school staff). While this division aligns with the internal workings of the school's administration, it fails to clarify the core educational values of the curriculum. Moreover, teacher development courses are not appropriate to include in the formal student curriculum; the curriculum is meant to serve students, not staff development. Teacher training should be handled separately from the student-centered curriculum. Additionally, the categories of courses may overlap in content.

In planning the curriculum, schools must reflect not only on the existing curriculum base but also on their educational philosophy and developmental goals. This requires a synthesis of established courses and the broader educational vision. "Using a more systematic and sustainable transformation approach is especially important, as it can alter both the learning experience and the course objectives." ① That is, A systematic and sustainable transformation approach is essential, as it can significantly reshape both the learning experience and the objectives of each course.Therefore, the curriculum system should be designed around student competency demands. The student competency framework should serve as a model to organize the school's curriculum. This study suggests that the school's curriculum structure can be conceptualized along at least two dimensions:

a) Fields of Competency: This refers to the areas targeted by the curriculum to develop core competencies. Drawing from the eight fields of the national high school curriculum, schools can create a common yet distinctive curriculum content structure that aligns with their competency framework. For example, common competencies might include humanities, scientific, and artistic literacy, while school-specific competencies could include survival skills, leadership abilities, and so on.

b) Types of Courses: This dimension categorizes courses based on content and the degree of integration between knowledge and skills. Possible categories include: extension courses, enrichment courses, integrated courses, inquiry-based courses, and self-directed courses.

---

① Huang, C. J. (2013). The Exploration of an Integrated Investigation Conceptual Framework for Curriculum Transformation. Curriculum and Teaching, 2013(3): 11.

Core competencies, especially fundamental ones, arise from the integration of knowledge, skills, and attitudes. Depending on the course type, the function of developing competencies will vary. A comprehensive knowledge system that integrates these elements can more directly support competency development.

These two dimensions can be represented visually in a two-dimensional diagram. In the vertical dimension, each course targets specific student competencies. The horizontal dimension integrates national and school-based courses, allowing flexibility. While even the basic curriculum will incorporate national elements, the school-based curriculum will increasingly feature content developed autonomously by the school. The mode of course implementation will also become more open and integrated.

This structure not only allows educational leaders to reflect on whether the curriculum offered to students is balanced and aligned with the school's educational intentions, but it also provides a clear curriculum map. Such a map shows how courses are designed to cultivate specific competencies and provides opportunities for reflection and adjustment where needed.

3.2 Transformation from Text to Experience: Teaching Understanding Directed Toward Student Competencies

The learning process for students involves transforming the textbook-based curriculum into an experiential curriculum. This process requires guidance, instruction, and support from teachers. When designing lessons, teachers must consider how to turn the "objectified" textbook curriculum into meaningful student experiences, building on their prior knowledge. This design process involves both the teacher's understanding of the curriculum content and their ability to effectively execute that understanding.

Recent years have seen significant changes in classroom teaching in China, with the introduction of new reform models. However, certain issues persist. For example, some teachers, relying on their existing teaching experience or merely following exam syllabi, reduce curriculum content to a few key points—such as specific knowledge, the derivation of formulas, or the application of rules. These approaches often overlook the deeper disciplinary thinking, methods, and broader social significance that the content may carry. Even in classrooms where teaching methods have been reformed, if a teacher's understanding of the curriculum content has not evolved, these reforms will have limited success in transforming student experiences.

Furthermore, while the use of guided learning plans has increased students' sense of purpose and autonomy, many of these plans are essentially pre-distributed exercises. For example, they might consist of theorems to memorize before class, exercises to complete in group discussions, or conclusions to present in class. With the growing use of multimedia technology in schools, much of this technology is still primarily aimed at helping students memorize and reproduce knowledge, theorems, and rules presented in the curriculum. Without appropriate teaching methods and tools, this content cannot achieve its educational goals, and students' understanding of the material remains superficial.

If teachers limit their understanding of the curriculum text and rely on methods that merely align with student learning characteristics, the teaching objectives cannot be fully realized. Thus, in the process of understanding, designing, and implementing the curriculum, teachers need to ensure that the curriculum text serves not as an end in itself but as a tool for the development of student competencies. The ultimate goal is to develop student competencies, with the curriculum text simply facilitating that goal. The effectiveness of this tool depends on how teachers approach and execute its development.

Teaching design should be guided by the goal of cultivating student competencies. This requires teachers to extract the educational potential embedded within the curriculum content. Competencies, a blend of character and ability, are formed through the interaction between students and their environment. A competency-driven curriculum should be experiential and integrative, engaging students fully and transforming textbook knowledge into experiential learning through active participation.

To foster student competencies, teachers must analyze not only the knowledge and skill gradients in the curriculum but also the potential for multi-dimensional and multi-level growth in student experiences. These experiences must align with the intended competency framework. Schwab refers to this latent potential as "curriculum potential," [①] which describes the "curriculum embedded in subject content that has the potential to help students grow and develop." Recognizing and extracting this potential is a critical first step in designing effective teaching. Only by extracting these elements can teachers gather valuable components to foster student competencies. Teacher-designed curricula often begin with an analysis of the textbook.

When designing lessons, teachers must uncover and organize the potential of the curriculum. According to American scholar Ben Peretz[②], curriculum design is enriched when multiple perspectives are applied, rather than a single, narrow viewpoint. Teachers, as "users and developers" of the curriculum, bear part of the responsibility for curriculum development. While teachers may not be involved in the curriculum's initial design phase, they have the autonomy and flexibility to adapt the curriculum during implementation. This allows them to infuse their own insights into the teaching process. As Bresler argues, teachers should not merely be faithful

---

① Schwabjj. The practical 3: translation into curriculum [J]. School Review,1973 (81):501-522.
② Ben-Peretzm. The concept of curriculum potential [J]. Curriculum Theory Network, 1975(2):151-159.

executors of the curriculum but should adapt it to fit the specific needs of their classroom environments.

To analyze the potential of the curriculum, scholar Deng Zongyi suggests four thematic clues that guide teachers in exploring the curriculum's latent educational value①:

1. Exploration Clue: Teachers should identify the core concepts within the curriculum content, explore how these concepts relate to other themes, and determine whether there are additional related topics worth exploring. This step involves understanding the main ideas and their interconnections.

2. Socio-Cultural Clue: Teachers should consider the significance of the curriculum's themes for students, society, and the world at large. This includes discussing how themes manifest in various socio-cultural contexts, exploring different perspectives, and fostering relevant attitudes and values.

3. Psychological-Epistemological Clue: This clue focuses on students' prior knowledge and skills. Teachers should think about what students need to know before engaging with the curriculum content and how this knowledge connects with students' previous learning experiences. The goal is to ensure that students can build on their existing knowledge and experiences.

4. Educational Transformation Clue: Teachers should focus on activities that will expand students' perspectives and provide opportunities for problem-solving, independent learning, and interdisciplinary exploration. This clue also considers how assessment methods can support teaching and how available resources can be used to achieve educational goals.

These four clues serve as a comprehensive framework for teachers to analyze the curriculum from multiple angles. Teachers can apply these clues

---

① Deng Z. Revisiting curriculum potential [J]. Curriculum Inquiry, 2011(3):538-559.

to interpret curriculum content more holistically, thereby enriching the teaching process. Different subjects and teaching styles may lead to different approaches to curriculum analysis, but the common goal is always to cultivate student competencies.

By adhering to this competency framework, teachers can avoid narrowing their focus to a limited range of content or oversimplifying their teaching methods. Instead, they are encouraged to engage students more deeply and provide transformative learning experiences that promote the development of essential skills and competencies.

3.3 Transformation of Commonality into Individuality: Student Development Plans Based on Student Competencies

Core competencies form the foundation of student competencies. These competencies represent the essential skills and attributes that all students should develop. However, the notion of common competencies does not imply that all students will attain them at the same level. For any given competency, different students will follow distinct paths to achieve it. The true value of the school curriculum lies in its ability to transform common competencies into individualized competency systems that cater to the unique characteristics and needs of each student. This transformation process addresses several key issues:

1. Implementation of Course Selectivity

In the latest curriculum reforms, elective modules have been integrated into high school courses, supplementing the traditional division between arts and sciences to better address the diverse needs of students. With recent adjustments to the college entrance exam system, the rigid arts-sciences division has been removed, giving students more flexibility to choose the subjects they wish to study. This shift marks progress in catering to students' individual competency inclinations. However, compared to high school systems in other countries or regions, applied courses remain relatively scarce in China. For instance, Hong Kong's new educational system has added a range of applied learning courses in fields such as creative learning, media and communication, business, management and law, services, applied sciences, and engineering and production. These courses are designed to meet students' diverse needs. High schools in mainland China could adopt similar approaches through school-based curricula, providing students with different "menus" of courses that cater to various competency inclinations. By offering such options, schools can help students pursue the same competencies but through different pathways tailored to their individual interests.

2. Layered Teaching

Layered teaching goes beyond simply grouping students by their learning levels or abilities and assigning them different content. It also involves offering various forms of content representation and teaching activities tailored to students' cognitive tendencies, interests, and prior knowledge. Strategies for layered teaching include adjusting the sequence of learning tasks, modifying the pace and timing of lessons, and varying student groupings based on different subjects or topics. Teachers can encourage students to present their learning or research findings in different formats, give targeted praise to specific students, and provide differentiated rewards. This approach fosters an environment where students can access and engage with the curriculum in ways that suit their unique learning profiles.

3. Providing Student Support Systems

As high school education continues to expand, its function and characteristics will evolve, with a growing emphasis on fairness in the educational process. Sociologist John Rawls' well-known principles of social justice highlight the importance of equality, respect for differences, and compensation for deficiencies[①]. In this context, high school education must address not only differences in the types of competencies students possess but also the disparities in their competency levels. For students facing academic challenges or developmental barriers, individualized support is crucial. However, the current educational system in China lacks personalized classes and specialized support teachers. To establish such systems, schools must ensure they have a sufficient number of qualified teachers, specialized resources, and structural adjustments in both teacher allocation and teaching management. From intent to plan, text to experience, and commonality to individuality: A unified Framework for Curriculum Transformation. The three transformations—moving from intent to plan, from text to experience, and from commonality to individuality—represent different levels of curriculum change. At each level, the framework of student core competencies plays a crucial role in guiding the planning and structuring of various curriculum elements. This approach ensures that the creation of new curricular forms is purposeful and directed. It prevents the gap between curriculum levels from becoming a process of diminishing returns, and instead helps to align educational practices with the broader goal of student competency development.

[Originally published in *Curriculum · Textbooks · Teaching Methods* in the November 2016 issue, authored by Lyu Lijie and Li Gang.]

① John Rawls. A Theory of Justice. Translated by He Huaihong, He Baogang, and Liao Shenbai, Beijing: China Social Sciences Press, 2009, pp. 50-57.

Part 3 Curriculum Implementation and Assessment

Chapter 9 Context-Based Teaching and Group Discussions—Reflections on Teaching Strategies in the New Curriculum

Under the guidance of the new curriculum, many teachers have reconsidered the essence of education and actively applied their insights in their classroom teaching. As key agents of change and partners in educational reform, experimental teachers provide valuable case studies for researching curriculum implementation. This section analyzes and reflects on two common yet often overlooked teaching phenomena within the context of the new curriculum.

1. Situational Teaching

What is situational teaching? Situational teaching theory, which emerged in the West in the 1980s, is rooted in cognitive psychology and transformative perspectives on knowledge. The core idea is that knowledge is inherently contextual—it is an activity, part of a larger social and cultural framework, and evolves through real-world application. The acquisition of knowledge is an interactive process between individuals and their environment rather than a mere accumulation of isolated facts. Situational teaching and learning differ from traditional methods in several key ways: A. promoting transfer: Situational cognition enables learners to understand the real-world relevance of their learning, exposing the challenges and context behind their thinking. Traditional learning, by contrast, often simplifies or idealizes knowledge, rendering it abstract and disconnected from practical application. As a result, students may acquire knowledge at a superficial level—primarily for classroom use or exam preparation—without developing the ability to apply it in real-life contexts. Their understanding of decontextualized knowledge is often limited to its literal interpretation, which restricts its usefulness to academic assessments rather than real-world problem-solving; B. Facilitating deeper understanding: Traditional learning environments frequently rely on artificial and overly simplified scenarios designed to align with predefined cognitive pathways. These pathways, structured by curriculum developers and teachers, assume universal validity, effectiveness, organization, and scientific rigor. However, research indicates that in everyday life, individuals tend to employ more practical, context-dependent strategies. For instance, when grocery shopping, people often rely on mental arithmetic or estimations, using environmental cues rather than rigid formulas[①]. This underscores the significance of situational learning: it fosters deeper, more meaningful engagement with content by mirroring authentic cognitive processes. C. encouraging subjective construction: In situational learning, students immersed in real-world contexts are more likely to develop curiosity, a passion for problem-solving, and a sense of responsibility. These intrinsic motivations drive students to explore, validate, and expand their knowledge, leading to the creation of personalized cognitive pathways. Such individualized learning trajectories are shaped by students' unique experiences, promoting deeper and more authentic understanding.

1.1 Classroom Observation Excerpts

Classroom Observation Excerpt 1: First-Grade Math Lesson

Lesson Content: Addition and subtraction of two-digit numbers without carrying or borrowing.

Teacher: "Do you know how many classes our school has in total?" (The teacher displays a slide with a photo of the school.)

(Students react with excitement and begin discussing.)

---

① Gao Wen. The Role of Context and Content in Situated Cognition: A Discussion on the Theoretical Foundations of Situated Cognition and the Design of Learning Environments, Part I [J]. Foreign Education Information, 1997(4).

Teacher: "Look at our beautiful school!" (Writes on the board: Six first-grade classes, eight second-grade classes, eight third-grade classes…) "Who can calculate the total number of classes?"

(A student blurts out, "Count the windows!" The teacher reminds students to raise their hands before answering.)

(The teacher guides the class through the addition process.)

Teacher: "Now, do you know how many teachers we have in total?" (Displays a group photo of teachers.)

Teacher: "This picture was taken on last year's Teachers' Day. Can you estimate how many teachers there are?"

(Students call out guesses: "150," "200," "300"…)

Teacher: "How can we accurately calculate the total number of teachers?"

A male student suggests: "We can add up the teachers from each class."

Teacher: "That method might not be the most efficient." (Writes on the board: 18 female math teachers, 20 male math teachers; 38 Chinese teachers, 10 male Chinese teachers and displays a table with teacher numbers by subject.)

(The class works together to solve the addition problem.)

Classroom Observation Excerpt 2: Second-Grade Math Lesson

Lesson Content: Recognizing coins.

(The teacher displays a slide showing a real-life scenario: A boy, Xiaoming, holding a banknote at the cashier, with a girl, Lingling, behind him carrying various coins.)

Teacher: "Xiaoming wants to buy a pencil, but the cashier doesn't have enough change. What should he do?"

A student suggests: "Go to the bank and exchange money!"

Teacher: (Gestures toward the image.) "Look closely—Lingling behind Xiaoming has a lot of loose change. What could Xiaoming do instead?"

Analysis of Situational Teaching

In both cases, the teachers employed situational teaching strategies to move beyond the traditional approach of "teaching formulas—memorizing formulas—practicing formulas." Their goal was to connect mathematical principles to students' real-life experiences, making lessons more engaging and dynamic. A review of their lesson plans, teaching methods, and post-lesson reflections suggests that both teachers reimagined the curriculum. Rather than serving as mere "vocal versions of the textbook," they embraced the concept of the "teacher curriculum," fostering an interactive, student-centered classroom. Moreover, the teachers' selection of situational contexts was highly effective. On one hand, they successfully linked real-world scenarios to the mathematical content. On the other hand, they chose familiar and relatable situations from students' everyday lives, which increased their engagement and sustained attention compared to traditional instruction. These observations align with the goals of the new curriculum reform. However, a deeper analysis reveals that the teachers' understanding of situational teaching requires further refinement. After all, situational teaching as a meaningful concept is not just a label. Ideally, situational teaching should evolve from merely embedding real-world examples into instruction to creating meaningful, context-driven learning experiences that encourage critical thinking and problem-solving.

In effective situational teaching, students should not be passive recipients of information but active participants in the learning process. They should engage with real-world situations, devise solutions to problems, seek meaningful information, and analyze, filter, and organize that information until they reach a resolution. This process should be open-ended, allowing students to construct personal meaning through interaction with the situation. The problem-solving tools, information sources, methods, and cognitive pathways should be tailored to the learner's individual needs and preferences. In Case 1, for example, the teacher introduced a situational problem about *"learning about our school,"* a topic well within the students' *zone of proximal development* and likely to spark enthusiasm for thinking and action. However, after posing the problem, the teacher immediately provided all the necessary numerical data (such as the number of teachers per subject). This approach limited the students' engagement with the problem and specifically undermined the connection between the students' thinking and the designed situation, as the teacher had already predetermined the conditions for solving it. The essence of situational teaching is not simply embedding a fixed problem-solving strategy within a narrative but fostering open-ended exploration that allows students to generate multiple solutions. This suggests that many educators misunderstand situational teaching, reducing it to a structured scenario where the solution path is already determined. In this case, although the teacher effectively used slides and photos to create an engaging scenario, the problem-solving process remained largely teacher-directed. A more effective approach would have been to extend the situation by encouraging students to investigate further—perhaps by visiting classrooms, conducting surveys, or even consulting the principal for data. Such an approach would have led to multiple solutions, deepened students' understanding of mathematical concepts, and enhanced knowledge transfer through hands-on learning experiences.

Historically, a *situational teaching model* influenced by Western education theories gained popularity in China during the 1980s, particularly in Chinese language instruction. In this model, teachers created scenarios from the text and stimulating students in the emotional experiences of authors. While this approach is valuable in the humanities, it does not fully translate to mathematics or the natural sciences, where situational teaching must go beyond creating an *emotional atmosphere* and instead promote active cognitive engagement. In subjects like math, situations should encourage students to think critically and solve problems, rather than merely absorbing information within a pre-structured scenario. Thus, in the context of curriculum reform and evolving instructional methods, educators must critically reflect on how to genuinely allow students to experience the value of mathematics. A deeper understanding of Western situational learning theories—particularly those that emphasize cognitive engagement and knowledge construction—could offer valuable insights into improving situational teaching practices in mathematics education.

2. Group Discussion

Group discussion is widely recognized as an effective method for learning and intellectual exploration. Its historical roots can be traced to ancient educational practices, such as Confucius' "dialectical questioning" and Socrates' "maieutic method." Institutions like the Yue Lu Academy in China and Plato's Academy in Athens were renowned not only for their discussion-based learning cultures but also for their lasting contributions to intellectual and cultural traditions. Discussion plays a crucial role in clarifying understanding, organizing thoughts, and fostering collective wisdom. However, as education systems evolved, the social effectiveness of education shifted. The traditional class-based system, which emphasized lecture-based teaching, improved efficiency but constrained students' creative thinking. In response to this, educational reforms in Europe and the United States during the late 19th and early 20th centuries, including the Dalton Plan and the Winnetka Plan, sought to decentralize learning and promote small-group discussions. Although modern education cannot fully replicate these ancient approaches, the underlying principles of discussion-based learning remain highly relevant and can be meaningfully integrated into contemporary classrooms.

Classroom Observation Record

Subject: Area and Perimeter Practice Activity

Classroom Interaction:

Teacher: (After a few review exercises) "Now, we will have a group discussion. Take out your paper squares. Each group of four students will work together to discuss: 'How many different rectangular shapes can you make with 16 squares?'"

Around 30% of students hesitated initially but soon began arranging their squares. However, 40% worked independently without engaging in discussion, while 10% appeared indifferent and distracted. The remaining 20% participated but struggled to articulate their reasoning, instead asserting individual viewpoints without meaningful exchange. The teacher circulated briefly among the front rows before returning to the podium after two minutes. Rather than soliciting responses from groups, she asked students to raise their hands and answer individually.

Analysis of Group Discussion Effectiveness

The scenario above is a common occurrence in classroom teaching, particularly in public lessons where group discussions are incorporated as part of instructional design. Traditionally, classroom instruction followed a teacher-centered model, where teachers controlled the learning process while students passively absorbed information. In contrast, the new curriculum emphasizes student participation and active engagement, positioning group discussions as a means to deepen understanding and enhance classroom interaction. However, in practice, such discussions often fall short of their intended purpose.

While many teachers attempt to foster engagement through group discussions, they frequently overlook the conditions necessary for meaningful intellectual exchange. The mere increase in student speech does not equate to effective discussion. For discussions to be meaningful, they must provide students with opportunities for both independent thinking and collaborative exploration, rather than merely serving as an extension of the teacher's pre-planned lesson. In the observed case, the discussion failed to generate critical debate or intellectual engagement. Many students showed signs of fatigue or disinterest, and the discussion did not influence the teacher's approach but rather functioned as a procedural step in fulfilling the lesson plan.

A key misconception lies in equating the quantity of student speech with meaningful participation. Genuine discussions are spontaneous, emerging naturally from the content or students' inquiries, rather than being rigidly structured to align with predetermined outcomes. When student agency is respected, discussions occur organically based on curiosity and engagement with the subject matter. Ideally, classroom discussions should not be constrained by the need to confirm correct answers but should instead foster critical thinking and problem-solving.

In this case, the teacher had predetermined the discussion topic, anticipating possible areas of difficulty or disagreement. However, this approach limited both the spontaneity and depth of student engagement. For a discussion to be truly meaningful, the question posed must be open-ended, allowing for exploration from multiple perspectives. In this instance, the problem of forming rectangular shapes had a fixed solution, reducing the discussion to an exercise in verification rather than an opportunity for creative reasoning. Consequently, the discussion lacked the intellectual dynamism necessary for deep learning.

Ultimately, group discussions should not be used merely to diversify teaching methods but should serve as an integral component of the learning process. Effective discussions provide students with the opportunity to express their ideas, engage with others, and construct their own understanding of the subject matter. For discussions to fulfill their pedagogical potential, they must be designed as platforms for inquiry and exploration, rather than as structured steps within a rigid instructional framework.

3. Reflection on the Implementation of the New Curriculum

The current curriculum reform represents an all-encompassing transformation, influencing various aspects of education, including curriculum management models, development processes, learning objectives, content, course structures, and pedagogical approaches. This shift challenges traditional educational paradigms, particularly those deeply embedded in teachers' practices and beliefs. While educators recognize the significance of these reforms and are actively adjusting their professional habits, the process of implementation remains complex, requiring continuous reflection and adaptation.

3.1 Curriculum Reform as a Transformation in Educational Philosophy

At its core, curriculum reform is not merely a structural adjustment but a fundamental shift in educational philosophy. Without a corresponding change in mindset, educators may only engage with the new curriculum at a superficial level. Certain long-standing beliefs and practices persist despite efforts to promote reform. Two common misconceptions include: One is changing teaching methods without changing content. That is, many teachers assume that reform is achieved simply by modifying their teaching methods—such as incorporating multimedia, posing more questions, enriching lesson designs, or varying instructional formats. While these adjustments are valuable, they often result in two distinct types of lessons: showcase lessons (for public demonstrations) and traditional lessons (for routine instruction). In both cases, the underlying content remains unchanged, still centered on the systematic transmission of knowledge and teacher authority. Superficial modifications in teaching style do not constitute true reform. Effective pedagogy requires that instructional methods serve the content meaningfully rather than merely appearing different on the surface. Another prevalent misconception is the belief that every lesson must simultaneously reflect all curriculum objectives, such as fostering problem-solving skills, emotional development, and student interaction. This approach places an unrealistic burden on teachers and leads to cognitive overload for both educators and students. Curriculum objectives should be viewed as progressive milestones, achieved over time rather than within a single lesson. When teachers attempt to incorporate every objective simultaneously, the result is often fragmented instruction that lacks coherence and depth. A more effective approach is to align individual lessons with specific, achievable objectives that contribute to students' long-term intellectual and personal growth.

3.2 Balancing Teacher Authority and Student Agency

A recurring challenge in curriculum reform is the perceived tension between maintaining teacher authority and fostering student agency. In reality, these two elements are not contradictory but rather interdependent. The role of the teacher and that of the student are not positioned in opposition; rather, they mutually reinforce one another. For decades, the traditional model of teacher-centered instruction has been criticized, leading to global efforts to redistribute classroom authority. However, despite shifting pedagogical trends, the teacher's role remains central. True reform does not entail the complete relinquishment of teacher authority but rather the development of a balanced dynamic where students take ownership of their learning while benefiting from expert guidance. Striking this balance is more complex than simply shifting power dynamics in the classroom. It requires deep subject knowledge, a strong sense of educational responsibility, passion for teaching, and the ability to assess and respond to classroom interactions with pedagogical tact. The teacher's role remains indispensable in cultivating an environment where students are engaged, independent thinkers while ensuring that learning remains structured and purposeful.

3.3 The Gradual Transformation of Teaching Practices

One of the defining characteristics of curriculum reform is the gradual evolution of teaching practices, which often lags behind theoretical understanding. Many educators intellectually acknowledge the value of the new curriculum but struggle to translate these ideas into practice. This phenomenon highlights a fundamental reality: conceptual awareness alone does not equate to effective implementation. Only through ongoing reflection and consistent application can theoretical insights develop into meaningful pedagogical changes. Like deeply ingrained habits, teaching practices evolve gradually. A teacher's instructional approach is shaped by years of experience and cannot be instantly transformed. The authentic role of a teacher emerges over time, refined through reflection, experimentation, and accumulated insights. As the saying goes, "Reform is a process, not an event" [①].Thus, while addressing the challenges of implementing the new curriculum is essential, it is equally important to maintain a long-term perspective. Overreacting to minor setbacks may hinder progress, whereas a commitment to continuous professional development fosters sustainable educational transformation.

---

① Fullan M. The meaning of education change [M]. New York: Teachers College Press,1982:41.

[Originally published in *Educational Development Research*, Issue 10, 2002 (by Lyu Lijie & Ma Yunpeng)]

Chapter 10 Designing the 'My Neighborhood' Thematic Unit through the Lens of Evolutionary Learning Theory

1. Insights from Variation Learning Theory

This study examines the thematic unit *My Neighborhood Relations* within the *Ethics and Society* curriculum, utilizing Variation Learning Theory as a guiding framework for instructional design. The primary objective is to deepen students' understanding of social complexities by centering on their cognitive development and perspectives. Through this approach, students are encouraged to analyze interpersonal conflicts from multiple angles, explore various strategies for resolving social issues, and ultimately cultivate the ability to lead calm, healthy, and fulfilling lives.

Ethics and Society is an integrated course designed for students in grades 3 to 6 of compulsory education. Grounded in children's living experiences, it introduces thematic threads that expand progressively from family, school, and community (hometown) to country and the world. This structured expansion enables students to engage with an increasingly complex social landscape, fostering both moral character and a sense of social responsibility.

Among the initial topics covered in this curriculum is *My Neighborhood Relations*, which becomes particularly relevant as children begin interacting with the broader community beyond their family and school environments. Neighborhood experiences leave lasting emotional and cognitive impressions, shaping children's moral values and understanding of social relationships. Positive neighborhood interactions contribute to the development of a healthy worldview. Even seemingly minor, everyday occurrences—if approached with careful reflection—can serve as valuable learning opportunities for problem-solving in real-life contexts.

However, conventional instructional designs often oversimplify the concept of neighborhood relations, reinforcing the familiar saying, "A close neighbor is better than a distant relative." While this saying promotes goodwill and mutual aid, it does not fully capture the complexity of neighborhood dynamics. Effective neighborhood relations involve not only kindness and cooperation but also tolerance, respect for shared spaces, and the ability to assert one's legal rights when necessary. Superficial moral lessons fail to equip students with the skills needed to navigate the intricacies of social interactions. The central challenge in designing this thematic unit is to move beyond moralistic teachings and instead use authentic neighborhood narratives to explore the multifaceted nature of social life. This approach enables students to critically reflect on interpersonal conflicts, assess diverse approaches to conflict resolution, and develop a well-rounded, constructive perspective on social interactions. The ultimate goal is to enhance students' cognitive skills, deepen their moral reasoning, and align instructional practices with the core objectives of the curriculum. To achieve this, the research team proposes using Variation Learning Theory as the foundational framework for redesigning the unit. By leveraging this approach, the instructional design can more effectively capture the richness of social interactions, present diverse perspectives, and foster a deeper, more meaningful engagement with real-world ethical dilemmas.

1.1 Overview of Variation Learning Theory

Variation Learning Theory, developed by Professor Ference Marton and his research team at the University of Gothenburg, originates from a phenomenography approach to understanding how individuals perceive and engage with the world. Marton posits that learning is "an intrinsic relationship between the individual and the world" (Lu, Pang & Zhi, 2006, p.

10), emphasizing that education should equip students with the cognitive tools necessary to navigate an increasingly complex society[①].

At its core, Variation Learning Theory asserts that effective learning occurs when students engage with subject matter from multiple perspectives. Marton suggests that learning is not merely about acquiring knowledge but about developing new ways of seeing by discerning and focusing on key aspects of an object simultaneously. It is through variation that learners can identify and distinguish essential characteristics of a concept. By encountering different variations of a concept within the same learning experience, students gain a more profound and nuanced understanding of its fundamental properties.

This theoretical framework aligns closely with Chinese educational traditions, particularly in disciplines such as mathematics, where instructional methods emphasize recognizing invariant principles across different contexts. Furthermore, the Hong Kong Institute of Education has successfully applied Variation Learning Theory across subjects such as Mandarin, English, and General Knowledge, adapting instructional strategies to cater to individual learning differences and fostering a deeper engagement with core content. Marton's theory identifies three distinct levels of variation that shape the learning process:

1. Variation in Students' Understanding of Learning Content

Educators must first identify students' misconceptions and learning difficulties to tailor instructional strategies accordingly. Understanding how students perceive the content is crucial for designing lessons that address their specific cognitive needs.

① Lü, Lijie. *Research on the Process of National Curriculum Design* [M]. Beijing: Educational Science Publishing House, 2008:23.

2. Variation in How Teachers Present Learning Content

Different educators approach the same subject matter in distinct ways. By sharing diverse instructional strategies, teachers can enhance pedagogical practices, enriching students' exposure to various perspectives on the same topic.

3. Variation in Learning Design to Foster Deep Understanding

Teachers must strategically determine which aspects of a concept should vary, which should remain constant, and how these elements interact to optimize student comprehension. Thoughtful instructional design ensures that variation is purposeful and enhances conceptual clarity rather than causing cognitive overload.

Neighborhood relations, as a reflection of social interpersonal dynamics, present a complex issue for children. By focusing on key aspects of the problem, understanding and evaluating it from various perspectives, and addressing key events, teachers can enhance students' cognitive abilities and improve the effectiveness of their teaching. Therefore, effective lesson design must build upon students' existing understanding of the issue, uncover different perspectives, and help them improve their cognitive quality, which will help them build problem-solving skills and develop a healthy moral perspective.

2. Theme Unit Design and Implementation under the Guidance of Variation Learning Theory

To explore neighborhood relationships effectively, the research team conducted pre-class surveys and found that many students had encountered real-life neighborhood conflicts. One commonly reported issue was "water leakage from upstairs affecting the downstairs". Based on this finding, the team selected the "leakage incident" as the entry point for analyzing neighborhood interactions and employed role-play to engage students in the discussion. However, classroom observations revealed several shortcomings in the original lesson design and student engagement. a. Dominance of Role-Playing. The role-playing activity took up most of the lesson time, leaving little room for student reflection or discussion. While engaging, it failed to deepen students' analytical skills beyond performance. b. Simplistic Understanding. Students' interpretations of the conflict were superficial. The role-playing exercises often repeated the same ideas, lacking variation in the depth of analysis and possible solutions. c. Limited Teacher Guidance. The teacher's involvement was primarily a one-sided moral summary at the end of the lesson. This resulted in passive value transmission, rather than fostering independent critical thinking and meaningful engagement with ethical dilemmas.

To address these issues, the research team redesigned the lesson using Variation Learning Theory as a guiding framework. The revised lesson retained its focus on "how to handle problems", for two primary reasons. One is that the issue is closely related to students' real-life experiences, making it a meaningful context for discussion. The other is that lesson provides an opportunity for students to explore varied perspectives on conflict resolution, shaping their understanding of neighborhood relationships. The revised design aimed to enhance students' cognitive engagement, enabling them to explore different conflict-resolution strategies and reflect on their implications for building a harmonious and fulfilling life. The revised course design under the Variation Learning Theory involved the following adjustment.

2.1 Introducing Variation in Learning Content

To deepen students' understanding of neighborhood conflicts, the research team introduced variation by modifying the "plot" of the leakage incident. By presenting different scenarios, students could experience the complexity of real-life conflicts and explore how different responses lead to different outcomes. The team designed three scenarios, each highlighting a distinct approach to conflict resolution.

Table 3-1

No.	Contradictory Event	Post-Event Life State	Student Reflection/Discussion Focus
1	Escalation and Coercion: After the Li family's house was flooded due to water leakage from the Wen family's apartment upstairs, Li's mother angrily confronted the Wen family and demanded excessive compensation. Under pressure, the Wen family agreed, but resentment remained.	The two families lived in ongoing hostility. Their children avoided each other, and the community atmosphere became tense.	"Has the Winner Really Won?" - Does forcing an outcome guarantee long-term happiness? How can we create a healthy and joyful community life?
2	Legal Intervention: After noticing water leakage from the Li family's apartment, the Wang family investigated the issue and gathered evidence. When the Li family denied responsibility, the Wang family sought resolution through property management and legal channels.	The issue was resolved fairly, but the Li family felt guilty about their earlier denial. The Wang family continued their normal life.	"Fair Resolution" - How do legal channels ensure fairness? How do we balance justice and social harmony?

No.	Contradictory Event	Post-Event Life State	Student Reflection/Discussion Focus
3	Mutual Understanding and Reconciliation: The Wang family, realizing their mistake, sincerely apologized and offered to compensate the Li family. The Li family, seeing the Wang family's goodwill, forgave them, leading to a strengthened neighborly bond.	The two families became close neighbors, supporting each other in daily life.	"I Am Sorry" - How does empathy and understanding contribute to a better community? What are the long-term benefits of resolving conflicts amicably?

These contrasting scenarios encouraged students to critically examine different conflict-resolution approaches, promoting a deeper and more nuanced understanding of neighborhood dynamics.

2.2 Focusing on Key Features of Learning Content in Discussions

Beyond introducing variation in content, the revised lesson placed a stronger emphasis on structured discussions to stimulate critical thinking. Instead of merely performing a role-play, students were:

Encouraged to compare different scenarios, identifying the advantages and disadvantages of each approach.

Guided to analyze the emotional, social, and moral consequences of different conflict-resolution strategies.

Asked to reflect on their own experiences with neighborhood relationships and discuss alternative ways to handle disputes in real life.

By incorporating Variation Learning Theory, the lesson design shifted from passive role-playing to active cognitive engagement, equipping students with the tools to analyze real-world social conflicts and develop ethical reasoning skills.

Through discussions, students summarize principles for managing neighborhood relationships based on each role-play. These principles contribute to fostering a healthy and joyful life. However, since principles may vary depending on the situation, teachers must provide appropriate guidance. This process unfolds through four stages:

Stage 1: Introducing Attitudes Toward Conflict Resolution

The teacher encourages students to reflect on their attitudes toward conflict resolution based on the previous lesson's role-play. To stimulate deeper thinking, the teacher poses thought-provoking questions that create cognitive and moral conflicts. Since the first practice lesson revealed a tendency toward aggressive problem-solving, students are asked to share real-life examples of neighborhood conflicts resolved calmly. The teacher follows up with reflective questions such as: "Why do people often solve problems calmly in daily life?", "What are the consequences of extreme problem-solving methods?" and "If two parties cannot reach an agreement, what alternative resolution methods could be considered?"

Stage 2: Role-Play and Impact Reflection

During the role-play, students explore how different conflict resolution approaches affect people's lives. In the first group's scenario, *"Has the Winner Really Won?"*, the Li family coerces the Wen family into paying compensation through threats. Although compensation is received, the outcome is a hostile relationship between the two families. This illustrates how resolving the issue in such a manner creates a tense living environment. Similar reflections are drawn from the second and third groups' role-plays.

Stage 3: Three-Dimensional Comparison and Reflection

Students compare the three role-plays and discuss their reflections with peers. The teacher leads a summary of the lessons learned, emphasizing the principles of problem-solving. Key participants, such as the mother from the Li family in Group 1, share their perspectives on how they felt after resolving the issue. Teachers guide students in articulating key conclusions:

Group 1 (Aggressive Approach): When one's rights are infringed, it is important to express dissatisfaction appropriately. Aggressive actions such as arguing, fighting, or threatening escalate conflicts and hinder the possibility of a healthy and happy life.

Group 2 (Legal Approach): Neighbors should uphold public morality and avoid causing inconvenience to others. When unintentional harm occurs, one should take responsibility and offer compensation. If the other party refuses to engage reasonably, legal intervention can be sought while maintaining a calm approach.

Group 3 (Understanding Approach): Neighbors should practice tolerance, mutual respect, and responsibility. Apologizing and fostering a harmonious relationship contribute to a healthy and happy neighborhood environment.

Stage 4: Deepening Understanding of Life Impact

This stage enhances students' awareness of how different conflict resolution methods shape life outcomes. The lesson highlighted that insufficient teacher guidance led to a lack of deep understanding of event variations. In future lessons, students are guided to compare extreme, legal, and understanding-based approaches to conflict resolution and observe their long-term consequences: hostile, normal, or harmonious relationships. The focus is placed on helping students understand that life is dynamic and that every action carries lasting consequences.

2.3 Variation at Different Cognitive Levels

A. Knowledge Explanation. The teacher provides lectures and presentations on essential life concepts, such as the impact of hostility on physical and mental health and fundamental legal knowledge related to neighborhood relationships. B. Emotional Engagement. To deepen students' emotional understanding, the teacher introduces engaging stories from the textbook, such as *The Different Sound of the Piano*. By reading with emotion, the teacher creates an atmosphere that fosters empathy and emotional resonance among students.

At the conclusion of the lesson, the teacher shifts the focus away from the water leakage event and presents various neighborhood dilemma stories using slides. These stories provoke cognitive and moral conflicts, encouraging students to apply their learned principles in real-world contexts. This process helps them recognize shared attributes across different events and enhances their problem-solving abilities.

3. Analysis and Conclusion

3.1 "Teaching" vs. "Insight" — Different Educational Outcomes

Students with limited life experience often struggle to gain deep insights from real-life social scenarios. A direct instructional approach may make students feel disconnected from real-life applications. The revised course design introduces the concept of *"post-life tense,"* emphasizing life before and after conflict resolution. This approach enables students to experience firsthand how their problem-solving methods shape their quality of life. Over time, students realize that while conflicts are inevitable, their approach to resolving them is a choice that influences long-term well-being.

Scenario	Conflict Resolution Approach	Life Outcome
Has the Winner Really Won?	Aggressive Measures	Hostile Life
Fair Resolution	Legal Measures	Normal Life
I'm Sorry	Understanding Approach	Harmonious Life

Figure 3-1 Behaviors and Results

3.2 The Theory of Dynamic Learning as a Theoretical Foundation

The theory of dynamic learning provides a framework for understanding complex social issues. Unlike other subjects, *Morality and Society* begins with real-life phenomena and explores both objective realities and the construction of personal value systems. Thematic units, particularly those addressing social conflicts, present transformed life scenarios within specific contexts. These units encourage value-based discussions, stimulate diverse perspectives, and guide students toward deeper reflection. By engaging in these structured discussions, students develop critical thinking skills and a broader worldview, making dynamic learning theory a valuable foundation for instructional design.

[This study was originally published in *Shanghai Educational Research*, Issue 3, 2008, by Lyu Lijie and Zhao Tongyou.]

Chapter 11 Collaborative Learning in Children: A Study on Homogeneous Grouping in Primary School

Cooperative learning emerged in the United States in the 1970s as an innovative teaching strategy designed to enhance the academic performance of all students. Beyond academic benefits, it aimed to foster positive and constructive interpersonal relationships among students from diverse racial backgrounds, ultimately working toward reducing racial divisions, discrimination, and social apathy in schools and classrooms. Scholars such as Slavin (R. E.), the Johnson brothers (D. W. & R. T. Johnson), and Sharan played a pivotal role in shaping cooperative learning by defining its core principles, group structures, and instructional strategies.

In China, the reform of basic education in 2001 introduced a focus on "autonomous, cooperative, and inquiry-based learning," bringing cooperative learning to the forefront of educational discourse. In recent years, schools have increasingly explored autonomous and personalized learning, with cooperative learning remaining a central component of these reforms.

While multiple definitions exist, this article defines cooperative learning as a teaching structure that emphasizes student-to-student interaction, supported by various educational theories, strategies, and methodologies. Over time, the value of cooperative learning has been widely recognized, yet several challenges persist—such as the effectiveness of collaboration, students' willingness to cooperate, ethical concerns, and the role of lower-achieving students within groups. As a pedagogical approach, cooperative learning represents a reasonable and progressive improvement over traditional methods; however, its successful implementation requires a systematic and context-specific theoretical framework to guide its practice.

1. Core Issues in Cooperative Learning within Classroom Instruction

Although many researchers acknowledge cooperative learning as an effective approach, it should not be considered a universal teaching method for every classroom. Since "no single teaching method is best under all conditions" and given that students' personalities, subject characteristics, and learning tasks vary, cooperative learning should be seen as one of several instructional strategies, rather than a one-size-fits-all solution.

When incorporating cooperative learning into classroom instruction, three key questions must be addressed: What types of course content are best suited for cooperative learning? What teaching and developmental goals can cooperative learning help achieve? How should cooperative learning be organized to maximize its effectiveness? These three dimensions (content suitability, instructional goals, and organizational strategies) form the foundation for effective implementation.

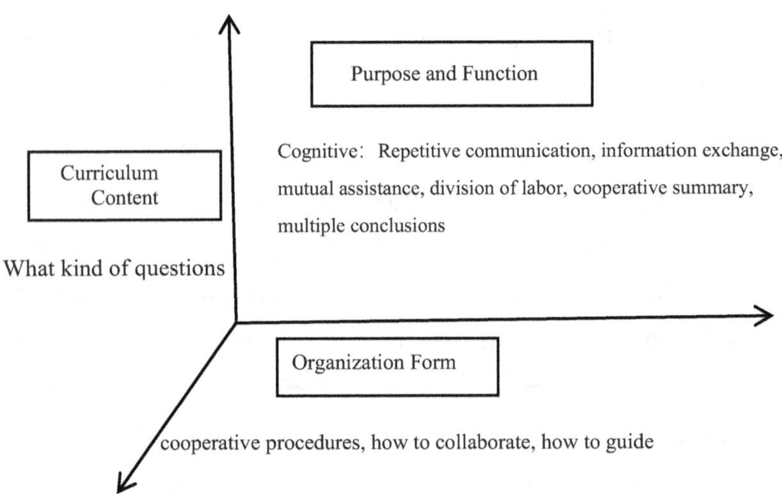

Figure 3-2: Three-dimensional Issues in Cooperative Learning

First, what types of course content are suitable for cooperative learning? This foundational question helps to determine the appropriate contexts in which cooperative learning can be effectively applied. Scholars such as Rachel A. Lotan have identified several key characteristics of cooperative learning tasks:

Open-ended learning tasks that encourage exploration and discussion

Diverse learning content that allows for multiple perspectives

Tasks requiring active interdependence, where students must rely on one another

Clearly defined individual responsibilities within the group

Explicit performance evaluation criteria to assess group outcomes

These characteristics ensure that cooperative learning fosters meaningful engagement rather than simply dividing tasks among students.

Second, what are the goals and expected outcomes of cooperative learning? Understanding the intended teaching outcomes is crucial for designing effective cooperative learning activities. These goals can be both cognitive and non-cognitive:

Cognitive Goals:

Enhancing memory retention through peer repetition

Encouraging information sharing and knowledge exchange

Promoting collaborative problem-solving and critical thinking

Structuring discussions to achieve multiple conclusions

Non-Cognitive Goals:

Increasing students' motivation to learn

Cultivating social and emotional skills such as teamwork, empathy, and responsibility

Western psychologists have classified different levels of cognitive engagement within cooperative learning. Robyn and colleagues (1998) identified six levels of cognitive language processing:

Repetition of information – Echoing what others say almost verbatim

Unstructured opinions – Thinking aloud without strong topic relevance

Specific viewpoints – Presenting factual information related to the topic

Evidence-based explanations – Providing logical reasoning to support claims

Generalizations – Deriving broader conclusions or principles from discussions

Evaluation – Comparing multiple pieces of evidence to reach an informed judgment

These classifications provide useful reference points for assessing the depth of students' cognitive engagement during cooperative learning activities.

Finally, how should cooperative learning be organized? The structure of cooperative learning significantly influences its effectiveness. Key considerations include:

Group Composition: Should groups be homogeneous (students with similar abilities) or heterogeneous (students with diverse abilities)?

Group Size: How many students should be in each group for optimal interaction?

Collaboration Strategies: What specific methods, procedures, and instructional strategies will foster effective teamwork?

Teacher's Role: How should teachers facilitate discussions and guide students through the process?

Research on group structure presents diverse perspectives: The Johnson brothers advocate for heterogeneous groups, arguing that they encourage deeper thinking and better explanations among students; John Baer, in contrast, supports homogeneous groups, suggesting that students with similar knowledge levels communicate more effectively; Lou et al. found that middle-ability students perform better in homogeneous groups, whereas low-ability students benefit from heterogeneous groups due to the support and guidance they receive from higher-achieving peers; Bennett et al. noted that low- and middle-ability students often struggle in homogeneous groups, while low-ability students may feel overlooked in heterogeneous groups. Some researchers argue that slower learners benefit from homogeneous groups, as they feel a greater sense of progress when working with peers at a similar level, rather than constantly comparing themselves to higher-performing students.

2. Exploring Homogeneous Group Formation in the Primary School *Moral Education and Life* Curriculum

The course of *Moral Education and Life* is an integrated, activity-based curriculum designed for younger primary school students. It emphasizes flexibility, openness, and comprehensiveness, encouraging active student participation throughout the learning process. Many of its tasks require group collaboration, are of low cognitive difficulty, and have strong real-life relevance, making this course well-suited for cooperative learning.

In the first semester of second grade, we conducted a cooperative learning experiment that focused specifically on homogeneous group formation. This study explores the advantages and challenges of using homogeneous groups and examines how teacher guidance can help address potential drawbacks. While Western empirical research presents conflicting views on the effectiveness of homogeneous versus heterogeneous groups, we selected homogeneous grouping based on the nature of the course's learning tasks. Over one semester, cooperative learning served as the primary instructional structure, with homogeneous grouping as the group formation method.

2.1 Anticipated Benefits of Cooperative Learning in the Thematic Unit

The semester's thematic activities included "How Big Is Our Body," "Playing with Autumn," and "Reading Exchange Meeting," among others. Taking "How Big Is Our Body" as an example, this unit is a secondary theme within the "Caring for Our Bodies" section of the second-grade, first-semester textbook from Beijing Normal University's edition of "Moral Education and Life."

The learning tasks for this unit were designed with three key principles:

Appropriate Difficulty Level – Tasks were structured to be manageable through group efforts, ensuring that students felt motivated and engaged.

Flexibility and Creativity – Group activities included open-ended tasks that allowed for creative exploration rather than rigid instructions.

Sustained Exploration – Thematic activities extended across multiple lessons, allowing students to build on prior knowledge and deepen their understanding over time.

The core activity required students to experience and visualize their body size by working together in groups. The process included:

Outlining the Body Shape – One student acted as a model, while the others traced their body outline on paper.

Designing and Decorating Clothes – The group collaborated to design outfits, fostering creativity and teamwork.

Reflection and Discussion – Students shared their experiences and observations with their peers.

This cooperative learning activity was carried out over four class periods, allowing students to engage deeply with the topic. The implementation of cooperative learning in this thematic unit led to both cognitive and non-cognitive benefits:

Cognitive Benefits

Encouraged personalized learning about body awareness and physical growth

Promoted active exploration through hands-on activities

Reinforced understanding through peer collaboration

Non-Cognitive Benefits

Increased motivation and interest in learning

Strengthened interpersonal communication skills

Enhanced confidence in self-expression and personal development

Overall, using homogeneous group formation in this primary school moral education curriculum fostered collaborative learning, creativity, and social development while ensuring that students engaged meaningfully with the subject matter.

2.2 Establishing Small Groups in Cooperative Learning

1. Group Size: 3-4 Members

Group size is a crucial factor in cooperative learning, as it directly affects the effectiveness of collaboration. Scholars such as W. Johnson and others argue that:

In a two-person group, students manage interactions only between themselves.

In a three-person group, six different interactions must be handled.

In a four-person group, this number increases to twelve.

As group size grows, the complexity of communication and coordination increases, requiring stronger interpersonal and group management skills. Based on this, Johnson et al. concluded that smaller groups are generally more effective.

Our observations in second-grade *Moral Education and Life* classes examined how different group sizes influenced students' cooperative performance. The results revealed:

Smaller groups (2 members): Activities progressed smoothly, but interaction opportunities were limited, leading to longer task completion times.

Larger groups (5+ members): Individual task loads decreased, but communication and coordination demand increased, reducing overall efficiency. Additionally, the "some do nothing while others do everything" phenomenon became more prevalent.

After analyzing these factors, we concluded that a group size of 3-4 members is the most reasonable and effective for second-grade students, balancing interaction, engagement, and task efficiency.

2. Voluntary Homogeneous Grouping

A widely accepted principle for group formation is "heterogeneous within groups, homogeneous between groups." Research suggests that heterogeneous groups encourage diverse perspectives, stimulate active learning, and deepen cognition. However, practical challenges exist:

In some classrooms, high- and medium-level students in heterogeneous groups do not show significant progress, while only low-level students benefit.

High-achieving students may be unwilling to assist lower-achieving peers, leading to unequal participation where some students dominate while others are ignored.

To address these challenges, we explored the potential advantages of homogeneous grouping. While homogeneous grouping is often used in high school settings to differentiate academic levels, it may lead to psychological concerns in younger students, such as feelings of inferiority or unhealthy competition.

To mitigate these issues, we implemented a voluntary grouping method based on the principle of "homogeneous by willingness, heterogeneous in other respects." Students selected their preferred partners, ideally forming groups of 3-4 members. The results showed that:

Most students grouped with friends of similar gender, personality, and academic ability.

Since students collaborated with trusted peers, they displayed higher motivation and enthusiasm for group tasks.

3. Observing and Analyzing Learning Performance in Homogeneous Groups

To evaluate the impact of homogeneous grouping, we selected three representative groups—Group A, Group B, and Group C—for detailed observation. These groups varied in their academic performance, social dynamics, and interaction styles, influencing their learning outcomes in different ways.

Group A: Four academically excellent, confident, and self-disciplined girls (A1, A2, A3, A4) who actively engaged and collaborated.

Group B: Three boys (B1, B2, B3) with average academic performance, typically passive in heterogeneous groups and hesitant to share opinions.

Group C: Four students (C1, C2, C3, C4) who were less motivated and had been assigned to their group by the teacher after voluntary grouping.

The data collection process included: recording the group interactions with a camera， capturing discussions using an audio recorder, documenting student performance after each class, and analyzing results at the end of each thematic unit.

While some critics argue that homogeneous groups primarily benefit high-achieving students while others lag behind, our findings suggested a more nuanced outcome. Each group demonstrated distinct developmental gains, indicating that homogeneous grouping can enhance collaboration when structured effectively, different student groups benefit in varied ways, depending on their academic background, motivation, and group dynamics.

Overall, this study highlights the potential of voluntary homogeneous grouping as a practical alternative to traditional heterogeneous group structures, particularly in early primary education settings.

Group A demonstrated exceptional collaboration from the outset. Their willingness to cooperate was evident in their organized approach to tasks and the high quality of their final product. Below is an excerpt from their first lesson on the unit “Taking Care of Our Bodies” under the theme “How Big Is Our Body?”:

A3: I will draw the legs.

A4: I’ll take care of this part.

A1: I’ll draw the body.

A2: Let's not do it like that; let's discuss it first. Look, here is our plan. Who will draw the head first?

A1: A3, you draw the head.

A3: Okay. ...

A4: Let's put all the colored pens together to use.

A3: Use my pens; there are more colors.

A1: Let's all use them together.

A4: We can use our own pens, and if any color is missing, we can borrow. How does that sound?

A2: Sounds good.

A3: That's settled. We've discussed it. Let's all sit down.

......

A4: Let's speed up, and we can add a crown. I'll do it.

A1: You can choose your favorite colors when coloring, just make sure the combinations look good.

A2: A1, you should make the final decision. I'm just the model.

A4: The pants don't look good. Let's make them red. Color lightly, don't press too hard.

A3: I'm not doing this very well.

A1: It's fine, we'll design it together.

A2: I'll help you later. My pens have special colors; everyone can use them.

A1: We should color in order so it doesn't get messy. A

4: We can also adjust it flexibly according to our earlier discussion.

A3: A2, thank you.

……

The final product of Group A was the best, which was exactly as expected. Several key elements contributed to their success: Mutual Agreement and Cooperation: Frequent phrases like "I agree," "I'll help you," and "Thank you" created a collaborative environment. Proactive and Constructive Contributions: Each member proposed constructive ideas, with phrases like "Let's discuss this" and "Let's speed up," reflecting their active engagement. In-Depth Understanding of the Task: The group's clear planning ("making good combinations" and "coloring in order") demonstrated not only high cognitive abilities but also advanced social development and teamwork awareness. Ultimately, Group A's work was of the highest quality, demonstrating effective cognitive and collaborative strategies.

Group B consisted of three boys with average academic performance. They were generally reserved and did not actively express their opinions. In heterogeneous groups, they tended to remain silent and take on passive roles. According to the transcript, the group's work progressed smoothly. They followed the teacher's instructions systematically: first by discussing the division of tasks, then outlining, and finally decorating the clothing. B2: Let's first decide who will outline the body. Raise your hand if you agree with B1.

B2: Let's first decide who will outline the body. Raise your hand if you agree with B1.

B1: I'll do the outlining.

B2: I'll color. Is that okay?

B3: Let's all color the outline together.

B2: We need to discuss what color goes where.

.....

B2: You tell us which part you want to color.

B3: I'll do the head, and then I'll help you with the body.

B2: What part do you want to do?

......

B1: I'll use red to mark the parts I'm responsible for.

B2: The head is a bit difficult. I'll mark it with green. Who wants to draw the left side of the body? Raise your hand. Who wants the right side?

B1: I'll draw these parts.

......

B2: I only have oil pastels, not watercolor pens.

B1: You can use the oil pastels to color mine.

B2: I have an idea, we could vote. B1 is the model, and if everyone likes his clothes, we'll use his clothes. If not, we can use someone else's.

B3: I think his clothes look good.

B2: Who agrees B3's clothes are good? Raise your hand... and who agrees with B1's? ... You can't vote for your own.

Since the three members of Group B are familiar with one another, they have developed a habit of communicating smoothly during daily play. As a result, the most notable feature of their task completion is a calm and democratic decision-making process. Key terms that frequently appear in their discussions include "together," "discuss," and "agree."

Among the group, B2's behavior is particularly noteworthy. Although B2 usually exhibits behavior similar to the rest of the group, he appears noticeably more relaxed in this familiar setting. He actively assumes the role of a "democratic leader," using the phrase "raise your hand" nine times in a single discussion. This suggests that he is not only attempting to guide and facilitate group cooperation but is also enthusiastically engaging others in the collaborative process. B2's leadership role emerges organically within the context of this small-group environment.

Group C consists of four students who are frequently criticized by the teacher for rule-breaking and occasionally disrupting their peers. In heterogeneous groups, they are often viewed as unwelcome members and are generally not expected to contribute significantly to group tasks, as long as they refrain from causing disruptions. Their initial collaboration, following the formation of the group, was notably unsteady. The following is an analysis of their classroom performance over the course of a semester, with a focus on their first lesson.

First Lesson Classroom Recording:

(While other groups are dividing tasks, C Group members do not respond, instead playing around and not paying attention to the task at hand. The group finally fails to decide who will be the model, and no one feels anxious about the unfinished task.)

Teacher: "Record the group's division of tasks on the card and discuss how to complete the task efficiently. Use pencils."

C1: "Let's choose C4."

C3: "Why should you decide?"

C1: "I just want it like this."

C2: "Forget it, let C1 do whatever. He's too domineering."

C1: "I'll find someone else to draw, not you (C2)."

C4: "I don't want to be the model."

C2: "If you don't, I will."

C1: "We all disagree with you being the model."

Teacher: "This isn't difficult. First, don't get upset, let's discuss again, okay?"

C1: "Task number 3 is mine."

C2: "I'm doing task number 2."

C4: "Who's doing task number 4?"

C4: "What number am I?"

C2: "I don't know. We're drawing clothes together, but there was no discussion."

C3: "What do you mean there was no discussion?"

C2: "I won't be in this group next time. This is so unlucky."

C3: "Why is C1 so domineering?"

C4: "Alright, you two draw the upper body, and I'll draw the clothes."

C1: "No."

(C2 wanders off again, joining another group to play. C1 remains distracted by his stationery, leaving only C3 and C4 to continue working.)

C2: "I'm back. What's this? It's terrible."

After Class Teacher Discussion:

Teacher: "How did today go? You performed well, right?"

C2: "I made a lot of mistakes. 50% was because of C1, 10% was because of me, and the rest was because of the others. I feel like C1 is too domineering. I see two duplicate tasks that need to be changed. He keeps pushing me and not letting me do anything."

Teacher: "Was it because you didn't communicate and discuss well?"

C2: "When the group was working, C1 didn't follow the planned division of tasks. He kept disrupting things. I didn't do too well either, but I kept trying to finish it, so I'm somewhat satisfied with that."

Teacher: "Is there anything else you want to say?"

C1: "I don't want to cooperate with C2. He's so annoying. He's always against me, and I have to keep giving in. But I thought about it, I shouldn't argue with him for so long."

Teacher: "That makes sense. If you hadn't wasted so much time arguing, you might have done better. It seems like it's important to discuss things when working in groups."

C4: "I feel really annoyed. Good friends shouldn't be like this. I'm not happy. I don't like it when group members argue. C1 always scribbles around; it shouldn't be like that."

Before the Second Lesson:

Teacher: "Are you going to argue again this time?"

C3: "I didn't argue last time."

C1: "I won't argue anymore. I'll be more considerate of C2."

C2: "I'll also tolerate him more."

C4: "I'll also tolerate both of them. I'll stop them from arguing."

C1: "I'll discuss more with everyone."

After Class Teacher Discussion:

Teacher: "How was the group activity today? What did you do?"

C2: "I outlined the edges and fixed the mistakes. I didn't argue with anyone. C1 didn't act on his own; when they told me to stop, I did. I'm listening to other people's opinions now."

C1: "I did well today. I didn't argue with C2. C2 said the blue watercolor pen was bad, so I used black. I'll listen to his opinion. We discussed it together. It feels really good. We're being patient. We can be good friends, but I don't know if C2 agrees."

C2: "Yes, I agree."

C3: "The thing I'm most proud of today is leading everyone to finish the task quickly and well. The two of them (C1 and C2) have changed a lot since last week. They don't argue anymore, almost never. I like being friends with them. I'd like to work with them again in the future."

C4: "I feel really good this week."

At the start of the first lesson, Group C's performance aligned with the teacher's expectations. They immediately became distracted and demonstrated little sense of responsibility for the task. However, this time, when no one took initiative, there was no one else to rely on. The four members were forced to begin working amid noisy arguments. Nearly every sentence they exchanged contained expressions of rejection -- "Why?" "I just want it this way," "Don't interfere," "Too domineering," "I don't want to," "I won't," "No," "Don't agree," and "I don't know."

In addition to their poor communication, they also lacked confidence in their ability to complete the task, which prevented them from discussing how to divide the work. C2, in particular, tended to shift blame for the group's failure, saying he was "unlucky" and that others were "too bad." There was no discussion about the task or any attempt to develop a work plan. The outcome of this process left everyone feeling frustrated.

After class, the teacher prompted them to reflect. Even without the teacher's continued intervention, the students themselves acknowledged that the arguments had made everyone feel "annoyed" and that "this isn't good." Before the second lesson, they made a conscious decision to "tolerate," "stop," and "discuss." The classroom atmosphere was significantly calmer compared to the first session. Afterward, they expressed satisfaction, noting that they had "not argued," "not acted independently," "stopped when told," and "listened to others' opinions," while also practicing patience and mutual respect. They felt the lesson "went really well" and shared that they "could be friends" and "would like to work with them again."

These changes, though modest, were unexpected and encouraging. The students in Group C recognized the challenges caused by their earlier behavior and proactively sought improvement. They developed simple but effective strategies such as "being patient" and "not acting alone," ultimately coming to appreciate the value of collaboration and change.

A Month Later:

In the second theme activity, still based on the previous groupings, the students in C Group were tasked with making a large toy.

C4: "What should we make? Let's discuss it."

C2: "I want to make a big house and stay inside."

C1: "I don't like that. Let's make a maze instead."

C3: "I don't think that works. Let's make a castle."

C4: "We'll need enough materials for that."

C1: "I don't agree with that."

C3: "So what do we do?"

C2: "Let's go with my idea."

C1: "If we do his, I'm not participating."

C3: "Don't be like that. Let's discuss it."

C4: "Yeah, let's vote by raising hands."

(After voting, C2 agrees with C1's idea.)

C1: "Look at my great work."

C2: "It's not that great. It's too rough, and the tape is uneven."

C1: "If you criticize it again, I won't hold back."

C2: "It's just not that great."

C3: "Let's get to work, everyone!"

C4: "Didn't we agree not to argue? Why have you forgotten? Let's discuss how to finish the toy."

C1: "Okay, I'll give in."

C2: "I'll apologize to everyone."

In the second task, C1 and C2 continued to act according to their personal preferences, without fully considering the opinions of the other group members. However, prompted by their peers' reminders, they adhered to the previously agreed-upon "raise-your-hand vote" rule. Phrases such as *"I'll give in"* and *"I'll apologize"* began to appear in their interactions, indicating an increased willingness to compromise. Although problems still arose, the students in Group C demonstrated notable improvements in social interaction and self-awareness. These adjustments reflected early signs of change and personal growth.

3. Reflections on Homogeneous Group Collaborative Learning

3.1 Student Engagement and Development within the Zone of Proximal Development (ZPD)

Across all groups, each student was actively engaged in their respective group's communication system, with no one being excluded or neglected. In homogeneous groups, where members shared similar abilities and motivations, peer interactions were frequent and meaningful. Unlike heterogeneous groups, where high-ability students often focus on assisting lower-ability peers, homogeneous groups enabled all students to concentrate on task completion, leading to greater efficiency and higher-quality work. Furthermore, in homogeneous settings, students could more easily emulate the behaviors and strategies of their peers, making the task material fall within their Zone of Proximal Development (ZPD). This fostered a conducive learning environment where students could build on each other's strengths and collaboratively address weaknesses.

3.2 Differences in Collaborative Methods and Work Quality

The collaborative strategies employed in homogeneous groups varied significantly across different ability levels. While Group A demonstrated high levels of efficiency and creativity, Groups B and C faced challenges in collaboration, particularly regarding leadership and task comprehension. Group B exhibited steady improvement but lacked deep cognitive engagement, whereas Group C initially struggled but made significant progress after self-reflection.

3.3 Developmental Focus Across Different Ability Groups

In homogeneous groups, students concentrated on overcoming their individual weaknesses, with each member's development centered on enhancing their social and cognitive skills. High-ability students in Group A refined their leadership and teamwork abilities, while Group B developed stronger communication and decision-making strategies. For Group C, the initial focus was on fostering social skills and cooperation before engaging more meaningfully with the task (see Figure 3-3).

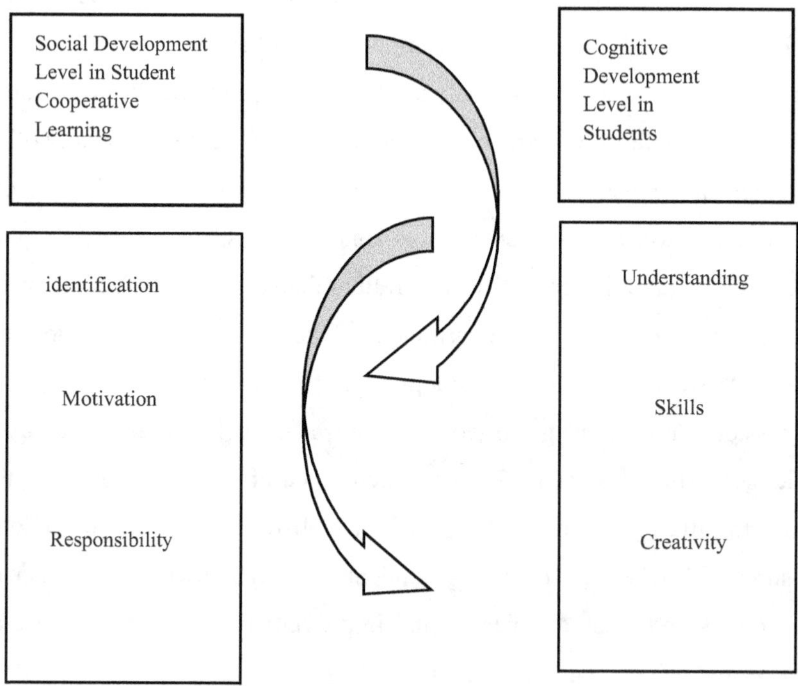

Figure 3-3: Structure of Growth Focus for Students in Homogeneous Groups

3.4 Teacher Guidance Based on Group Characteristics: Focusing on Key Intervention Points

In homogeneous groups, students display varying levels of ability, learning needs, and challenges. Consequently, teachers must tailor their guidance strategies to address the specific needs of each group. High-Ability Students: These students typically do not seek teacher assistance. When the teacher circulates, guidance for these students primarily involves providing general advice or additional resources to deepen their understanding. The teacher's role is more focused on enrichment opportunities rather than direct intervention. Intermediate Students: Students with moderate academic abilities and more introverted personalities can complete learning tasks independently but may require additional encouragement to remain engaged and take initiative during group activities. Teachers should provide positive reinforcement and occasional prompts to build their confidence in contributing to discussions and tasks. Developing Students: Groups consisting of students who are still developing academically or socially often encounter challenges related to cooperation, such as unclear task division, lack of motivation, and frequent interpersonal conflicts. These groups require more time and attention from teachers. Rather than directly intervening in the subject matter or offering overly critical feedback, teachers should adopt the role of a "part-time tour guide," stepping in at critical moments during task progression and offering targeted guidance to help students navigate challenges. This approach requires patience, careful observation, and the ability to allow students the space for self-reflection and behavioral adjustment. Teachers can encourage students to recognize the significance of their actions and celebrate incremental improvements, fostering a sense of progress and achievement.

As discussed earlier, this study relies on cooperative learning within thematic units of the *Morality and Life* curriculum. While the effectiveness of homogeneous grouping depends on various preconditions, it remains a valuable organizational method, particularly when teaching objectives emphasize social development and active participation. When based on students' willingness to collaborate, homogeneous grouping proves to be an effective structure for fostering engagement, cooperation, and positive social interaction within the classroom.

Chapter 12 Exploring the Logic behind Model Selection in Teaching Reform

The 2001 *Outline for the Reform of Basic Education Curriculum (Trial)* proposed the need to "change the current situation in which curriculum implementation excessively emphasizes passive learning, rote memorization, and mechanical training." Instead, it advocated for students to actively participate, engage in exploration, and develop hands-on skills. The goal was to cultivate students' ability to collect and process information, acquire new knowledge, analyze and solve problems, and enhance their communication and collaboration skills. Similarly, *the National Medium- and Long-Term Educational Reform and Development Plan Outline (2010-2020)* emphasized the necessity of "deepening educational and teaching reforms, innovating teaching methods, exploring multiple cultivation approaches, and promoting heuristic, inquiry-based, discussion-based, and participatory teaching to help students learn how to learn." These policy documents share a common reform objective—emphasizing student autonomy in the classroom and fostering their learning abilities, practical skills, and innovative capacities.

In recent years, some schools, based on their unique practical environments and real-world needs, have introduced teaching reform concepts such as student-led learning, learning-driven instruction, and pre-lesson self-study. These approaches have been framed as distinct "models" of teaching reform. Many schools are actively experimenting with and refining their teaching reform models, often drawing inspiration from successful case studies.

1. The Pursuit of Change in Models and Forms

Student-centered teaching models share a common historical background, with reform goals and slogans reflecting a consistent push for change. However, due to differing reform foundations and contextual factors, schools often implement reforms in varied ways, resulting in distinct models of change. For instance, some classrooms emphasize students constructing conclusions through inquiry. In these settings, teachers pose questions, and students explore answers collaboratively in groups. The focus is not merely on arriving at definitive answers but on fostering critical thinking and analytical skills through the learning process. Other classrooms, particularly those following a small-class or personalized teaching philosophy, prioritize addressing student differences. These classrooms emphasize autonomous learning and group discussions to ensure each student's experiences and learning pace are respected, with differentiated instruction catering to individual needs. Many schools adopt a model where student-centered activities are followed by teacher summaries. In this model, students first engage in independent study, often using provided learning materials to grasp textbook content. They then discuss challenges encountered with peers, while the teacher offers guidance as needed. At the end of the lesson, the teacher summarizes the key points. In some cases, school leaders impose time limits, such as restricting the teacher's summary to "ten minutes" or allowing students to provide the summary instead. These classrooms emphasize clear learning objectives, foster student autonomy, and seek to enhance the overall effectiveness of student engagement.

Across these various models, a common feature is the high level of student participation, with student-centered activities dominating classroom time. The integration of methods such as autonomous learning and group work helps break away from rigid, traditional teaching methods. However, these reform-oriented models represent just one aspect of the broader educational reform landscape, which remains inherently diverse and complex. Despite this diversity, all these models share certain core characteristics. Emphasis on Student Autonomy: Since the late 20th century, educational reform in China has consistently aimed to shift the focus toward students as active participants in the learning process. Improvement-Oriented Reform: The legitimacy of these models lies in their ability to address existing challenges and enhance teaching methods to meet reform objectives. Through iterative reform experimentation, educators gain deeper insights into different teaching styles, thereby resolving practical classroom challenges and aligning with broader educational aspirations. As schools seek to replicate successful case studies, certain patterns have emerged in the process of imitation: Mandating a standardized teaching model across all grade levels and subjects within a school. Structuring classroom activities into fixed sequences with predetermined time allocations, such as implementing a "learning first, teaching second" approach that restricts lecture time. Prioritizing models that emphasize both student engagement and the reinforcement of textbook knowledge, favoring those with apparent "practical utility". While these models share common features, they stem from diverse philosophical foundations and reform intentions. Despite being presented as innovations, their implementation often oversimplifies the original ideas, transforming them into rigid routines that, over time, become institutionalized procedures.

2. Reflections on the Choice of Teaching Models

2.1 Does the Selected Model Align with Its Underlying Educational Philosophy?

A teaching model serves as a tangible representation of a broader educational philosophy, designed to translate abstract principles into actionable classroom practices. Each model is rooted in a specific theoretical framework and was originally developed with distinct pedagogical goals. While the model's creators often ensure a strong alignment between philosophy and practice, this alignment may weaken as the model is adopted in different educational settings. Therefore, it is crucial for educators to grasp the foundational philosophy behind a model to prevent it from devolving into a rigid set of prescribed procedures. Reducing a model to a formulaic routine can strip it of its intended pedagogical objectives and responsiveness to students' needs. To preserve its transformative potential, educators must approach the model with an understanding of its guiding principles rather than merely adhering to its surface-level structure.

2.2 Does the Model Prioritize "Practical Efficacy" at the Expense of Deeper Learning?

Many student-centered reform models follow a predictable pattern: students engage in self-study, participate in peer discussions, and conclude with teacher-guided practice or summary. While this approach encourages student participation and aligns with conventional learning goals—such as content mastery and knowledge retention—it may fail to achieve the broader aims of educational reform. The true objective of reform is not merely to enhance knowledge acquisition but to cultivate deeper learning experiences, critical thinking, and creativity. However, in practice, the emphasis on practical efficacy often results in a reversion to traditional educational values under the guise of innovation.

2.3 Does the Teaching Method Align with the Intended Learning Sequence?

Each teaching method has inherent strengths and limitations. In standardized models, teaching methods are often rigidly structured, dictating the flow of classroom activities. For example, a fixed sequence of self-study, discussion, practice, and summary can limit teacher flexibility and constrain the depth of content exploration. While guided self-study fosters student initiative, it may also narrow the scope of learning and inhibit creativity. Even widely adopted strategies like group discussions can become repetitive or superficial if applied indiscriminately. Strict adherence to a prescribed sequence may lead to missed opportunities for deeper inquiry and critical engagement. To foster meaningful learning, teachers must remain adaptable, ensuring that instructional methods are thoughtfully aligned with lesson objectives and responsive to students' evolving needs.

2.4 Does Student "Subjectivity" in Learning Necessarily Fulfill Its Intended Purpose?

In traditional teaching models, teachers hold primary control over discourse, determining both the content and pace of instruction. In contrast, reform-oriented models—such as the "learning first, teaching second" approach—seek to diminish teacher dominance by limiting direct instruction and deferring teacher summaries. However, does this structural shift inherently fulfill the reform's educational goals? The essence of subjectivity lies in the development of the learner as an active participant in their own education. If this developmental depth is absent, merely altering the structure of instruction does not achieve meaningful reform.

Some reform proponents advocate for teachers to "speak as little as possible" in the classroom, but this should not be misinterpreted as an argument for minimizing instruction. Teaching is not synonymous with lecturing; rather, it encompasses a broader spectrum of pedagogical strategies, including creating meaningful learning contexts, stimulating inquiry, guiding exploration, and providing formative assessment. Student-centered teaching is not a passive process; it requires continuous teacher intervention, adaptation, and scaffolding to ensure that learning objectives are met.

3. Attention to the Prerequisites for Choosing Teaching Models

The core figure of empiricism, John Dewey, discussed teaching methods in Children and Curriculum. He argued that "Children and curriculum are only the two poles of the educational process, and a straight line may be drawn between the two points. The current level or standpoint of the child, as well as the facts and truths within the disciplines, can determine the teaching method. Teaching is an ongoing reconstruction that extends from the child's present experience to the organized truths represented by the disciplines."[①] Dewey emphasizes that the "standpoint" of the child is the starting point for teaching, but what determines the teaching method? It is the relationship between the child's current "standpoint" and the "facts and truths within the discipline" that guides the teaching method. The purpose and significance of teaching are to move the child from their "current experience" toward the "experiences represented by each discipline."

The reasonableness of teaching must consider whether students' subjectivity is manifested in the classroom, and it must also assess what kind of "facts and truths within the discipline" their subjectivity is pointing to, as well as what kinds of "disciplinary experiences" have been achieved. First, the "disciplinary experience" here should not only refer to the quantity and solidness of knowledge acquired. Second, disciplinary experience will not naturally emerge simply because students are the subject; as Dewey notes, "emptiness can only produce emptiness; it cannot create something from nothing. Inexperienced students can only produce immature results." Dewey cautions that if we merely return children to their existing selves and expect them to extend from there to new truths or behaviors, it is impossible.[②]

Therefore, the premise for choosing teaching models and methods is to analyze the possibilities that the curriculum can bring to students. Teachers must first understand the potential teaching purposes and functions embedded in the content and then, based on their knowledge of the learners, their own understanding, and the educational and teaching context, interpret,

① John Dewey. The Child and the Curriculum. Translated by Lin Baoshan and Kang Chunzhi, Taipei: Wunan Publishing, 1990, pp. 112, 116.
② Jiang Shanye. Concise International Encyclopedia of Education: Curriculum [M]. Beijing: Educational Science Press, 1991: 11.

transform, and organize these into the teaching objectives and values they pursue.

3.1 Curriculum Potential Analysis

What is the experience represented by each discipline? In the classroom, students are not only experiencing disciplinary knowledge but also elements of the curriculum that can promote their growth. Schwab, Peretz, and others have proposed the concept of "curricular potential." Schwab believes that the potential of the curriculum is embedded in the disciplinary content, providing possibilities for student growth and development. Peretz defines curriculum potential as "all learning experiences derived from specific sources aimed at achieving broad educational objectives."①

In practice, some teachers believe that "if students can understand the textbook content by themselves, I really don't need to explain it." If the learning experiences students require are merely tasks like "what is the content" or "how to answer questions," this assumption may seem reasonable. As Peretz puts it, "Teachers' daily experiences often narrow their perspectives on utilizing the full potential of curriculum materials. Teachers tend to focus on the obvious explanations of the textbook, especially the parts they are already familiar with… hence the need to increase teachers' awareness of the opposite aspects of curriculum materials."②

The concept of curriculum potential suggests that teaching objectives are not simply stated in the text of the textbook, nor are they fixed or unchangeable; they need to be uncovered by teachers. Teaching design must consider whether students can obtain knowledge, how they will obtain it, and what exactly they are supposed to learn. According to Schwab's view, when

---

① Jiang Shanye. Concise International Encyclopedia of Education: Curriculum [M]. Beijing: Educational Science Press, 1991: 11.

② Schwab. J. J. The practical 3: translation into curriculum [J]. School Review,1973 (81):501-522.

a discipline's content is transformed into curriculum content, it involves three potential dimensions of meaning: the theme, the source, and understanding.①

The theme dimension refers to the central meaning and significance expressed by the content materials, which are evident and easily detectable. The source dimension refers to the methods and principles behind the generation of the disciplinary content. Disciplinary experts use specific methods and principles to organize disordered knowledge into a coherent form, and every piece of disciplinary content contains specific methods and principles for its formation. The third dimension is understanding, which refers to the complex organization of disciplinary content. To understand it, one must apply principles, approach it from multiple perspectives, ask different questions, and use different thinking methods. For instance, when scientific material enters the curriculum, the curriculum or teaching designer can choose its theme dimension to provide learners with descriptions and explanations of related phenomena, or they can focus on a principle or method required to understand the material and use it as the learning content, thus teaching students how to make judgments. For example, if the source dimension of poetry is chosen as the learning content, students can practice writing poetry and analyzing poems to discover the characteristics of poetry. This not only helps students understand the characteristics of poetry but also enables them to develop skills in analyzing and creating poetry. This dimension holds latent value for the learners.

Regarding this issue, some scholars suggest that although German pedagogical theory has different conceptual systems, it also emphasizes the analysis of the curriculum's potential, particularly in terms of teaching design. German educational theory views teaching content as knowledge, experiences, and wisdom that have been specially selected and organized to

① Deng Z. Constructing chinese didactics: (re)discovering the German didactics tradition [J]. Jahrbuch fur Allgemeine Didaktik (JfAD), 2012(1):108-128.

achieve educational objectives, serving as a medium for promoting human development, liberation, and freedom. Teaching content contains educational potential that needs to be discovered and realized during teaching.

"In order to fulfill this task, teachers must analyze and interpret the meaning of these contents when designing lessons." As the first step in teaching design, teachers must understand the educational intentions embedded in the curriculum content by its designers and reflect on the reasons behind selecting particular content. German scholar Klafki provides a framework for teachers to analyze content during teaching design, which includes five steps:

1. Value of the content: What rules, methods, techniques, or attitudes does this content provide to the learner?

2. Current significance: What meaning do the experiences, knowledge, abilities, or skills that students gain from this content have?

3. Future significance: What impact will this content have on students' futures?

4. Content structure: How is the content structured? How do various content parts relate to each other? Are there different levels of content and value?

5. Educational representativeness: For students of a specific age group, what cases, phenomena, specific scenarios, experiences, people, and factors are interesting, inspiring, acceptable, and understandable? ①

3.2 Different "Sources" of Disciplines Have Different Teaching Values

Schwab emphasizes the "source" in a discipline, meaning that "each subject content contains certain methods and principles for forming that

① Klafkiw. Didactic analysis as the core of preparation of instruction [J]. Journal of Curriculum Studies,1995(1):13-30.

subject content," which is a potential that can be excavated in the curriculum. This potential is different, forming different subject characteristics. This difference is both a limitation in teaching design and a possibility for teaching meaning. Subject curricula come from one or more disciplines, naturally bearing the inherent attributes of the discipline itself. The knowledge and experience of these disciplines are produced through different methods, or in other words, different research methods. In teaching, when understanding and interpreting these subject contents, we should also follow the specific thinking characteristics, expressive characteristics, and communicative characteristics of these subjects. For example, in the humanities, the Chinese language has both aesthetic and interpretive characteristics. It requires understanding the meaning of a text, while also experiencing and expressing beauty through emotional rendering; moral formation is based on reflective experience or speculation. Mathematics, on the other hand, is a kind of mathematical logic, a Cartesian tradition[①], a strict deduction in the mind; while natural sciences (like physics and chemistry) are based on inductive experiments. In the same teaching model, assuming these disciplines are the same would result in using the same expression and thinking methods. For instance, if in a Chinese language class, the main task for teachers and students is to find the thread of the article's writing and identify words that describe the thread, even if this is done in a self-directed manner or through discussion, it is still using a mathematical knowledge formation method. The understanding and aesthetic value that Chinese teaching should have will be lost. It is precisely because an object does not possess all attributes that it can be what it is and thus have its own value. Each subject curriculum has its own unique characteristics, and it is only through this that teaching can have its own function. As a result, teaching itself becomes rich, complex, and full of charm.

---

① Wu Guosheng. Science and Humanities [J]. Chinese Social Sciences, 2001(4): 10-13.

3.3 Teaching is the Teacher's Unique Educational Creation

The main carriers of the curriculum are the curriculum standards and textbooks. However, when compilers translate their understanding of the curriculum into text, the meaning is often diminished. In teaching, if the primary goal is merely to understand the words in the textbook and master the knowledge points, the scope of understanding will inevitably be limited. Teaching should not—and cannot—be reduced to a simple restatement of the content in the textbooks because the guiding factor in the teaching process is the "present." Teachers have the ability to unearth the hidden potential of the curriculum—those aspects within the textbooks that may not be explicitly stated, those generated during teaching, and those that the textbooks intended to convey but failed to communicate directly. These elements can all become integral parts of the teaching content. In this sense, teaching is the most active process in realizing the full potential of the curriculum. For example, Chinese language teaching expert Dou Guimei discusses her lesson preparation process and proposes four levels of analysis:

a. Analyze what the text actually says: Teachers must first clarify the original text—read it thoroughly, understand it, and deeply grasp its meaning. As independent readers, teachers should engage with the text critically, imagining and analyzing it, rather than simply adopting others' interpretations.

b. Analyze what the text aims to convey: This step involves understanding why the text expresses itself in a particular way. To do this, teachers must consider relevant background factors, such as the author's life, the historical context of the writing, the social influences at the time, and the characteristics of the literary genre.

c. Analyze what the text can communicate: Different individuals interpret the same text in various ways. Factors such as reading levels, personal experiences, intellectual backgrounds, and even differing social or historical contexts can yield diverse interpretations. These multiple perspectives help teachers achieve a more nuanced understanding of the text.

d. Analyze what the text should convey: At this stage, the teacher must consider the text from their own pedagogical standpoint. "Remove the need to reconstruct the author's psychological experience" and instead think about how to transform their own reading experience into something accessible and understandable for students. Dou Guimei emphasizes that a teacher's goal is "to understand the author better than the author himself."①

If the first three steps involve the teacher's interpretation, selection, and organization of the curriculum potential, the fourth step is the teacher's transformation of that potential. Teachers need to reinterpret, transform, and organize the teaching content based on their understanding of the learners, their own interpretations, and the broader educational context.

3.4 The Meaningful and Creative Nature of Teaching Models

The development of teaching models is contingent on specific contexts. To effectively learn a model, one must understand the underlying values and core concepts, which often require a certain degree of abstraction and should be accompanied by creative actions, rather than simply following a prescribed procedure. This process involves practice, experimentation, and reflection. For instance, some educators in China have undergone a transformation in their approach, shifting from using "phases" and "models" to "modules" during their teaching reform journey. At the outset of the reform, they proposed six teaching phases that reflected the needs of student-centered learning: self-study and questioning, communication and presentation, interactive exploration, in-depth explanation and guidance, corrective feedback, and application transfer. After a period of exploration,

① Dou Guimei. Being a Teacher with Professional Dignity [M]. Guilin: Li River Press, 2007: 24.

they adapted the phases into six modules to prevent the rigidity often associated with models. This shift allowed teachers to use these phases in a more flexible, dynamic, and combinatory manner. Testing a model helps practitioners explore the ideas behind it, transforming unclear or abstract concepts into practical, replicable structures. As educators internalize the meaning and value of the reform, they transcend rigid models and embrace a more varied and complex teaching style, while still adhering to the fundamental principle of student-centered learning. Therefore, the models used in reform serve as temporary frameworks to convey ideas and provide “rules” for those still unfamiliar with the underlying concepts. Once these ideas are understood, practitioners should be given the freedom to design their own rich, multidimensional classrooms. Consequently, the reform process must allow space for those who fully grasp the ideas to innovate and develop their own teaching practices.

[The original article was published in *Educational Theory and Practice*, 2014, Issue 31 (by Feng Qi, Lyu Lijie, Yuan Qiuhong)]

Chapter 13 Advancing Tradition: The Development of School-based Curricula on Traditional Culture

In March 2014, the Ministry of Education issued the *Guidelines for Improving the Education of Excellent Traditional Chinese Culture* (hereinafter referred to as the "*Guidelines*"), which advocated for the integration of traditional cultural education into the primary and secondary school curriculum, offering a top-down framework to promote this effort in schools. In January 2017, the General Office of the CPC Central Committee and the State Council released the *Opinions on Implementing the Project of Inheriting and Developing Excellent Traditional Chinese Culture* (hereinafter referred to as the "*Opinions*"), marking the first time a central government document was solely dedicated to the inheritance and development of traditional Chinese culture. This document established both the foundation and strategic direction for the implementation of traditional culture education.

Traditional Chinese culture is a vital source of national cohesion and creativity and serves as a fundamental pillar of national and cultural confidence. As the primary channel for talent cultivation, school education plays a crucial role in the transmission of traditional culture. Currently, many schools integrate traditional culture through national curricula, school-based courses, and extracurricular activities. The curriculum serves to shape the cultural framework and personality traits of each generation. In this sense, the type of traditional culture presented in the curriculum influences students' understanding, value orientation, and cultural identity related to traditional Chinese heritage.

This study, as part of a broader research initiative, investigates the current status and challenges of school-based traditional culture courses nationwide. It aims to offer practical insights and strategic recommendations for optimizing such curricula. In this context, school-based traditional culture courses refer to those autonomously developed and sustainably implemented by schools, with a focused emphasis on themes related to excellent traditional Chinese culture.

1. The Educational Implications and Curriculum Value of China's Fine Traditional Culture

1.1 Educational Significance and Curriculum Value of Excellent Traditional Chinese Culture

The inheritance and development of traditional Chinese culture are not only imperative for enhancing China's cultural soft power and strengthening cultural confidence, but they are also intrinsic to cultural continuity itself. This process conveys the enduring value of the cultural lineage that binds the nation together. The vitality of a national cultural identity depends on the reciprocal interaction between collective cultural norms and individual beliefs. On one hand, individuals rely on cultural frameworks to regulate their behavior and attain symbolic recognition, identity, and value alignment with cultural ideals[①]. On the other hand, these interactions cultivate citizens who possess a strong sense of national responsibility and who, through their character and capabilities, contribute to the evolution and enrichment of national culture[②]. Within this dynamic, education plays a dual role: it both nurtures individual development through traditional cultural values and serves as a transformative force in shaping and renewing societal culture. In

① Clifford Geertz. The Interpretation of Cultures. Translated by Naribilig, et al., Shanghai: Shanghai People's Publishing House, 1999, pp. 56-57.

② Qin, Guangguang, Feng, Li, & Chen, Pu. *Dictionary of Cultural Studies* [M]. Beijing: Central University for Nationalities Press, 1988:108.

other words, education not only guides and disciplines individuals through exposure to traditional culture but also fosters the proactive engagement of individuals in its continuation and innovation.

In daily life, students encounter diverse cultural expressions that lead to differences in lifestyle, behavioral norms, and patterns of thought. Through education, students interpret these cultural variations, make informed decisions, and adjust their behavior accordingly- resulting in a diversity of values and actions across groups. Under the guidance of high-quality education, the deep structures of excellent traditional Chinese culture-such as values, psychological traits, and emotional patterns-become the core elements of national identity and social cohesion. Students are thereby equipped to understand these elements intellectually, internalize them as personal values, and embody them in their behavior. This process fosters collective identity, emotional attachment, and strengthens national unity at a spiritual level.

Thus, education is not only the primary mechanism for transmitting and developing traditional culture, but also the key to sustaining cultural continuity. It facilitates the transition of traditional culture from being merely "taught" to being consciously "carried forward."

1.2 Curriculum as a Pathway for Cultural Education, and School-Based Curriculum as a "Node" within the Cultural Context

The curriculum serves as a critical pathway for cultural education. From the perspective of what students should internalize through their curricular experiences, the curriculum must develop a distinct structural character and provide rich cultural resources that enable students to achieve inner growth while embracing cultural norms①. Within China's national curriculum system,

① Dewey B.J. Democracy and Education: an introduction to the philosophy of education [J]. American Journal of Sociology,1916(1):40-49.

subjects such as Chinese language, history, moral and legal education, music, physical education, and art systematically incorporate elements of traditional Chinese culture. However, culture is a multifaceted social construct encompassing literature, art, science, morality, and more. Its transmission involves not only the transfer of knowledge and information but also the conveyance of values through emotional engagement, as well as the cultivation of cultural understanding and identity through experiential and comparative processes.

School-based curricula, in contrast to the standardized national framework, are typically developed based on the humanistic atmosphere, regional resources, and historical heritage of individual schools and local communities[①]. These curricula are uniquely positioned to reflect localized cultural features. While the national curriculum provides the foundational framework for Chinese cultural education, school-based curricula function as "nodes" where this cultural framework is localized, contextualized, and brought to life.

Moreover, cultural identity develops through a gradual and deepening process. Without personal emotional resonance and localized grounding, it is difficult to sustain recognition of the deeper structures of excellent traditional Chinese culture. By drawing on diverse local resources and engaging students in step-by-step learning experiences, school-based curricula serve as essential nodes within the broader cultural context, playing a distinctive and irreplaceable role in fostering cultural understanding and emotional connection.

---

① Lü, Lijie, & Yuan Qiuhong. The Logic of Curriculum Organization in School-Based Curriculum Development [J]. *Educational Research*, 2014(9):96–103.

2. Research Design and Methods

This study explores the scope and characteristics of school-based courses on traditional Chinese culture in primary and secondary schools across China. It focuses on dimensions such as course quantity and typology, regional features, organizational structures, teaching quality, and external influencing factors including public attention, resource utilization, and teacher capacity. A mixed-methods research design was employed, incorporating public opinion analysis, questionnaire surveys, individual interviews, and classroom observations.

To ensure representative sampling, a stratified approach was used based on China's "Seventh Five-Year Plan" regional division—namely, the Eastern, Central, and Western regions. The sample comprised 45 schools from the Eastern region, 43 from the Central region, and 32 from the Western region. Between October 2018 and January 2019, two rounds of surveys were conducted in primary and secondary schools located in 12 provinces, municipalities, and autonomous regions. The study collected 120 curriculum plans (or course syllabi), 1,542 teacher questionnaires, 6,874 elementary student questionnaires, and 5,356 secondary student questionnaires. Additionally, interviews were conducted with 10 school principals and 24 teachers, and 16 classroom observations were completed. This comprehensive dataset enabled a systematic analysis of the current implementation status of school-based traditional culture courses in China.

2.1 Survey on the Basic Characteristics of School-Based Traditional Culture Courses

The research team pre-processed and consolidated the 120 curriculum documents, analyzing key aspects such as the proportion of traditional culture courses, course typology, organizational formats, and evaluation mechanisms. The data were visualized using the *sunburst R* package (), which generated sunburst charts to display hierarchical relationships. Additional descriptive analyses were conducted using R's built-in statistical functions, and results were reported in terms of means and percentages.

2.2 Analysis of Teachers' and Students' Attitudes

To assess the attitudes of teachers and students toward school-based traditional culture courses, validated scales were developed and piloted in the first round of the survey. The teacher attitude scale was based on the 1959 attitude framework by Katz et al., which conceptualizes attitude as an organized set of cognitive, affective, and behavioral predispositions toward a particular object (e.g., person, event, or concept). Accordingly, the scale measured three dimensions: cognitive understanding, emotional response, and behavioral intention regarding traditional culture education[①].

The student satisfaction scale was adapted from the causal model of customer satisfaction developed by Dr. Claes Fornell of the National Quality Research Center, University of Michigan. This model was tailored to assess student satisfaction with traditional culture courses and included constructs such as expectation, perceived quality, perceived value, and loyalty toward the course experience[②].

The student cultural identity scale was constructed based on the psychological structure of ethnic cultural identity. It measured three dimensions: symbolic cultural identity (recognition of cultural symbols), cultural practice identity (engagement in cultural activities), and value identity (internalization of cultural values)[③].

---

① Li, Jie. *Research on the Current Situation and Transformation of College Students' Life Attitudes* [M]. Shanghai: Shanghai People's Publishing House, 2015:54–55.

② Liu R, Jung L. The commuter student and student satisfaction [J]. Research in Higher Education,1980(3):215-226.

③ Wang, Pei, & Hu, Fawen. National Cultural Identity: Connotations and Structure [J]. *Journal of Shanghai Normal University (Philosophy and Social Sciences Edition)*, 2011(1):101–107.

All questionnaires in this study employed a 5-point Likert scale for responses. The teacher attitude scale and student satisfaction scale were designed as self-report instruments, while the student cultural identity scale adopted a situational judgment test format. The internal consistency of each scale was assessed using Cronbach's Alpha, calculated through R language functions. As shown in Table 3-2, all three scales demonstrated strong internal reliability, with Cronbach's Alpha coefficients exceeding 0.75.

To examine the validity of the three questionnaires, the Kaiser-Meyer-Olkin (KMO) function in the psych package (https://cran.r-project.org/web/packages/psych/) was first used to calculate the KMO values for each questionnaire. The results showed that the KMO values of the three questionnaires were all above 0.8, indicating suitability for exploratory factor analysis. In addition, the built-in factanal function in R, the factor. analysis function, and the fa function in the psych package were used to perform orthogonal rotation based on the principal axis method. The standardized factor loadings of the three questionnaires ranged from 0.568 to 0.871, and the total variance explained exceeded 75% (see Table 1), as shown in Table 1.

In summary, the second round of the questionnaires demonstrates relatively good validity. Based on the evidence of good reliability and validity of the questionnaires, cluster analysis was conducted on each group dimension using R. A heatmap was drawn using the pheatmap package to depict the group distribution of teachers' attitudes and students' course satisfaction in relation to their sense of cultural identity with traditional culture (https://cran.r- web/packages/pheatmap/index.html).

Table 3-2: Reliability and Validity Test Results for the Scales

Scale Name	Grade Level	Cronbach's Alpha	KMO Value	Total Explanation Rate
Teacher Attitude	All	0.940	0.961	82.836%
Student Course Satisfaction	Elementary	0.922	0.945	86.497%
	Secondary	0.833	0.901	84.742%
Student Cultural Identity	Elementary	0.804	0.869	78.839%
	Secondary	0.777	0.827	76.438%

2.3 Constructing a Model for Course Satisfaction and Cultural Identity

From the standpoint of students' curricular experiences, the curriculum should establish a distinct structural personality and offer rich cultural resources, enabling students to achieve internal transcendence while engaging with cultural norms. As such, the curriculum serves as a vital conduit for cultural education, and through school-based courses on excellent traditional Chinese culture, students can develop a sense of cultural identity. To investigate the relationship between student satisfaction with traditional culture school-based courses and the formation of cultural identity, this study employed Structural Equation Modeling (SEM) using Amos 21.0 software. SEM is a robust analytical technique that integrates path analysis and confirmatory factor analysis within a multivariate framework. The model was estimated using the Maximum Likelihood (ML) method.

After several rounds of estimation, refinement, and recalibration, a final model was obtained with strong fit indices: $\chi^2/df = 3.12$ (< 5), GFI = 0.957 (> 0.90), CFI = 0.931 (> 0.90), RMSEA = 0.067 (< 0.08).

These results indicate an acceptable and well-fitting model. The model illustrates the impact of traditional culture school-based curricula on fostering cultural identity among students. The findings are expected to inform practical and effective recommendations for optimizing such curricula to better cultivate students' cultural identity aligned with excellent traditional Chinese culture.

2.4 Public Opinion Landscape and Spatial Autocorrelation Analysis of Traditional Culture Education

Although social attention does not directly determine the implementation of school-based traditional culture courses, it exerts a subtle yet pervasive influence on all stakeholders—students, teachers, principals, and curriculum designers—thereby shaping the practice and outcomes of traditional culture education and indirectly affecting students' cultural identity. This underscores the critical role of public opinion in both the implementation and efficacy of such educational initiatives.

To assess the national landscape of public opinion, the researchers analyzed media coverage of traditional culture education from 2014 to 2018, sourcing data from major outlets such as People's Daily Online, Xinhua News, Sina, and numerous provincial and municipal education websites.

To capture the regional distribution and characteristics of public discourse, all collected news texts were imported into NVivo software. Using open coding, the researchers identified and categorized "free nodes" based on traditional culture education themes—such as cultural carriers (e.g., Confucius, Kunqu opera, shadow puppetry, classical Chinese studies) and cultivation pathways (e.g., national curriculum integration, study tours).

In order to quantify and compare public attention to traditional culture education across different provinces and municipalities, the research team developed the Traditional Culture Education Public-sentiment Competitiveness Index (TCEPCI), referencing established data processing approaches in research management. The formula for calculating a region's TCEPCI is presented as follows:

$$\text{TCEPCI for a province} = \sqrt{\frac{\text{Number of traditional culture education carriers in a certain province}}{\text{Average number of carriers in 31 provinces}} \times \frac{\text{Number of traditional culture cultivation paths in a certain province}}{\text{Average number of cultivation paths in 31 provinces}}}$$

Due to the diversity of the educational carriers and cultivation paths in traditional culture, it is difficult to rationally quantify the public opinion force in each province and city. However, this formula allows the index for each province to be derived objectively by comparing it with the national average. All calculations were completed using R language. Next, the TCEPCI index was input into ArcGIS software's Getis-Ord General G module for global spatial autocorrelation analysis. In the global autocorrelation computation of the G index, a p-value ≤ 0.05 indicates statistical significance. A positive Z value means that there is a clustering effect in the spatial distribution of research competitiveness in China's counselor studies. If the ratio of the observed G index to the expected G index is greater than 1, it indicates that high-value clusters are present; if it is less than 1, it shows low-value clusters. [①]However, if the ratio equals 1, it indicates that both high and low-value clusters exist within the spatial region. In such cases, further local spatial autocorrelation computation is needed for further analysis. To assess the local spatial autocorrelation strength of the public opinion competitiveness of traditional culture education, the researchers used LISA (Local Indicators of Spatial Association) to analyze the local spatial autocorrelation. The simulation was set to run 999 times, and the results were presented as a map

① Getis A, Ordjk. The analysis of spatial association by use of distance statistics [J]. Geographical Analysis,1992(3):189-206.

showing the regions and types where clustering effects occurred. This analysis was used to predict the future trend of public opinion on traditional culture education in various provinces and cities.

3. Research Results and Analysis

3.1 Current Status of Traditional Culture-based School Curricula

Among the 120 schools surveyed across 12 provinces and municipalities, 107 schools reported implementing school-based curricula, and 92 of these specifically offered traditional culture-based courses. In total, 321 traditional culture-oriented school-based courses were collected, demonstrating a considerable volume and nationwide presence of such curricula. These courses were categorized into three main types: "Dao" (principles), "Qi" (practical skills), and Comprehensive courses. "Dao" courses involve abstract cultural content, grounded in clear and systematic ideological frameworks. These are further subdivided into three thematic areas: history, classical texts, and moral education. "Qi" courses emphasize practical, lifestyle-related, and folk elements of traditional culture. These include 21 subcategories such as tea ceremony, etiquette, music, chess, calligraphy, and painting (see Figure 3-4 for details). Comprehensive courses integrate both "Dao" and "Qi" elements, adopting a thematic, cross-disciplinary approach that combines *cognitive, experiential,* and *exploratory* learning strategies for students. After classification, 78 courses fell under the "Dao" category, 245 under "Qi," and 7 were categorized as comprehensive. These courses cover a broad spectrum of traditional Chinese cultural expressions—ranging from philosophy and literature to rituals and customs—demonstrating considerable educational potential and cultural value. However, curriculum analysis also revealed several noteworthy concerns. In some cases, schools exhibit content misalignment or excessive emphasis. For example, certain schools require students—by as early as third grade—to memorize entire classical texts, including Di Zi Gui, San Zi Jing, Qian Zi Wen, Da *Xue*, *Zhong*

Yong, and *Meng Zi*, placing a potentially undue burden on young learners. Some schools heavily incorporate Confucian principles, particularly the doctrine of the Zhong Yong (Doctrine of the Mean), stressing balance and moderation, but often in ways that lack pedagogical balance or adaptability to students' developmental needs. Others organize experiential rituals, such as bowing before statues of Confucius or tying wish ribbons on a "Top Scholar Bridge" prior to entrance examinations as symbolic acts of cultural prayer for academic success. Cultural inheritance entails not only preserving traditional values but also engaging in a selective adaptation process, wherein schools must discern and transmit the most socially relevant and educationally meaningful elements of traditional culture to align with contemporary developmental goals.

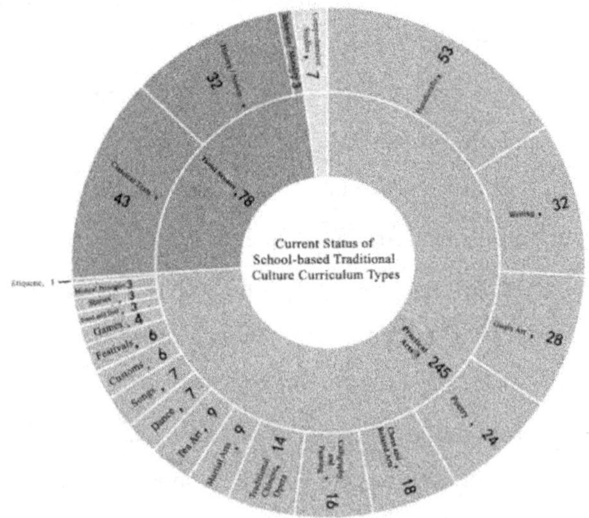

Figure 3-4: Sunburst Diagram of the Categories of Traditional Culture-based School Curricula Offered

Curriculum design is the process of cultural selection. The curriculum shapes students' understanding of traditional culture, and through school education, especially school curricula, cultural inheritance and continuation are achieved. This process is also a selection process for traditional culture. What traditional culture should be preserved, continued, or developed in school curricula constitutes future generations' understanding of traditional culture. From this perspective, school curricula represent the understanding, selection, and restructuring of traditional culture; curricula are the transformation of culture. Therefore, it is necessary to explore and define the common values of traditional culture-based courses. In the rich and diverse forms of curricula—ranging from content fields, literacy functions, cultural background, and historical origins—we need to analyze, identify, and grasp the unity of values and objectives within traditional culture-based curricula, thereby establishing a "diverse yet unified" ideological positioning for these courses.

Traditional culture-based school curricula rely on local resources for implementation, but time allocation and methods still appear insufficient overall. In curriculum implementation, schools across different regions make full use of local cultural resources to offer traditional culture-based school curricula with regional characteristics. For example, the Into the Old Summer Palace course in Haidian District, Beijing; the Shadow Puppetry course in Gansu; the Into Confucius course in Linyi, Shandong; the Waist Drum course in Shaanxi; and the Blue Bamboo Carving course in Changzhou, Jiangsu. These courses leverage local resources, considering students' living environments, and play a unique and dynamic role in education. However, the survey also reveals that a common challenge faced by these traditional culture-based school curricula is the issue of ensuring sufficient class hours. Over 80% of primary schools can meet the required 12 class hours per year for traditional culture-based school curricula, but most secondary schools can only meet 4 hours per year. This is because secondary school schedules are very tight, and students report that school-based courses are often replaced by subjects like mathematics and physics. Additionally, in terms of course implementation methods, 53.66% of primary and secondary school students only engage with the courses in the classroom. Only 1% of students have visited places such as communities, memorial halls, folk museums, museums, and Confucian academies more than four times as part of their school-based curriculum. Traditional cultural content has already been systematically presented in national curricula, particularly in subjects like Chinese, History, Moral Education, and Arts. How does the traditional culture content in school-based curricula relate to the national curriculum? If the school-based curriculum merely supplements or extends the national curriculum content, how appropriate is this increase in quantity? If more is better, the vast and rich nature of Chinese culture could lead to unlimited course content. Particularly when the school-based content is unrelated to the senior high school entrance exam or the college entrance exam, it is naturally seen as an academic burden by both students and teachers, leading to resistance to its true implementation. Therefore, the focus of traditional culture content in school-based curricula should not be on the quantity of knowledge or information, but rather on experiencing and practicing culture through a comprehensive, experiential, and hands-on approach. It should integrate existing knowledge and information to understand the culture, foster students' curiosity, and encourage them to perceive the existence of traditional culture in created contexts and environments.

3.2 Depiction of the Main Participants in Traditional Culture-based School Curricula

The depiction of the current status of the teacher-student groups is based on a heatmap clustering technique using the K-means algorithm, which calculates average distances from a given dimension's central value. This algorithm generates clusters without distinguishing between positive or negative outcomes. Each small square within a cluster represents the score of a teacher or student on a particular dimension relative to the average score for that dimension, with darker colors indicating higher scores and lighter colors indicating lower ones. Each row shows the score of an individual teacher or student across various dimensions, and the dendrogram on the left indicates the clustering results for each teacher or student.

1. Clustering Analysis of Teachers' Attitudes Toward Traditional Culture-based School Curricula

The survey on teachers' attitudes toward traditional culture education primarily measured three aspects: cognition, emotion, and behavior. In general, teachers show strong emotional recognition and make efforts to implement traditional cultural education through their actions. However, their overall understanding of traditional culture education remains somewhat shallow. Interviews revealed that teachers recognize the necessity and urgency of offering traditional culture-based school curricula, with 91.77% of teachers willing to uphold traditional cultural principles throughout their careers. However, many schools only have a small number of full-time teachers or rely on part-time instructors for traditional culture-based school curricula, and most of these teachers lack a comprehensive grasp of traditional culture's core principles. Consequently, while teachers are quick to respond positively to the Outline policy, they are constrained by the lack of full-time specialists, limited professional development opportunities, and insufficient external support, leading to a situation where their efforts do not fully align with their intentions. Based on specific variations in cognition, emotion, and behavior, teachers can be categorized into five groups: "Mediocre Teachers," "Active Teachers," "High-quality Teachers," "Aspirational Teachers," and "Executional Teachers" (as shown in Figure 3-5).

"Mediocre Teachers" perform moderately across cognition, emotion, and behavior, often adopting a "getting by" attitude, and account for approximately 8.33% of the tot"l. "High-quality Teachers" excel in all three dimensions. "Active Teachers" (23.56% of the group) perform well emotionally and behaviorally but have weaker cognitive understanding—they are enthusiastic about teaching traditional culture yet struggle to deepen their grasp due to external constraints. Unlike "Aspirational Teachers", they not only embrace the subject emotionally but also actively apply it in teaching. Finally, around 17.38% are "Executional Teachers", who engage with traditional culture curricula solely due to school policies or mandates, without genuine acceptance or internalization.

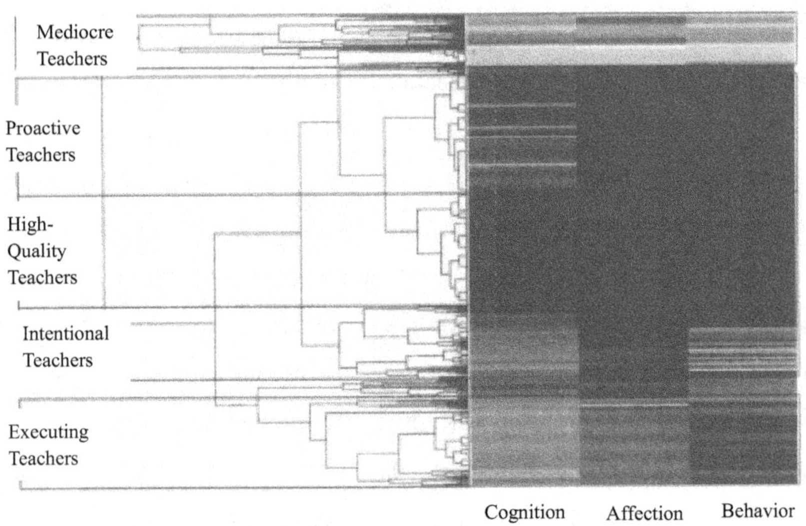

Figure 3-5: Group Clustering of Teachers' Attitudes Toward School-Based Curricula on Traditional Culture

2. Cluster Analysis of Student Satisfaction with School-based Curricula

From the current general situation of student satisfaction with traditional culture-based school curricula, it is evident that students have high expectations. However, their abilities to perceive and engage with the teaching content or methods are relatively weak, leading to varied perceptions of the value gained from the course (learning outcomes) and student loyalty. This suggests that Chinese traditional culture remains a core value pursued by students in their learning and daily lives. School-based curricula should not merely “tell” information, “preach” values, or “implant” mystical knowledge of traditional culture. Rather, they should teach students how to make choices in a multicultural context, discover beauty in familiar cultural elements, and develop a sense of belief.

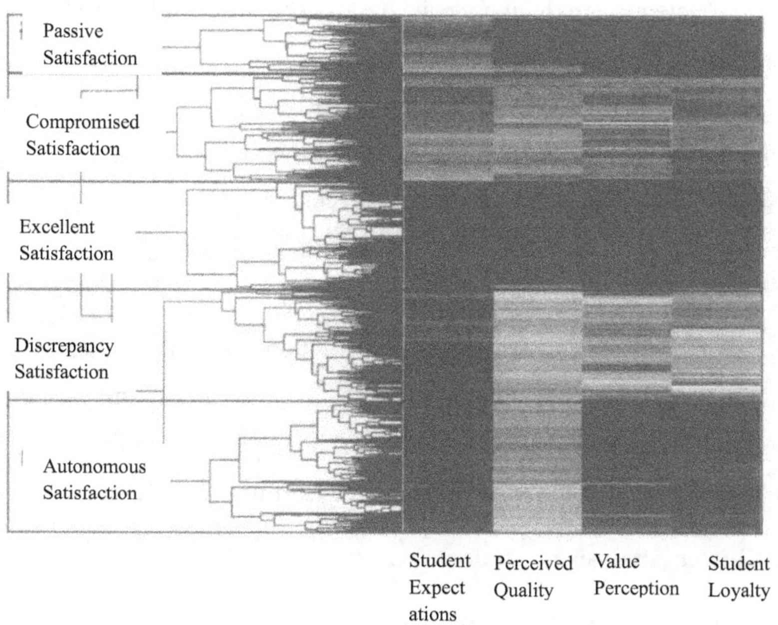

Figure 3-6: Clustering of Primary and Secondary School Students' Satisfaction with Traditional Culture-Based School Curricula

Based on specific differences in students' satisfaction across four dimensions of the course, they can be classified into five types: “Passive Satisfaction,” “Compromised Satisfaction,” “Excellent Satisfaction,” “Discrepancy Satisfaction,” and “Autonomous Satisfaction” (as shown in Figure 3-6). The proportion of students in the “Passive Satisfaction” category is relatively low, at 9.39%. These students generally have average expectations for the traditional culture-based school curricula, but due to receiving carefully designed and appropriately implemented lessons from teachers, they experience a higher perceived quality, value recognition, and student loyalty. On the other hand, the "Compromised Satisfaction" group exhibits a generally average response across all four dimensions, showing a low and unbalanced level of satisfaction with the traditional culture-based school curriculum. The "Excellent Satisfaction" and "Discrepancy Satisfaction" categories exhibit opposite trends. The former refers to students whose relatively high expectations are met, resulting in satisfaction across all dimensions. In contrast, the "Discrepancy Satisfaction" group represents students whose expectations were not fulfilled, creating a large gap between their anticipated outcomes and actual results. This discrepancy leads to lower satisfaction with the course and a lack of loyalty to it. Both of these categories account for approximately 20% of the total student population. Additionally, there is another category, "Autonomous Satisfaction," in which students start with high expectations. Although they do not experience high-quality teaching in the implementation of the course, they achieve a relatively high level of satisfaction through their independent learning and research efforts.

3. Cluster Analysis of Students' Cultural Identity

The formation of students' cultural identity is often a spiral process that evolves from the superficial perception of cultural symbols to the internalization and experiential understanding of cultural essence. This process is not solely influenced by school education, but also by various factors from family and society. The current overall picture of students' cultural identity shows significant differences, with considerable variation between groups, but clear similarities within each group. Individuals, when accepting implicit norms of national cultural concepts, not only understand and identify with group paradigms but also shape their individual understanding of culture based on their life experiences and growth.

Therefore, individuals generate a "homogeneity" similar to the ethnic group while also forming "heterogeneity" in their personal

interpretations of culture. [①] Based on differences in cultural symbol identification, cultural identity, and value-based cultural identity, the students can be categorized into five types: "Deep Identity," "Equal Identity," "Passive Identity," "Cognitive Identity," and "Superficial Identity" (as shown in Figure 3-7).

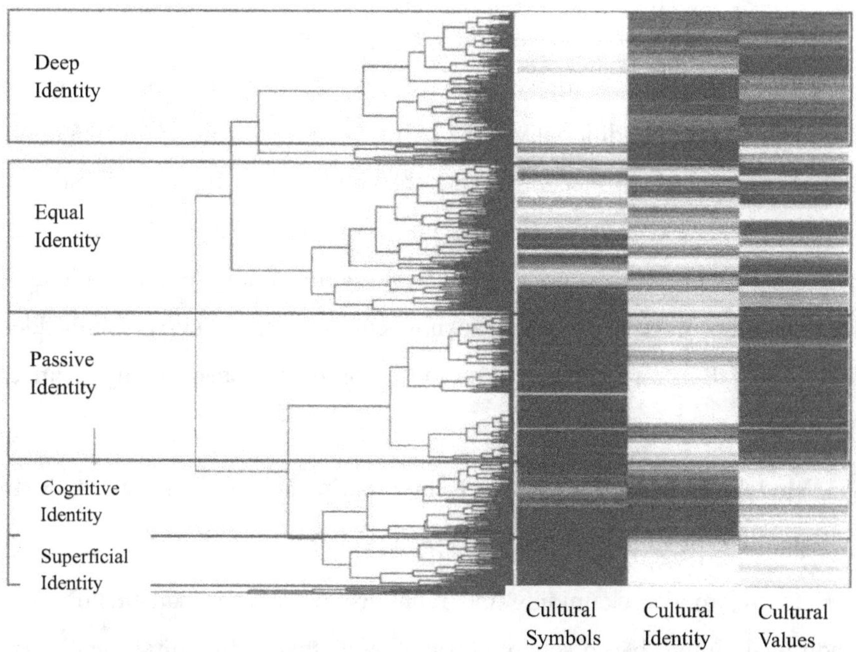

Figure 3-7: Clustering of Primary and Secondary School Students

Among these, "Deep Identity" and "Superficial Identity" show opposite trends in cultural symbol recognition. While students may not remember the specific meanings of certain cultural symbols, they have already understood and internalized the essence of traditional Chinese culture through prior learning and immersion. This type of student is more commonly found in the

① Han, Zhen. Characteristics of Cultural Identity of Overseas Chinese in the Era of Globalization [J]. *Academics in China*, 2009(2):25–32.

upper grades of secondary school, accounting for 23.48% of the overall student population. Students categorized as "Equal Recognition" demonstrate average performance across the three dimensions, showing only a vague, outline-level understanding and recognition of traditional Chinese culture. "Passive Recognition" students, on the other hand, have passively absorbed various aspects of traditional cultural education, resulting in an understanding and recognition of the representative symbols and basic concepts of the culture. However, they have not truly internalized these beliefs into emotional attachment or transformed them into subjective identity recognition. As a result, their cultural identity recognition remains relatively low. Additionally, there is another category, "Cognitive Recognition," which accounts for about 10% of the overall student population. These students, having undergone some level of study, have performed well in recognizing cultural symbols and cultural identity. However, they have yet to deeply acknowledge the spiritual values embedded in traditional culture. This type is more commonly seen among younger students.

3.3 Model Construction of the Relationship Between Student Course Satisfaction and Traditional Cultural Identity

In the model examining the relationship between satisfaction with traditional culture-based school curricula and students' cultural identity (as shown in Figure 3-8), the average variance extracted (AVE) values for each latent variable were calculated to be greater than 0.5. Additionally, the parameters of the model were found to be significant at the level of $P \leq 0.05$ (except for the correlation between student expectations and value perception). This indicates that the dimensions of the model possess good internal logic.

From the model diagram and the overall summary of the correlation coefficients, it can be observed that the satisfaction with traditional culture-based school curricula suggests that the implementation of these courses can enhance students' cultural identity. Indeed, the development of students' recognition of outstanding Chinese traditional culture is not solely confined to the implementation of school-based curricula. It also depends on the infiltration of national curricula in school education, as well as the collaborative educational forces of social and family education. However, the construction of this model illustrates that traditional culture-based school curricula are an appropriate and effective pathway for enhancing students' cultural identity.

The relationship model on the left side of the diagram, which links course satisfaction, reveals that students' perceptions of teaching methods and content in traditional culture-based curricula determine their learning outcomes. That is, the perceived quality has a decisive effect on value perception, with a direct effect of 0.62. Moreover, the level of students' value perception plays a decisive role in their course loyalty, with a direct effect of 0.69. Additionally, student expectations have a certain influence on perceived quality, value perception, and student loyalty, though the effect is relatively weak, particularly in the aspect of value perception (the direct effect is only 0.28).

Thus, although the survey indicates that most students have expectations regarding the content of traditional culture, it is their personal perception and outcomes from traditional culture-based curricula that truly influence their satisfaction with the course. This finding highlights the need, when designing and implementing traditional culture-based school curricula, to promote embodied and diverse teaching methods, as well as the appropriateness and timeliness of teaching content. It is essential to fully consider students' experiences and rootedness, and to improve the curricula in a timely manner, thereby enhancing students' perceived quality of these courses. In turn, this will improve their value perception, ultimately increasing their satisfaction with the courses.

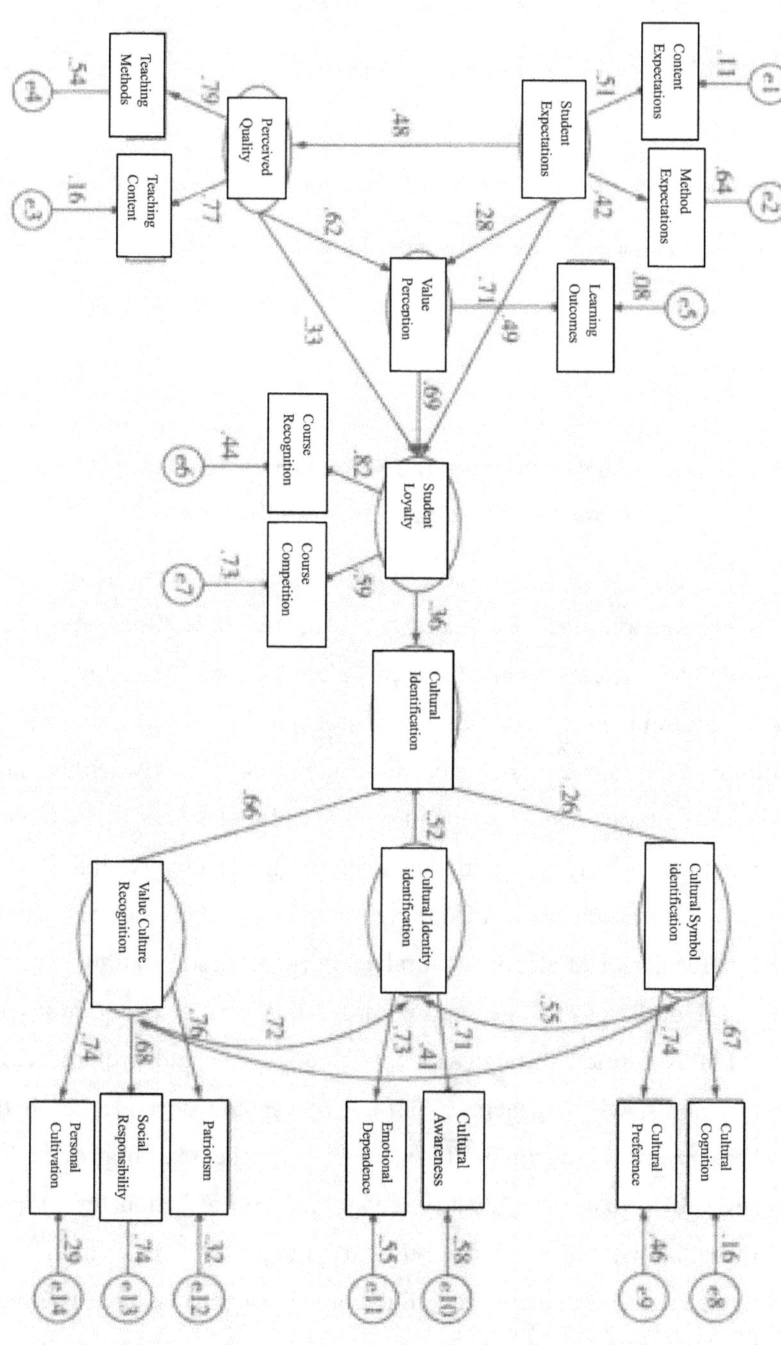
Content Expectations
Method Expectations
Student Expectations
Perceived Quality
Teaching Methods
Teaching Content
Value Perception
Learning Outcomes
Student Loyalty
Course Recognition
Course Competition
Cultural Identification
Value Culture Recognition
Cultural Identity identification
Cultural Symbol identification
Personal Cultivation
Social Responsibility
Patriotism
Emotional Dependence
Cultural Awareness
Cultural Preference
Cultural Cognition
e1
e2
e3
e4
e5
e6
e7
e8
e9
e10
e11
e12
e13
e14
.11
.64
.51
.42
.48
.28
.79
.77
.54
.16
.62
.71
.08
.49
.33
.69
.82
.44
.59
.73
.36
.66
.52
.26
.72
.55
.41
.74
.68
.76
.73
.71
.74
.67
.29
.74
.32
.55
.58
.46
.16

e1: Content Expectation e2: Method Expectation — Academic Expectation

e3: Teaching Method e4: Teaching Content — Perceived Quality

e5: Learning Achievement — Value Perception

e6: Course Recognition e7: Course Competition — Student Loyalty — Cultural Identity

e8: Cultural Cognition e9: Cultural Preference — Cultural Symbol Recognition

e10: Cultural Awareness e11: Emotional Dependence — Cultural Identity Recognition

e12: National Sentiment e13: Social Responsibility e14: Personal Cultivation — Value Cultural Recognition

Figure 3-8: Model of Primary and Secondary School Students' Course Satisfaction and Cultural Identity Perception

Additionally, according to the cultural identity model on the right side of the model construction, we can clearly see that the three dimensions of the relationship with the generation of student cultural identity, from high to low, are value cultural identity, cultural identity recognition, and cultural symbol recognition. At the same time, the correlation coefficients between the three are 0.55 for cultural identity recognition and cultural symbol recognition, 0.72 for cultural identity recognition and value cultural identity, and 0.41 for cultural symbol recognition and value cultural identity. It can be seen that the actual test results of students' cultural identity generation align with the theoretical hypotheses. The generation of cultural identity is not an instant process, but is formed through students' recognition and preference for cultural symbols, which generates self-awareness and dependence on the cultural environment they are in. It is a continuous process of improving and promoting self-formation of identity recognition and affection for Chinese excellent traditional culture through the differentiation of multiculturalism. Based on this, students achieve recognition of the essence of Chinese national cultural spirit, which involves understanding the value culture in Chinese excellent traditional culture, such as "promoting benevolence, emphasizing the people, keeping trust, advocating righteousness, valuing harmony, and seeking great unity." In summary, the generation of cultural identity is a layered, progressive process. This requires us to focus on the requirements of the "Outline" in curriculum design and implementation, promoting its vertical coherence, and gradually enabling students to move from the symbolic recognition of traditional cultural objects to the conceptual understanding of the spiritual dimension.

3.4 Dynamic Changes in Public Opinion Regarding Traditional Cultural Education Activities in Schools

We organized and analyzed 1684 valid news reports from 2014 to 2018 related to traditional cultural education policies and activities conducted by basic education schools across provinces and cities. In terms of quantity, the number of reports related to traditional cultural education from 2014 to 2018 were 119, 146, 263, 432, and 724 respectively. It can be seen that since the Ministry of Education promulgated the "Outline" in 2014, the number of public opinion reports has generally shown an increasing trend year by year, and the growth rate has significantly accelerated since 2017. The year 2017 became a special time point mainly due to the introduction of the "Opinions" document. Provinces and cities have strengthened their focus and attention to traditional Chinese culture education to implement the basic ideas of the "Opinions," greatly enhancing publicity efforts and providing guidance in policy interpretation, specific requirements, goals, tasks, and practical strategies. This also fully demonstrates that adhering to policy guidance is a fundamental feature of the local implementation of traditional cultural education, and the guiding role of policies has played an active role in the implementation of traditional culture education across regions.

Through quantitative calculation, it can be found that provinces such as Chongqing (3.949), Sichuan (3.466), Shandong (3.370), Henan (3.171), and

Anhui (2.898) have relatively high TCEPCI levels and good competitive power in traditional culture education public opinion. Among them, Shandong, Henan, and Anhui have strong advantages in the diversity of educational carriers through the development and utilization of their intangible cultural heritage resources, while Chongqing and Sichuan have exerted efforts in the diversity of educational paths, resulting in high competitiveness. Furthermore, from the overall measurement results, it can be seen that the current public opinion competitiveness in traditional culture education in China presents a significant spatial distribution pattern of large differences. So, is there a "knowledge spillover" of educational methods and resource exploration between adjacent provinces, leading to a spatial agglomeration effect? According to the ArcGIS measurement, the global autocorrelation Z value is 3.228, and the P-value is $0.001 \leq 0.001$, which indicates that the public opinion competitiveness in traditional culture education has shown significant spatial agglomeration. The ratio of the G index to the expected G index is 1, indicating that there are high-value agglomerations between provinces with strong competitiveness, as well as low-value agglomerations between provinces with weak competitiveness. Subsequently, using TCEPCI values for local spatial autocorrelation testing, it was found that provinces such as Henan, Anhui, and Zhejiang, along with the surrounding areas (i.e., the Central Plains region and the Yangtze River Delta region), exhibited high-high agglomeration effects, while Xinjiang, Tibet, and surrounding areas showed low-low agglomeration effects. The Guizhou province and its surrounding areas demonstrated low-high agglomeration effects.

The public opinion reports on traditional culture education are often a process of news publicity based on the enhancement of practical approaches, and they mostly contain information about relatively excellent or distinctive traditional culture education carriers and methods. These reports can also influence practice by nourishing and inspiring the ongoing practice, reflection, and improvement of traditional culture education. As the spatial agglomeration effect occurs, the traditional culture educational carriers and paths concentrated in high-high agglomeration areas are promoted and mutually influenced. Under the influence of this knowledge spillover effect, theoretical research and practical adjustments of traditional culture education will continue to inject new insights, thus continuing to seize the "high ground" and "opportunities" of traditional culture education. In addition, the low-high agglomeration area in Guizhou may, through the knowledge accumulation, communication, sharing, and achievements spillover of surrounding provinces with strong public opinion power in traditional culture education, produce a "ride-along effect," ①and it can be predicted that in the near future, the public opinion strength of traditional culture in this region will also experience a certain degree of growth, which will promote the development of traditional culture education.

4. Discussion: Focus Areas for Improving the Quality of Traditional Cultural School-based Courses

The value of a curriculum lies in its shaping of students' physical and mental development. The value of traditional culture school-based courses lies in helping students understand and appreciate Chinese excellent traditional culture, reflect on the uniqueness of their own culture, and establish a connection to their national roots, thus gradually forming cultural identity. In order to improve the quality of such courses and promote students' cultural identity, the following aspects need to be considered.

---

① Sun, Yangchun, & Zhu, Lianhua. The "Spatial Spillover" and Dilemma of Local Higher Education Returns [J]. *Higher Education Exploration*, 2016(10):52–55.

4.1 Grasping the Appropriate Form of Traditional Cultural School-based Courses

Traditional cultural education is realized through multiple forms, such as national curriculum, school-based curriculum, and school activities. We need to consider: where does the function of school-based courses lie, and what form should they take? The national curriculum presents traditional culture through courses like Chinese, history, and art, forming a content system of traditional culture in various fields, characterized by systematicness and structurality. The function of school-based courses is to continue these contents or to make them more three-dimensional and "alive." Therefore, traditional cultural school-based courses should present integrated, specialized, and diversified forms. Traditional cultural school-based courses should not simply supplement traditional culture in the national curriculum in terms of quantity; hence, more content does not necessarily mean better, nor is more "traditional" always correct. The fundamental goal is to shape students' basic cultural structure on the premise of acceptance. On the "object" level, it is necessary to experience traditional cultural objects, techniques, customs, and food. The cultural system is different from the knowledge system. It needs to first take concrete forms, such as stories, techniques, knowledge, and objects, and then abstract into the emotional and value systems behind them. Without the "object," the "way" is too abstract, becoming preachy, and only the "object" culture, without its core essence, merely inherits tradition without culture. The "object" is the foundation of experiencing the "way," and the "way" is the ultimate goal of education. Meanwhile, traditional cultural forms in school-based courses can vary, and different cultural forms need to seek the same cultural essence, which requires teachers to guide students to perceive this essence through the experience of objects, techniques, customs, and food. This essence can be the "spirit" of the greater self, such as patriotism and responsibility, or the "flavor" of the smaller self, such as gentleness, harmony, nature, wisdom, and courtesy in how to regard nature, society, and others. By seeking commonality in differences, a rich, diverse, yet unified and harmonious educational ecology in traditional cultural education can be formed.

4.2 Further Clarify the Responsibilities and Functions of Local Curriculum Management

In 2001, the Ministry of Education issued the "Outline of the Curriculum Reform of Basic Education (Trial)" which further clarified the three-tier curriculum management structure at the national, local, and school levels. However, the practices of local curriculum management departments regarding their responsibilities, powers, and functions are not consistent across regions. Some localities mainly communicate and publicize the national curriculum policies and related documents, while others directly develop local curricula and textbooks, requiring schools to implement them. Simply communicating and publicizing national policies cannot fulfill their management functions; without the participation of schools and teachers in the development of local curricula and textbooks, the regional advantages of curriculum implementation may not be fully utilized, and teachers' ability to implement curricula may not be enhanced. To promote the development of school-based curricula, including those related to traditional culture, it is necessary to further clarify the responsibilities and functions of local curriculum management. First, local curriculum management should fulfill the function of planning and formulating local curriculum programs. Local curricula are not merely a transmission of national requirements but should combine national demands with the needs and goals of local curriculum development to generate localized curriculum programs. Secondly, local curricula should be responsible for supervising the basic standards of national curricula and overseeing their implementation. Thirdly, they should coordinate regional curriculum resources. For school-based traditional culture courses, this function is especially crucial. Local cultural departments, cultural figures, and media organizations should be coordinated to introduce local traditional cultural resources, promote exemplary case schools, and establish regional traditional culture promotion platforms, all of which can strongly support school curriculum development. Finally, local curriculum management should provide professional guidance to schools and teachers, offering support in areas such as helping schools and teachers select and identify traditional culture, providing curriculum development techniques, and ensuring appropriate methods for curriculum implementation.

4.3 Traditional Culture in the Curriculum Should Be Integrated into Contemporary Ethical and Aesthetic Commonalities

The formation of Chinese traditional culture has been a long process, with a diverse range of types and content. Mainstream culture, folk culture, and regional culture have all merged together. The question of which content can and should enter the curriculum system is a prerequisite for ensuring the quality of such school-based curricula. This cultural selection process is a systematic project for society as a whole, not something any single school can undertake. However, as institutions representing the state in nurturing youth, schools must transmit content that aligns with basic value norms and meets moral, ethical, and civil standards. As scholars from the social curriculum school believe, school curricula are a form of cultural reproduction, and they should play a guiding role in social culture. ①

Traditional culture courses originate from traditional culture, but at the same time, curricula are actively identifying and screening traditional cultural content. The traditional culture included in the curriculum shapes young people's understanding of traditional culture and depicts the public image of

---

① Michael Apple. *Ideology and Curriculum*. Translated by Huang Zhongjing, Shanghai: East China Normal University Press, 2001, pp. 37-41.

traditional culture. This "reproduction" of traditional culture in cultural transmission requires us to carefully consider the cultural selections made in the curriculum. Traditional culture is not a propaganda tool, nor a management instrument. What it transmits should be something to aspire to, something that makes young people proud and committed to passing it on. Traditional culture is not a fixed concept; it is inherently in a process of evolution and development. Each era of culture is the continuation of past culture, with each era having its own innovative cultural essence. The so-called traditional culture is the tradition that has been selected, integrated, and transformed by the times. "Our doubts, interests, criticisms, and disputes about tradition are all due to our confusion, perplexity, and expectations about the present and the future... Tradition can become the tradition of every generation, having different meanings for different generations, because tradition allows each era to extend it through its own understanding and interpretation, just like the rebirth of a phoenix after its transformation." [①]Traditional culture courses are a process of interpreting and extending traditional culture. They need to screen expressions from ethical systems like "filial piety, respect for elders, and reverence for teachers," using modern mainstream forms of interpersonal communication, psychological contracts, and aesthetic standards. They also need to transform the understanding of the core values such as "benevolence, people-centered, integrity, justice, harmony, and great unity" in light of modern national forms and value beliefs.

4.4 Traditional Culture in the Curriculum Should Form an Individual Cultural Schema with World Civilizations

School education completes its nurturing function through the curriculum. The curriculum system constructs students' knowledge system and value system, and it profoundly influences their cultural system. The

① Yin, Ding. The Destiny of Understanding [M]. Beijing: SDX Joint Publishing Company, 1988:2.

premise of cultural identity is cultural recognition, which comes after understanding the differences between one's own national culture and other ethnic cultures. It is only after this that a person can form recognition of their unique cultural identity. The curriculum structure in schools does not exclude, but rather equally values, other cultural forms and modes of civilization, as this provides students with a broader cultural understanding. International understanding and global competence are essential literacy for students' future survival and development. Understanding other cultures and experiencing the unfamiliar and the unknown are unavoidable parts of life for today's students. Through various media, firsthand experiences, and the dissemination of knowledge, today's students live surrounded by a rich and diverse cultural environment.

Regarding the development of ethnic and group cultures, the interplay between cultural identity and cultural change is precisely the inevitable process of cultural self-reflection, self-renewal, and creative development. As for individual culture, individuals, with their sense of cultural belonging, interact and develop in various global cultural circles, also needing recognition of elements from other cultures. The traditional culture within the school curriculum and its international perspective must coexist, but the cultural needs of different cultures should be integrated into the psychological structure of one's national cultural identity. This integration is difficult to standardize or unify in a fixed psychological schema. The curriculum merely provides the elements for forming such a schema, and each individual's cultural psychological structure must be completed through diverse, differentiated, and evolving experiences in school and social life.

Chapter 14 Constructing Dimensions for Quality Assessment of Basic Education Curriculum Development in the Context of Educational Equity

The quality of a nation's education should not be evaluated solely by students' academic achievements; the quality of the educational process itself is a fundamental dimension of educational excellence. The curriculum is the primary vehicle for talent cultivation in basic education. It reflects the goals of national educational policy and the developmental objectives of each educational stage. As such, the development of the basic education curriculum is a vital indicator of the overall quality and equity of a country's education system.

Since the release of the Outline for the Curriculum Reform of Basic Education (Trial) in 2001, followed by several landmark policy documents—such as the National Medium- and Long-Term Education Reform and Development Plan (2010–2020), the Opinions on Deepening Comprehensive Reform in the Education Sector (2013), and the Opinions on Fully Implementing the Fundamental Task of Moral Education and Deepening Curriculum Reform—China has consistently prioritized curriculum development as a central issue in its basic education reform agenda. Ensuring the quality of basic education curriculum development remains a critical and ongoing focus of educational research and policy implementation.

1. The Development of Basic Education Curriculum as an Important Dimension for Measuring Educational Quality and Equity

Educational Equity as a Foundation for Quality Education. Educational equity is the cornerstone of social equity. It emphasizes fairness—not just in terms of quantity, but also in the relationships among members of society across the educational process, from starting points to outcomes, ensuring that every individual receives what they need to thrive. Fairness involves balancing rights, responsibilities, and benefits among all stakeholders, enabling harmonious and just coexistence.

The 17th National Congress of the Communist Party of China emphasized education as a key to improving people's livelihoods and achieving social equity, affirming that "education is the foundation of national rejuvenation, and educational equity is the basis for social equity." The Education Planning Outline further elevated equity as a strategic priority, stating, "Promoting fairness is a basic national education policy," and "Improving quality is the core task of educational reform and development." Together, these policy positions clarify that promoting educational equity and improving educational quality are dual goals and fundamental responsibilities of China's basic education reform[①].

Scholars in China widely recognize three dimensions of educational equity:

A. Equity at the starting point – equal access to educational opportunities.

---

① Tan, Songhua, & Wang, Jian. The Pursuit of Quality Educational Equity [J]. *People's Education*, 2011(18):5–9.

B. Equity in the process – equal quality in the teaching and learning experience.

C. Equity in the outcome – equitable attainment of educational goals.

In recent years, national education policies have focused strongly on ensuring that every child receives equal access to education, which is essential for acquiring basic skills, integrating into society, and achieving a fulfilling life. Equal educational opportunity is, therefore, a foundational step toward social justice and a prerequisite for realizing starting point equity.

As the education system has expanded and universalized nine-year compulsory education, the central tension has shifted from inadequate access to a mismatch between educational supply and demand, particularly the insufficient supply of high-quality education. Consequently, quality equity has become a deeper and more urgent goal in the pursuit of educational fairness. What does quality equity mean? Globally, since the 1960s, countries have progressively broadened their understanding of educational equity—from a narrow focus on equal access and starting points, to concerns about equity in outcomes, and eventually to attention to the quality of the educational process itself. This evolution reflects a consensus: true educational equity requires not only equal opportunities and rights, but also equally high-quality educational experiences, ensuring students can achieve comparable standards of learning and development.

Notably, scholars in China generally agree that identical educational outcomes are neither realistic nor necessary. Rather, equity in outcomes should be assessed based on whether students meet acceptable standards of achievement, aligned with curriculum goals. More critically, attention must turn to the educational process, which has a profound and lasting impact on students' growth and long-term potential.

The quality of the educational process includes the internal dynamics of teaching and learning: the school environment, instructional quality, pedagogical strategies, student engagement, and classroom interactions. While difficult to measure directly, this process-oriented dimension shapes students' developmental trajectories in ways that standardized outcomes cannot capture. To approximate it, education systems often rely on input indicators—such as funding, infrastructure, teacher qualifications, and resource allocation—as proxy measures. While essential, these inputs are necessary but not sufficient; they do not, by themselves, guarantee high-quality or equitable educational experiences.

The quality of curriculum development is a key benchmark for evaluating the quality of the educational process. As the core medium through which educational goals are operationalized, the curriculum reflects national policy intentions, educational values, and pedagogical philosophies. It determines what knowledge is valued, how it is taught, and how students experience learning.

From what schools aim to teach, to what teachers are able to and actually do teach, to the strategies employed and the ways students engage with content—every element of the educational experience is shaped by the curriculum. Some scholars view curriculum as a broad and intangible force embedded in the entire educational process—shaping learning in subtle yet powerful ways. Others conceptualize it more concretely as a set of structured goals, content, and expected outcomes. Either way, curriculum lies at the heart of schooling, and the effectiveness of curriculum development is a direct indicator of a school's educational quality.

In short, curriculum development quality reflects both the system's commitment to educational equity and its capacity for educational excellence. Achieving a high-quality, equitable curriculum is thus not only a technical task, but also a moral imperative for fostering a just and thriving educational system.

2. The Quality Assessment of School Curriculum Development Based on Equity

2.1 The Connotation of Curriculum Development

Curriculum development is a multifaceted concept, encompassing diverse interpretations across historical, procedural, and evaluative dimensions. Firstly, curriculum development can be understood as the historical evolution of the curriculum—an examination of how curricula change over time, along with the educational ideologies, orientations, and characteristics that define each period. Secondly, it can be conceptualized as a sequential process, involving multiple interconnected stages such as curriculum research and formulation, policy dissemination and interpretation, school-level implementation and adaptation, innovation, evaluation, and feedback. These stages reflect the dynamic and cyclical nature of curriculum advancement.

In the context of this discussion, curriculum development refers specifically to the performance and status of the curriculum at various levels within a defined period. It includes both factual elements (what is being taught, how it is structured and implemented) and value judgments (the extent to which it meets educational goals and ethical standards). As one scholar aptly stated, "Curriculum is not a product of speculation but the result of action." [①] Therefore, curriculum quality must be traced through practical actions and institutional behaviors at all levels of the education system.

In the domain of quality management, two definitions of quality are particularly instructive. The first asserts that a product's quality is determined

---

① Huang, Zhengjie. *Curriculum Design* [M]. Taipei: Donghua Bookstore, 2002:85.

by whether it meets user needs and ensures satisfaction; the second emphasizes that quality implies the absence of defects, or conformity to required standards[①]. When these principles are applied to curriculum development, a high-quality curriculum is one that: aligns with national educational objectives; addresses student needs across diverse contexts; meets prescribed standards for content, structure, and outcomes. Thus, curriculum is not only a structured "product" intended for student learning and development—it is also a strategic resource invested in the educational process. It should therefore uphold the principles of equity and social fairness.

Sociologist John Rawls's theory of social justice, particularly his first principle of equal basic liberties and his emphasis on respecting individual differences and compensating for disadvantage, provides a valuable framework for examining curriculum development from an equity perspective.

From this standpoint, assessing curriculum quality requires clarity on what "equality" means in practice. Just as educational processes and outcomes cannot be identical across all regions, schools, or student populations, the curriculum must strive to ensure equity in access, content, and delivery. This requires acknowledging and addressing variations in environmental conditions, resource availability, and institutional capacity.

In an equitable curriculum development model:

A. Equal educational opportunity entails universal access to foundational learning resources and curricular content;

---

① Research Group on Educational Quality Standards, Chinese Academy of Educational Sciences. National Standards for Educational Quality and Their Formulation [J]. *Educational Research*, 2013(6).

B. Differentiated support addresses disparities in learning contexts, ensuring all students have the conditions necessary for meaningful participation;

C. Responsive implementation adapts curricular content and pedagogy to local realities, enabling schools to uphold both national standards and contextual relevance.

In recent decades, China's education reform policies have paid sustained attention to issues surrounding curriculum development in primary and secondary schools. These policies embed both normative principles—such as moral education, student-centered learning, and competency-based approaches—and actionable guidelines for school leaders, teachers, and education administrators.

Key documents that have guided this curriculum reform movement include:

The *Outline for the Curriculum Reform of Basic Education (Trial)* (2001);

The *National Medium- and Long-Term Education Reform and Development Plan (2010–2020)*;

The *Decision of the Third Plenary Session of the 18th CPC Central Committee on Major Issues Concerning Comprehensively Deepening Reforms* (2013);

The *Opinions of the Ministry of Education on Deepening Reform in the Field of Education Comprehensively* (2013);

The *Opinions of the Ministry of Education on Fully Deepening Curriculum Reform to Implement the Core Task of Moral Education* (2014).

These policy documents articulate evolving understandings of curriculum development and outline behavior norms that guide practice across different levels of the education system. Together, they form a policy foundation for assessing the quality and equity of school curriculum development in contemporary China. A policy matrix summarizing the curriculum-related provisions in these key documents is presented in Table 3-3.

Table 3-3 Curriculum Development Points in Key Documents

Level	Core Content Summary	Value Points
School Education	Principles and orientations: educational equity, balanced resource distribution, reducing dropout rates, lessening academic burdens, emphasizing socialist core values, focusing on capabilities, promoting holistic development, quality assessment	Educational equity, cultivating moral character
School System	Small class teaching in compulsory education, comprehensive quality assessment, student development guidance in high school, promoting the diverse development of high schools	Balanced development in compulsory education, choice in high school education
Curriculum Setup	National curriculum standards, development of local and school-based curricula, designing curriculum difficulty appropriately, ensuring full provision of music, PE, and arts teachers, strictly implementing required courses, offering elective courses, encouraging research-based learning, community service, and social practice	Implementing national curriculum, developing local and school-based curricula

Teaching	Optimizing knowledge structure, enriching social practice, enhancing capability development, fostering independence and initiative, encouraging inquiry and exploration, respecting personalities, addressing differences, creating supportive educational environments, using technology, reducing homework and exams, nurturing student interest and hobbies, strictly following curriculum plans	Reforming teaching concepts, reforming teaching methods
Evaluation	Reforming the exam and enrollment system, academic proficiency exams, comprehensive quality assessment, implementing high school proficiency tests and comprehensive quality assessments	Reforming evaluation methods
Student Literacy	Fostering student competencies such as innovation, practical abilities, scientific and cultural literacy, environmental awareness, aesthetic appreciation, proactive learning attitudes, basic knowledge, skills, information gathering and processing abilities, problem-solving and analytical abilities, communication and collaboration skills	Focusing on core student competencies
Resources	Diversified textbooks, curriculum resource development, teacher training, expert guidance, school-family cooperation	Textbook construction, enhancing teacher professional competence

The value points embedded in curriculum policy reflect national expectations for primary and secondary school curricula and serve as essential standards for evaluating curriculum quality. Key among these are educational equity, balanced allocation of resources, and a commitment to moral education and the socialist core values—principles that fundamentally guide curriculum development.

The educational system emphasizes holistic student development during the compulsory education stage and promotes flexibility and individual choice in high school, providing institutional support for curriculum innovation. In terms of curriculum structure, it is essential to ensure the rigorous implementation of the national curriculum while simultaneously encouraging the development of local and school-based curricula. Moreover, reforming teaching philosophies, instructional objectives, and pedagogical methods plays a critical role in enhancing students' overall competencies. Finally, curriculum development must be supported by reforms in examination and evaluation systems, as well as improvements in textbooks and ongoing teacher professional development.

2.2 Curriculum Quality Assessment Orientation

An analysis of educational policy from an equity perspective reveals key orientations for curriculum quality assessment:

1. Alignment with Educational Goals

The curriculum should reflect contemporary societal values and embody the nation's current educational objectives. The core mission of moral education and the promotion of socialist core values must be realized through school curricula. Furthermore, curricula should align with the developmental focus of each educational stage—for example, emphasizing equity and holistic growth in compulsory education, and stressing flexibility and differentiation in high school to accommodate students' diverse needs.

2. Implementation of Curriculum Plans and Standards

The national curriculum plan delineates the overarching goals and structure for education at the primary and secondary levels. Discipline-specific standards translate these plans into actionable frameworks, encompassing knowledge progression as well as embedded values and attitudes. These curriculum plans and standards are direct extensions of national educational policy. Adherence to them ensures that all students have equal access to quality educational content, a cornerstone of educational equity.

3. Respect for Student Differences

Equity in education does not imply uniformity but rather appropriateness—providing each student with an education tailored to their individual needs. As agents of the state, schools and teachers must acknowledge and accommodate differences in students' environments, cultural backgrounds, academic levels, and interests. The curriculum should therefore allow for course selection and personalized learning paths, particularly for under-resourced schools or students facing greater challenges.

4. Satisfaction with the Educational Process

Curriculum quality is also reflected in the educational process itself, notably in aspects such as safety, clarity, well-being, and balanced workload. Just as the quality of a product is measured not only by its functionality but also by its ability to meet users' needs for comfort, safety, and aesthetics, the "user experience" in education—namely the learning experience—deeply influences both students and teachers over time. This can be evaluated through the satisfaction and attitudes of those involved. For instance, students should feel that the curriculum is appropriately challenging and manageable; their emotional experience in class should be positive; and both students and parents should recognize the curriculum's value and relevance.

3. Levels and Key Points in the Assessment of School Curriculum Development Quality

3.1 Curriculum Performance Levels

To assess the quality of school curriculum development effectively, it is crucial to differentiate the various levels at which curriculum manifests. Scholars such as Goodlad, Posner, and Brophy have proposed distinct conceptual frameworks to categorize these curriculum levels. For instance, Goodlad delineates five levels: the ideal curriculum, written curriculum, perceived curriculum, implemented curriculum, and experienced curriculum. [①]Posner, on the other hand, categorizes curriculum into official, actual, hidden, null, and extracurricular curricula [②]A significant issue highlighted in Posner's framework is the phenomenon of curricular parallelism within the actual curriculum, wherein the official curriculum, the taught curriculum, and the tested (or acquired) curriculum often coexist but are not necessarily aligned. Brophy provides a more nuanced and detailed framework of curriculum in practice, identifying seven distinct levels[③]: The official written curriculum, the curriculum interpreted by school principals or curriculum committees, the unofficial but formally enacted school-level curriculum, the curriculum shaped by teachers' beliefs, the curriculum planned by teachers, the curriculum actually taught by teachers, and the curriculum experienced by students.

Brophy's typology highlights the complex and layered nature of curriculum enactment, encompassing texts, beliefs, and actions across multiple stakeholders—governments, schools, teachers, and students. His

① GoodlADJI. Curriculum inquiry: the study of curriculum practice [M]. New York: McGraw-Hill,1979.
② Posner, George J. Analyzing the Curriculum. Translated by Qiu Guangpeng, Han Miaomiao, and Zhang Xianrong, Shanghai: East China Normal University Press, 2007, p. 13.
③ Brophyje. How teachers influence what is taught and learned in classroom [J]. The Elementary School Journal,1982(4).

framework comprehensively reflects the dynamic processes and transformations involved in curriculum transmission and implementation.

Within the context of China's curriculum system, school curriculum development can be viewed as the process initiated after the publication of the national curriculum framework and subject-specific standards. This process encompasses school-level curriculum planning, the categorization and offering of courses, the curriculum as perceived and designed by teachers, its actual implementation in classrooms, and the curriculum as received and assessed among students.

Moreover, curriculum development can also be conceptualized as a form of public policy implementation. Accordingly, evaluation should not only determine whether the intended outcomes have been achieved, but also investigate various influencing factors such as stakeholder roles, target groups, available resources, and implementation strategies. As with policy evaluation, curriculum quality assessment must involve both empirical judgments (what is) and normative judgments (what ought to be), focusing on goal attainment, impacts, and implications for future development. (See Table 3-4)

Table 3-4 Levels of Curriculum

<table>
<tr><th colspan="2">Curriculum Levels / Curriculum Subjects</th><th>Goodlad</th><th>Brophy</th><th colspan="2">Posner</th></tr>
<tr><td colspan="2"></td><td>Ideal Curriculum</td><td>/</td><td colspan="2">/</td></tr>
<tr><td rowspan="4">Actual Curriculum</td><td rowspan="2">Official</td><td>Written Curriculum</td><td>Official Curriculum</td><td colspan="2">Official Curriculum</td></tr>
<tr><td>/</td><td>Curriculum Interpreted by Official</td><td>/</td><td rowspan="3">Actual Curriculum</td></tr>
<tr><td>School</td><td>/</td><td>School Set Curriculum</td><td>/</td></tr>
<tr><td></td><td>Perceived Curriculum</td><td>Teacher's Beliefs Curriculum</td><td>/</td></tr>
</table>

Curriculum Levels / Curriculum Subjects		Goodlad	Brophy	Posner	
	Teacher	/	Teacher's Planned Curriculum	/	
		Implemented Curriculum	Teacher's Implemented Curriculum	Taught Curriculum	
	Students	Experienced Curriculum	Student's Acquired Curriculum	Tested Curriculum	
	Curriculum Related to Stakeholders	/	/	Hidden Curriculum	
		/	/	Extracurricular Curriculum	
		/	/	Blank Curriculum	

3.2 Key Points in Large-Scale Curriculum Development Surveys

Large-scale curriculum development surveys across different countries often share common focal points. Following China's 2001 curriculum reform, a nationwide investigation was launched to examine the state of curriculum implementation. The major areas of focus included: the actual status of reform implementation, the attitudes of teachers and school principals toward the reforms, and key factors influencing the success or failure of curriculum implementation. ①

Similarly, in countries such as the United States, Japan, and the United Kingdom, comprehensive educational reforms were accompanied by large-scale curriculum evaluation studies. For example, in the United States, one prominent area of investigation has been the alignment between classroom instruction and curriculum standards. Improving the quality of basic education has long been a policy priority for U.S. federal and state governments. In August 1989, a conference of state governors held in Virginia issued a joint call for the federal government to establish national

① Ma, Yunpeng, & Tang, Lifang. Current Situation and Countermeasures of Curriculum Implementation: Analysis and Reflection Based on Some Pilot Area Evaluations [J]. *Journal of Northeast Normal University (Philosophy and Social Sciences Edition)*, 2002(5):124–129.

educational goals and uniform curriculum standards for key subjects in K–12 education. The aim was to ensure equal access to high-quality education for all students. This initiative received strong support from then-President George H. W. Bush.

In 1992, the National Education Standards and Testing Council was established at the federal level. Task forces for subjects such as English, mathematics, science, history, and geography were formed to develop national curriculum standards. [①]Later, in 2002, the No Child Left Behind Act (NCLB) was passed, imposing stringent accountability measures on schools that failed to meet prescribed educational benchmarks.

To support the monitoring of curriculum alignment and teaching effectiveness, the Wisconsin Center for Education Research (WCER), in collaboration with the Council of Chief State School Officers (CCSSO), developed a large-scale classroom survey tool known as the Survey of Enacted Curriculum (SEC). The SEC is designed to measure the degree of alignment between classroom instruction and curriculum standards [②], particularly in elementary and middle school classrooms.

The SEC framework analyzes instructional content along two core dimensions: content topics (themes), and cognitive demand levels. Teachers report the amount of classroom time devoted to each topic and cognitive level. This data is then used to evaluate how effectively instruction matches the expected curriculum standards and to assess the overall quality of the teaching process. The SEC has been in use in the United States for more than 15 years and has been adopted by over 30 states, making it a critical tool in large-scale curriculum research and quality assurance.

---

① Lü, Lijie. *Research on the Process of National Curriculum Design* [M]. Beijing: Educational Science Publishing House, 2008:23.

② Chen, Shuqing, Wang, Xiuhong, & Luan, Huimin. Construction and Inspiration of the "SEC" Curriculum Implementation Survey Model under the Perspective of Basic Education in the United States [J]. *Journal of Northeast Normal University (Philosophy and Social Sciences Edition)*, 2015(3).

In recent years, the United Kingdom has undertaken large-scale curriculum development reviews and reforms. In 2011, to align with national curriculum revisions, the Department for Education launched a comprehensive survey and review of curriculum development across primary and secondary schools. This initiative engaged a wide range of stakeholders—including teachers, principals, parents, students, and representatives from higher education and broader society—through official websites, mass media, and targeted questionnaires. The review assessed whether the existing curriculum effectively supported students' understanding of various subjects, promoted mastery of core knowledge in English, mathematics, science, and physical education, and allowed teachers adequate flexibility in curriculum design and delivery. It also evaluated whether the curriculum provided students with a world-class education. Insights from the review informed efforts to enhance national curriculum standards and improve transparency for parents regarding what their children should be learning, enabling better home-school collaboration.

In Japan, curriculum reform has similarly involved systematic monitoring by the Ministry of Education, Culture, Sports, Science and Technology (MEXT), using academic assessments, instructional surveys, and data analysis. In 1996, Japan's Central Education Council issued a landmark advisory report, *The Desired State of Education for the 21st Century*, emphasizing life skills development and individualized, autonomous learning within a relaxed educational environment. Following this, the 2002 implementation of the *Learning Guidance Guidelines* brought reductions in content volume, course difficulty, and instructional hours. However, concerns arose regarding a potential decline in academic standards. In response, the 2008 revised *Learning Guidance Guidelines* re-emphasized the importance of foundational knowledge and skills and increased total instructional time. To support reform monitoring, MEXT has since conducted annual surveys comprising two parts: academic achievement tests and curriculum implementation studies. [1] The former assesses student proficiency in core subjects—such as Japanese, social studies, mathematics, science, and English—at the upper primary, junior high, and senior high school levels, with results analyzed by content area and compared across years. The latter investigates key issues including instructional time allocations, the delivery of integrated studies, elective course implementation, and the effectiveness of personalized learning support. For high schools, surveys also examine credit requirements, subject offerings, and instructional hours across general, vocational, and comprehensive tracks. These data-driven evaluations provide targeted policy guidance and inform continuous curriculum adjustments.

Overall, the common goal of these large-scale curriculum development surveys is to understand the curriculum implementation process in order to monitor and ensure the quality of education and teaching. The main criterion for judging the quality of teaching is the national curriculum standards. The key points of the surveys focus on whether the school's curriculum arrangement is aligned with the core content of the curriculum plan and standards, as well as examining students' performance and attitudes during the course of curriculum implementation. This is used to verify whether school education, especially classroom teaching, adheres to the principles of educational reform and meets basic educational quality standards. Due to the relative independence of the teaching process and the large number of classrooms, these surveys are conducted using different methods.

---

① National Institute for Educational Policy Research, Ministry of Education, Culture, Sports, Science and Technology of Japan. Survey on the Implementation Status of School Education Curricula in Primary and Secondary (High) Schools [EB/OL]. [2015-11-01].

4. Constructing Dimensions for the Evaluation of Basic Education Curriculum Development Quality

Referring to the theory of curriculum development levels and based on the actual situation of school curricula in China, the first and second level indicators for evaluating the development of basic education curricula are established to describe the process and stages of school curriculum development. Based on the analysis of curriculum development quality orientation and the analysis of curriculum development levels and key points, the hierarchical structure, dimensions, and elements for evaluating the quality of basic education curriculum development are established (see Table 3-5).

Table 3-5: Dimensions for the Evaluation of Basic Education Curriculum Development

Primary Indicator	Secondary Indicator	Primary Indicator	Secondary Indicator
1.School Curriculum Plan	1.1 School Curriculum Planning	**3. Student Experience Curriculum**	3.1 Courses Acquired by Students
	1.2 National Curriculum Implementation		3.2 Student Engagement with the Curriculum
	1.3 (Local) School-Based Curriculum Development		
	2.1 Teacher's Curriculum Beliefs		4.1 Curriculum Stakeholders: Principals, Teachers
	2.2 Teacher- Planned Curriculum		4.2 Target Group: Students

Primary Indicator	Secondary Indicator	Primary Indicator	Secondary Indicator
2.Teacher Curriculum		**4.Influencing Factors**	4.3 Curriculum Resources: Textbooks, and School Physical Resources
	2.3 Teacher-Implemented Curriculum		4.4 Implementation Methods: Supporting Systems, Teacher Training, Academic Research

In the curriculum indicators, the elements for evaluating curriculum development are constructed and organized within evaluation orientations such as implementation plans and standards, curriculum development levels, user satisfaction, user costs, and protective measures.

Here is the translation of the provided text:

4.1 Implementation of Curriculum Plans and Standards

The implementation of national curriculum plans and standards by schools and teachers is a fundamental line of defense to ensure the quality of the educational process. Whether or not the national curriculum is executed serves as a deeper, process-oriented indicator of whether educational stakeholders are providing equal educational opportunities for students. Observational elements under this dimension include: whether schools have accompanying curriculum systems, the implementation of national curricula, students' mastery of the national curriculum, the quantity of locally developed school-based curricula, whether teachers' instructional designs align with curriculum standards, and whether the general teaching methods and organizational forms in the classroom are consistent with the curriculum philosophy. These factors measure whether schools and teachers provide students with curriculum content based on policies and standards, ensuring that students are given equal educational content during the educational process.

4.2 Curriculum Development Level

In this dimension, the level of curriculum development is described through the degree of implementation and the focus on differences. The degree of implementation includes: the rationality and systematization of the school curriculum system, the principal's awareness of curriculum planning, the principal's attitude towards the curriculum, teachers' beliefs about curriculum goals and teaching methods, the general teaching methods and organizational forms in the classroom, how teachers use textbooks, and teachers' emotional investment in the curriculum. These indicators can be integrated into various curriculum implementation models, such as Hall's "adoption model based on attention," ① for more systematic, specialized research. The focus on differences includes: the availability of elective courses in high school, themes of locally developed school-based curricula, the value recognition of locally developed school-based curricula, differences in the teaching methods used by teachers in different classes, and the availability of alternative textbooks. These factors reflect the awareness and actions of schools and teachers regarding differences in students' needs during the curriculum development process.

4.3 User Satisfaction

User satisfaction refers to the satisfaction of stakeholders such as principals, teachers, students, and parents with the curriculum. Key elements include: the principal's attitude toward national and school-based curricula, the value and difficulty of the national curriculum, teachers' recognition of the current curriculum, students' feelings about the classroom, students' interest and needs regarding the curriculum, and parents' satisfaction with the curriculum.

---

① Hallge, Hordsm. Change in schools: facilitating the process [R]. New York: State University of New York Press,1987:84.

4.4 User Costs

User costs refer to the investments made by students and teachers during the curriculum development process. Key elements include: the time students invest in the curriculum, the methods of student engagement (such as extra tutoring), students' emotional investment in the curriculum, the time and workload teachers invest in the curriculum, teachers' emotional investment, and the frequency of teacher training.

4.5 Safeguarding Measures

Safeguarding measures primarily refer to the methods of curriculum promotion and the resources necessary for curriculum development. Curriculum promotion includes relevant policies and systems related to curriculum development, such as whether the examination and evaluation system is consistent with the curriculum development requirements, whether teacher training and development can effectively enhance teachers' professional abilities, and whether academic research on curricula contributes to curriculum development. Essential resources for curriculum development include the quality of textbooks, financial resources for schools, and the availability of school facilities, grounds, and equipment necessary for curriculum development.

These elements aim to assess the performance of the curriculum across different levels during the school education process and the resulting impact. This evaluation helps to explain the internal operations of school education during the process of educational development, providing insights into the quality of the educational process. Despite the relative independence of the school education process, given the large number of basic education schools, these elements should be converted into tools for large-scale surveys.

Through big data analysis and comparative descriptions, these tools can help illustrate the forms of the educational process.

[Original Source: *Educational Research*, 2016, Issue 8 (Lyu Lijie, Ma Yunpeng)]

Part 4 Teachers and the Curriculum

Chapter 15 The Characteristics and Limitations of Collective Decision-making in Teacher Curriculum Design

1. Teacher's Curriculum Decision-Making

What is curriculum decision-making? The *Concise International Encyclopedia of Education* defines curriculum decision-making as "a judgment on the purposes and means related to education or socialization, which is usually made within the scope of schools and centered around the curriculum." In this context, "judgment" refers to "the result of conscious thought, representing an intention to act in a specific way or to generate a desired outcome." ①Curriculum decision-making, therefore, is a deliberative process involving thoughtful selection and evaluation of curricular matters. The decision-maker may be an individual, a group, or a collective entity.

Smith emphasizes that curriculum decisions are made within each teacher's operational space—this space represents the boundaries of autonomy as perceived by the teacher. ②Teachers make curriculum decisions on a daily basis, and their perceptions of curriculum standards, teaching materials, student needs, and other factors vary, resulting in different levels of curriculum control. Since the implementation of recent curriculum reforms in China, teachers' curricular autonomy has expanded, thereby increasing their "freedom limits" in decision-making. The dynamic interplay between teachers' "operational space" and their professional "judgments" is a topic worthy of close examination.

---

① Jiang, Shanye. *Concise Encyclopedia of International Education: Curriculum* [M]. Beijing: Educational Science Publishing House, 1991.
② Zhou, Shuqing. *Curriculum Development and Teacher Professionalism* [M]. Taipei: Taiwan Higher Education Cultural Enterprise Co., Ltd., 2004.

1.1 Levels and Types of Teacher's Curriculum Decision-Making

Curriculum itself exists across multiple levels, and so does curriculum decision-making. Goodlad proposed four levels of curriculum decision-making: societal, institutional, instructional, and experiential. Eisner added that any curriculum plan involves decision-making in five fundamental areas: the prioritization of educational purposes, B. curriculum content, C. learning opportunities, curriculum presentation, and student response and evaluation methods.①

In comparison, Klein's (1991) framework offers a more detailed classification. He divides curriculum decision-making into two domains: the levels at which decisions are made, and the central issues addressed in curriculum decisions. The levels of decision-making, according to Klein, follow Goodlad's framework and are subdivided into seven potential levels: academic, societal, formal, institutional, instructional, operational, and experiential. This sequence is arranged according to the proximity to the student or the focus of the curriculum. decision. Curriculum decisions at different levels concern nine elements: curriculum goals, content, resources, activities, teaching strategies, assessment, student groups, time arrangement, and spatial arrangement. According to Klein, these seven levels and nine elements form a bi-dimensional matrix of curriculum decision-making. ② Teachers, as curriculum decision-makers, may influence several levels. For example, as parents, their attitudes impact curriculum decisions at the "societal" level, or they may participate in national or regional curriculum design, influencing curriculum decisions at the "formal" level. However, when considering teachers solely in their role as educators, the primary focus

---

① Xu, Bimei. *Pursuing Excellence: A Case Study of Teacher Professional Development* [M]. Translated by Chen, Jing & Li, Zhongru. Beijing: People's Education Press, 2003.

② Klein. Mf. A conceptual framework for curriculum decision making [J]. The Politics of Curriculum Decision-making.Albany:State University of New York,1991.

is on curriculum decision-making at the "institutional," "instructional," and "operational" levels.

Calderhead classified teacher decision-making into three types based on the characteristics of daily decision-making. The first type involves extensive thinking, identifying feasible alternatives, and evaluating possible outcomes, which corresponds to reflective decision-making. The second type is immediate decision-making, which occurs spontaneously in response to unexpected events. The third type consists of regular, frequently occurring decisions that may even become automated or routinized, known as routine decision-making. When classroom issues deviate from expectations, teachers must make immediate decisions; however, if issues are recurrent, teachers will simply make routine decisions.①

1.2 Changes in the Focus of Research on Teacher Curriculum Decision-Making

1. The Relationship Between Teacher Decision-Making and Student Learning Outcomes

These studies emerged before the 1970s, under the influence of methodologies such as positivism and behaviorism. In order to demonstrate the professionalism of teachers, researchers employed research methods like correlation analysis and experiments to prove the relationship between teacher behavior and student achievement. The assumption behind this research was that teacher behavior, as a form of stimulus, inevitably led to changes in students' cognitive and understanding processes.

① Xu, Bimei. *Pursuing Excellence: A Case Study of Teacher Professional Development* [M]. Translated by Chen, Jing & Li, Zhongru. Beijing: People's Education Press, 2003.

2. How Teachers Make Decisions

With the development of cognitive psychology, after the 1970s, researchers became dissatisfied with reducing classroom teaching to a technical process. They began to focus on the underlying causes of teacher behavior, i.e., how teachers think, and how they make decisions. The focus of research shifted to understanding the decision-making process. Researchers abandoned quantitative methods and adopted descriptive methods. By providing teachers with materials such as classroom recordings (either their own or others'), teachers were asked to describe their thought processes at the time. These studies often compared novice teachers with experienced teachers to examine how teachers understand, attribute, think, judge, and evaluate. The results revealed differences in thinking, feelings, and behaviors between novice and expert teachers. Expert teachers were able to recognize typical situations and categorize students during their thought processes. Researchers thus became convinced: "Clearly, cognition can change behavior. Classroom decision-making research describes teaching behavior at the cognitive level. Teachers can analyze, compare, and model their teaching based on this, and using psychological methods to study classroom decisions will undoubtedly help teachers improve their teaching."①

3. Teacher Growth in Groups

With the shift in the concept of knowledge and the growing understanding of the complexity of educational practices, the focus of research has shifted from summarizing a fixed body of knowledge and technical rules for teachers to helping teachers develop by revealing the hidden factors of teacher beliefs, emotions, and practical knowledge. These studies often employed phenomenological research methods, demonstrating

---

① Calderheadj. A psychological approach to research on teachers' classroom decision- making [J]. British Educational Research Journal,1981(1).

the complexity of teacher work through descriptions of lived experiences. Furthermore, after the 1990s, researchers began to pay attention to the group factors influencing teacher development. What factors influence teachers' curriculum decision-making and actions? In addition to stable individual factors, group and situational factors are also influential. A dual analysis of individual and group learning emerged, focusing on how professional communities can promote teacher learning. "Taking learning communities as the unit of analysis, examining how professional communities promote teacher learning." ①Teachers grow through interactions with others and learn through the interaction between individuals, groups, and situations.

2. Teacher Collective Curriculum Decision-making: Forms and Characteristics

Teacher collective curriculum decision-making refers to the process by which a group of teachers collaboratively identifies feasible plans and assesses potential outcomes. This also includes the "automated and routine" decisions that the group collectively agrees upon. In China, much of teacher collective curriculum decision-making takes place during the collective lesson preparation process. Although not all teachers are involved at this stage, its existence is already an undeniable fact. In recent years, collective lesson planning has gained significant attention domestically, but opinions on its effectiveness are divided. In fact, since collective lesson planning is not a fixed form, debates surrounding it often involve opposing viewpoints. Even for the same form, the real-life operational context may differ. Therefore, before discussing its significance and limitations, it is important to clarify the various forms of teacher collective curriculum decision-making in educational practice.

① Liu, Xuehui, & Shen, Jiliang. Retrospect and Reflection on Teacher Cognition Research: Implications for Teacher Education [J]. *Theory and Practice of Education*, 2006(6):46–49.

2.1 Forms of Teacher Collective Curriculum Decision-Making

In the context of ongoing curriculum reform, teachers increasingly engage in various forms of collective curriculum decision-making. These forms reflect differing degrees of participation, autonomy, and professional depth. Six common types can be identified:

1. Holistic Interpretation Type

This form typically occurs at the district or municipal level, where subject leaders or expert teachers provide centralized explanations of curriculum objectives and content for a specific grade. Since the implementation of the new curriculum standards, these sessions have expanded to include interpretation at the standard level—clarifying the nature and goals of the subject and emphasizing a student-centered teaching philosophy. However, due to the large number of participants and the top-down nature of these sessions (often managerial or training-oriented), communication tends to be one-way. As a result, individual teachers' "operational space" for autonomous curriculum decision-making is constrained.

2. Process Agreement Type

This form is most common at the school level, typically within grade-level or subject-based teaching groups. It is also the most debated form of collective decision-making. Teachers jointly plan the semester's teaching progress, allocate instructional time, and identify key learning points and difficult content areas. A widely adopted practice is "division of labor with collaborative sharing", where each teacher is responsible for preparing a specific portion of the content, which is then shared during group meetings. The collective critiques and revisions foster shared ownership, though differences in instructional philosophy may also lead to controversy.

3. Lesson Study Type

Lesson study, as a collaborative and research-driven approach, has gained prominence under curriculum reform and is widely regarded as the most effective form of curriculum decision-making. Within subject research groups, teachers jointly design lessons by discussing instructional content, classroom organization, teaching resources, presentation methods, and time management. One teacher conducts the lesson while others observe, followed by reflective group discussions and plan revisions before a second implementation. In some cases, lesson videos (from expert teachers or foreign classrooms) are used as study materials for analysis and professional dialogue. This form emphasizes subject-specific pedagogical knowledge and revolves around the integration of curriculum goals, content, and methods with student-centered principles. It is intellectually demanding and contributes to the professional growth of teachers.

4. Problem-Solving Type

This type arises in both formal and informal contexts when teachers encounter difficulties in instruction. These may include misunderstandings of subject knowledge, unexpected classroom incidents, or challenging student behaviors. Teachers work together to analyze the issues, discuss multiple perspectives, and co-construct potential solutions. This collaborative, inquiry-based approach reinforces the practical and adaptive nature of curriculum decision-making.

5. Curriculum Development Type

As schools strive to establish unique educational identities under the new curriculum reform, many engage in the development of school-based curricula that reflect local characteristics and strengths. This often requires reconfiguring the school's overall curriculum structure and, in some cases, developing original teaching materials or textbooks. Although not all teachers are involved in this process, those who do gain deeper insight into the curriculum's underlying logic. With expanded decision-making space, teachers are compelled to reconsider curriculum from multiple dimensions—including educational aims, disciplinary structure, student interests, available resources, and the specific expertise of the teaching staff. This reflective process enhances their curricular agency and deepens their understanding of their educational role.

6. Feedback Adjustment Type

This type of collective decision-making often arises organically from ongoing practice. In forms such as lesson study or problem-solving discussions, consensus may not be initially achieved. Teachers may instead implement tentative strategies or explore different approaches in their classrooms. Based on post-implementation feedback and reflection, they collaboratively assess outcomes and make adjustments accordingly. This cyclical, data-informed decision-making process exemplifies adaptive professionalism and continuous improvement in teaching practice.

2.2 Characteristics of Teacher Collective Curriculum Decision-Making

Teacher collective curriculum decision-making is a complex and multifaceted process influenced by interpersonal, institutional, and professional dynamics. The following four characteristics capture the key dimensions of how teachers engage in collaborative curriculum work:

1. The Quality of Teacher Collaboration Determines the Effectiveness of Collective Curriculum Decision-Making

High-quality teacher collaboration is foundational to effective curriculum decision-making. Recent critiques of collective lesson preparation in schools often point to a lack of genuine and meaningful cooperation among teachers. Collective curriculum decision-making is not merely a technical procedure; it is deeply embedded in school culture, interpersonal relationships, and psychological factors.

First, the school's cultural climate plays a decisive role. In environments where competition outweighs collaboration—where teachers are preoccupied with academic rankings or high-stakes evaluations—professional dialogue is often stifled, and collaborative efforts become superficial. Sustained, high-quality collaboration requires a stable developmental environment that prioritizes professional growth over survival.

Second, leadership style significantly affects the collaborative process. Effective curriculum decision-making should encourage shared dialogue and the exchange of ideas rather than enforce top-down authority. However, many teachers report that collective lesson preparation is often dominated by a single leader, leaving little room for dissenting views or creativity. The effectiveness of such collaboration depends on how group leaders position themselves, facilitate discussion, motivate participation, and earn the trust of group members.

Third, individual teachers' motivation and professional capacity are also critical. Teachers who lack intrinsic motivation or a sense of responsibility may disengage from the process, relying excessively on others' contributions—a phenomenon perceived by peers as "free-riding." While "borrowing" ideas from colleagues is a valid and even encouraged form of professional learning, chronic disengagement may erode collective morale. Ultimately, the aim of collaborative curriculum work is to share and co-construct professional knowledge for the benefit of all students.

2. Teacher Collective Curriculum Decision-Making Operates at Hierarchical Levels

Curriculum decision-making involves multiple hierarchical levels. Building on Klein's categorization of curriculum issues, the scope of teacher involvement in decision-making in China typically spans the textbook level, subject knowledge level, subject-specific pedagogy level, and curriculum development level.

At the textbook level, decision-making often focuses on content sequencing, difficulty control, and pacing—procedural decisions that structure teaching tasks but offer limited professional depth. This work is also referred to as the "distribution of teaching tasks"①

At the subject knowledge level, teachers explore foundational disciplinary questions to enhance their understanding of curriculum content, which serves to bridge the gap between academic knowledge and classroom application.

The subject-specific pedagogy level is regarded as the core and most effective layer of curriculum decision-making. Drawing on Shulman's (1986) concept of pedagogical content knowledge (PCK), teachers consider how best to transform subject matter into teachable content through the use of examples, illustrations, instructional strategies, and assessment methods. ②PCK is not a static body of knowledge but a dynamic, practice-based expertise that links subject knowledge, textbook content, student characteristics, and teaching style.

At the curriculum development level, teachers contribute to the design of school-based curricula—participating in philosophical debates, textbook compilation, and institutional curriculum planning. While this level is not yet widely practiced in China, it represents a critical space for teacher agency and school-level innovation.

---

① Chen, Guisheng. Analysis of "Collective Lesson Preparation" [J]. *Chinese Journal of Education*, 2006(9):40–41.
② Shulman, Lee S. Theory, Practice, and the Professionalization of Education. *Comparative Education Research*, no. 3, 1999, pp. 36-40.

3. Individual Needs Vary in Collective Curriculum Decision-Making

Teachers' engagement with and benefits from collective curriculum decision-making differ based on their stage of professional development. Generally, teachers fall into three categories: novice, experienced, and expert.

Novice teachers tend to benefit the most from collaborative decision-making. Although they may possess strong academic backgrounds, they often lack the ability to translate disciplinary knowledge into practical classroom applications. For them, collective lesson planning and pedagogical discussions provide concrete guidance, modeling, and structure.

Experienced teachers, who are already familiar with basic teaching procedures, seek deeper engagement with subject-specific pedagogy. They value opportunities to address complex instructional challenges, participate in case discussions, and refine their teaching strategies.

Expert teachers often view collective curriculum decision-making as a platform for mentoring others and experimenting with innovative practices. They seek intellectual stimulation and empirical validation for their teaching ideas and welcome discussions that explore curriculum at conceptual or philosophical levels—areas less likely to attract the attention of novice or mid-career teachers.

4. Collective and Individual Curriculum Decision-Making Are Interdependent

Despite the collective nature of curriculum planning, the classroom remains the site of individual teacher autonomy. The implementation of the curriculum ultimately depends on each teacher's interpretation and adaptation of collective decisions. Thus, collective curriculum decision-making should serve as a framework for guidance, not a constraint on pedagogical creativity.

When collective decisions are overly prescriptive, they can suppress individual teaching styles and innovation. Conversely, if they are too vague, they offer little direction or professional support. The ideal balance lies in providing shared understandings and guiding principles—particularly through in-depth discussion of key issues—while preserving space for individual teacher reflection, agency, and contextual adaptation.

3. Limitations in Teacher Collective Curriculum Decision-Making That Need to Be Overcome

Despite the growing recognition of the value of collective curriculum decision-making, several structural and cultural limitations hinder its effectiveness. Addressing these limitations is essential for enhancing the quality and impact of collaborative curriculum work in schools.

3.1 Overcoming Limitations on Individual Expression within Collective Curriculum Decision-Making

In the absence of an ideal school culture, institutional structures are often tasked with guiding teacher collaboration. While the collective agreement on key points and instructional challenges is not inherently problematic, its implementation must avoid restricting teacher autonomy and creativity.

Pedagogical key points and difficulties do not exist independently of the learner; rather, they should be identified from the perspective of students' cognitive structures and learning needs. Key content includes knowledge, skills, and methods that are foundational to students' future development, requiring teachers to engage in historical inquiry and maintain a broad, integrative perspective. Difficulties, conversely, should reflect anticipated challenges based on students' current understanding. However, when collective planning becomes rigid—dictating uniform key points, difficulties, and teaching procedures—it risks homogenizing classroom instruction and stifling pedagogical differentiation. While collective curriculum decision-making serves to establish foundational curricular coherence, individual teacher decision-making on top of this foundation is essential for high-quality, context-responsive implementation.

To balance standardization with autonomy, some schools have adopted dual-lesson plan systems, where teachers develop both a collective lesson plan and an individualized version. In the latter, teachers are encouraged to adapt, extend, or replace parts of the shared plan with original ideas, fostering innovation while preserving core curriculum integrity.

3.2 Overcoming the Limitations of Various Curriculum Decision-Making Methods

Different forms of collective decision-making offer distinct benefits and limitations. The process-oriented method provides teachers with a general framework for lesson preparation based on established procedures. However, its reliance on pre-defined steps—often grounded in prior experience—may disengage teachers, particularly experienced ones who find the approach repetitive and uninspiring.

In contrast, the case study-based method anchors discussions in authentic classroom practices. It encourages reflection and deep analysis but is time-consuming and typically limited in scope, making it difficult to address the full breadth of the curriculum. The curriculum development-based method encourages teachers to think beyond immediate practice, expanding their professional vision and encouraging role shifts (e.g., from executor to designer). Yet, not all teachers currently have access to such opportunities, and even within these methods, passive participation can reduce their impact to mere formalities.

No single decision-making method can meet the diverse needs of all teachers. The key challenge lies in cultivating a positive cultural environment that supports genuine engagement. School leaders and professional experts play a crucial role by participating actively in discussions, providing oversight, and—most importantly—posing reflective, thought-provoking questions that elevate the quality of dialogue. Moreover, curriculum decision-making must be tightly linked to implementation. Routine classroom observations function not only as a form of professional development but also as an assessment of the effectiveness of curriculum decisions, ensuring that discussions translate into meaningful teaching practices.

3.3 Overcoming the Limitations of Uneven Information Flow in Communication

Curriculum decision-making is inherently dialogic, involving interactions with texts, students, peers, and one's prior experiences. Yet, within group discussions, dominant discourses often emerge, influenced by participants' experience levels, content knowledge, personality traits, or hierarchical status. While such dominance can streamline decision-making, it also risks marginalizing alternative viewpoints, especially those of novice teachers. For experienced and expert teachers, collective discussions remain valuable, as familiarity does not always equate to mastery. Many habitual practices, while seemingly effective, may be unexamined assumptions or even misconceptions. Collective reflection provides an opportunity to surface and reassess these practices.

Novice teachers, though less experienced, often approach curriculum with greater openness and fewer fixed patterns, making them more receptive to new ideas. However, they may lack the confidence or opportunity to express their views in hierarchical group settings. To address this, there is a need to establish structured mechanisms within collective discussions that actively solicit and value diverse perspectives, especially those from newer teachers.

[The original text was published in *Curriculum, Teaching Material and Teaching Method*, Issue 12, 2008 (Lyu Lijie & Chen Jianhong)]

Chapter 16 Drivers of Change in Teachers' Curriculum Actions

— A Curriculum Narrative from a *Morality and Life* Teacher's Perspective

Morality and Life is an integrated subject within the reformed basic education curriculum in China, designed for students in Grades 1 and 2 of primary school. Aimed at young learners transitioning into school life, the course supports students in adapting to their new social environments, cultivating healthy lifestyles, and fostering civic values. Rooted in children's real-life experiences, the course adopts a life-oriented approach to moral education that emphasizes meaning-making through experience and activity—an approach central to its educational philosophy.

Due to practical factors such as staffing constraints, this subject is frequently taught by the homeroom teacher. Yet this raises important questions: How do homeroom teachers perceive the significance of this course? Do they teach it with intentionality, and can they authentically embody its values? The following narrative, shared by Teacher Shi from a primary school in Nanguan District, Changchun, during a peer observation discussion, offers a first-hand account of one teacher's evolving engagement with the *Morality and Life* curriculum.

1. Teacher Shi's Experience with *Morality and Life*

At the outset, I must admit I did not teach Morality and Life seriously. I suspect many teachers might have had a similar experience. As a Chinese language teacher and the class's homeroom teacher, I often used the moral education period for spelling tests or extra exercises, especially when the principal was not around.

Having long served as a homeroom teacher for lower grades, I found the role both exhausting and filled with countless minor yet time-consuming tasks. At the start of the semester, complaints from students flooded in. During class, two students might start arguing:

"Teacher, he drew in my book!"

"He pushed me!"

The next day, I might receive a call from a parent: "Teacher, could you change my child's seat? His deskmate keeps bullying him." Even during lineup, issues such as pushing and shoving frequently arose. The class lacked cohesion, and I began to question whether I wanted to remain a homeroom teacher. Though these issues might seem trivial to teachers, they were deeply significant to the children—and thus demanded my attention.

Amid this frustration, I came across Unit 2 in the Morality and Life textbook, titled "Our Class Has Many Stories." The illustrations immediately caught my eye. The scenarios depicted—children complaining, small disputes—were familiar and mirrored the challenges in my own classroom. I realized this was an opportunity to engage the students meaningfully.

I transformed the students' daily complaints into a series of short stories. While the characters were fictional, the students recognized themselves in them. I asked them questions like: "Which character in the story do you like? Which one don't you like? Why?"

To my surprise, their responses were thoughtful, almost as if they were recognizing their own shortcomings. In the days that followed, the frequency of complaints gradually decreased—though not entirely.

Encouraged by this, I continued using the textbook in subsequent classes. One week, I organized a class session on the playground with two games: a three-legged race and a partner relay in which two students carried a ball between their backs. These activities were designed to foster teamwork, cooperation, and mutual support. As expected, some students performed well, while others struggled—dropping the ball or falling. Some blamed their partners:

"It's your fault! If it weren't for you, the ball wouldn't have fallen!"

Rather than scolding them, I brought the class back to reflect. I asked the successful teams to share their strategies and prompted others to consider why they hadn't performed well. The students responded earnestly. I concluded the lesson with the story, "One chopstick breaks easily, but ten chopsticks won't bend." They understood the message instantly.

During a later class, one student asked: "Teacher, will we still have to do spelling next time? Will the Chinese class monitor still collect our books?" At that moment, I felt a deep sense of guilt. I hadn't realized how much the students cherished the Morality and Life class. I had, unintentionally, deprived them of an experience they truly valued. I even felt apologetic toward the principal.

Inspired by this realization, I decided to plan a more meaningful activity for the third week. I prepared colorful cards and asked each student to make a "love card" and a "thank-you card." They wrote about classmates they had conflicted with or wanted to thank, and then exchanged cards. Later, several parents shared that their children were reluctant to throw the cards away—even though they were simple handmade notes—while more expensive musical cards given at Christmas were quickly discarded. It was then that I felt the real power and potential of moral education.

Among our grade-level team, several colleagues also teach Morality and Life, and we collaborate well. Each brings unique strengths:

Teacher Li is imaginative and perceptive, almost like a director, guiding our conceptual development.

Teacher Zhou is tech-savvy and excels at sourcing online materials.

I myself enjoy making teaching aids and crafts.

We divide our responsibilities accordingly. For each unit, Teacher Zhou handles research, Teacher Li offers conceptual guidance, and I focus on practical aspects, such as creating materials. This collaboration has significantly improved the quality and enjoyment of our moral education lessons—for both teachers and students.

2. Analysis of the Case Story

2.1 Teacher Shi's Reflection on Her Curriculum Practices

Human behavior is often goal-oriented, and teachers are no exception. In practice, educators tend to prioritize content and instructional activities that yield immediate, measurable outcomes. Within the current educational climate—where exam scores frequently serve as the primary indicator of teaching success—it is common for teachers and schools to emphasize testable subjects. In this context, subjects like *Moral Education and Life*, which are difficult to assess using conventional examinations, are often undervalued in daily teaching practice.

As a class teacher, Teacher Shi admitted to using moral education classes for dictation or workbook exercises—activities more directly linked to measurable academic performance. Although she was aware this was not ideal, her behavior reflected a widespread practice among her peers, revealing a pragmatic approach shaped by institutional expectations.

However, her teaching trajectory shifted when she encountered increasing behavioral challenges in her second-grade class. Students frequently quarreled, lodged complaints, and accused each other of bullying. The learning environment became overwhelming and disorderly, with a seemingly endless stream of interpersonal issues that demanded her attention. While these problems may appear trivial to adults, they held significant meaning for the children and required immediate and thoughtful intervention.

It was during this period of disorientation that Teacher Shi rediscovered the potential of the *Moral Education and Life* textbook, specifically the second unit, titled *"Our Class Has Many Stories."* The illustrations and scenarios in this unit closely mirrored the real-life experiences unfolding in her classroom. Recognizing the alignment between the curriculum content and her students' social-emotional needs, she chose to implement the unit's activities to address ongoing conflicts and alleviate her teaching burdens.

After applying the curriculum in practice, she observed a noticeable reduction in negative student behaviors. This outcome encouraged her to further explore and extend the curriculum. She experienced a moment of pedagogical reflection, realizing the intrinsic value of the course and expressing regret for having previously neglected its potential. Her growing recognition of the curriculum's positive impact not only changed her instructional approach but also led to increased engagement from students and appreciative feedback from parents. One parent's remark—that the activities were "effort-saving"—resonated with her as validation of the course's effectiveness and her own evolving teaching philosophy.

2.2 The Three Shifts in Teacher Shi's Curriculum Focus

Teacher Shi's narrative reveals three key shifts in her curriculum orientation and teaching philosophy, each marking a deeper engagement with both the subject content and her students' developmental needs.

From Neglect to Practical Engagement: Initially, Teacher Shi did not implement the curriculum as intended, using the class period for unrelated academic tasks. Her first significant shift occurred when she began using the textbook as a resource to resolve classroom conflicts. The stories she created from the students' complaints served not only as behavioral interventions but also as entry points into meaningful moral inquiry, enabling students to recognize and reflect on their actions.

From Activity Facilitation to Reflective Learning: The second shift emerged when she moved beyond storytelling to organizing cooperative games that required collaboration and mutual support. Through experiential learning—such as the three-legged race—students encountered the challenges of teamwork firsthand. This phase emphasized learning through doing, followed by guided reflection. It encouraged students to think critically about their behaviors and relational dynamics, fostering a deeper understanding of cooperation and empathy.

From Managing Behavior to Cultivating Relationships: In the third stage, Teacher Shi introduced activities like writing "love cards" and "thank-you cards," which prompted students to reflect on past conflicts, express gratitude, and take emotional responsibility. These activities went beyond behavioral management and focused on emotional growth, moral development, and the cultivation of positive interpersonal relationships. This phase marked a transition toward a more holistic and affective dimension of moral education.

These three pedagogical shifts also corresponded to the developmental stages of the students' social and emotional learning:

Initial Stage (Storytelling): Introduced basic moral concepts such as right and wrong.

Intermediate Stage (Experiential Learning): Fostered understanding of cooperation and mutual support through direct participation.

Advanced Stage (Emotional Reflection): Facilitated deeper personal reflection, emotional expression, and moral internalization.

For Teacher Shi, this progression mirrored her own professional growth. Initially, her approach aimed to resolve immediate classroom management problems. However, as she gained insight into the students' needs and the curriculum's potential, her focus shifted toward designing activities that supported long-term social and emotional development. Her deep familiarity with her students, coupled with her reflective and creative teaching methods, became key drivers of this transformation.

Ultimately, this case illustrates how curriculum implementation is not solely a matter of following prescribed content. Instead, it is deeply shaped by the teacher's evolving understanding of students, the teaching context, and the curriculum's educational philosophy. Teacher Shi's story exemplifies how meaningful shifts in teaching practice can emerge through lived experience, reflective inquiry, and responsive curriculum engagement (see figure 4-1).

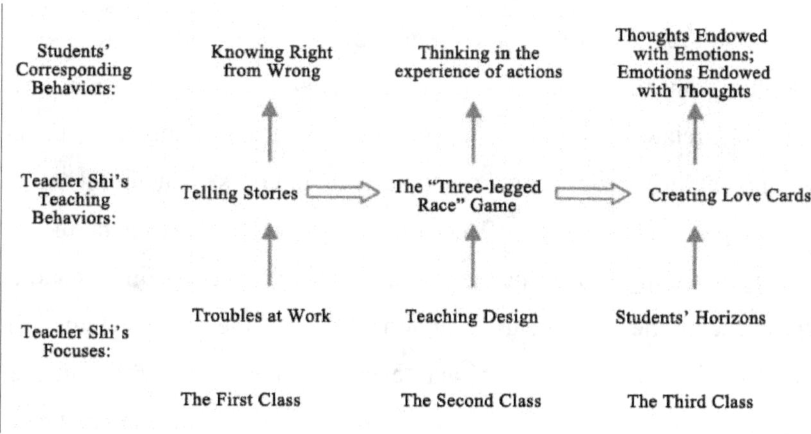

Figure 4-1

2.3 Teacher Shi's Course Implementation Shows Different Stages

Teacher Shi's course implementation process is quite typical. Many teachers have had "similar experiences" to hers: from initially resisting and not implementing the course, to applying and experimenting with the new curriculum, and finally to independently and effectively implementing the new curriculum, even creatively. The stages of course implementation described here align closely with the eight stages of curriculum implementation — "Non-use, Orientation, Preparation, Mechanical Use,

Regularization, Refinement, Integration, and Innovation"[①]. However, their theoretical framework does not explain the key point of how teachers transition from non-use to initial attempts or mechanical use of the new curriculum. In other words, just because a teacher has not used a new curriculum does not automatically mean they will move through the phases of "orientation, preparation," and "mechanical use." Hall's stages of curriculum implementation are idealized and theoretical. What motivates teachers to abandon their previous working habits and try unfamiliar actions whose outcomes are unpredictable? After teachers mechanically use the new curriculum, what drives them to continue its use, refine it, and reach a level of regularity or even sophistication? In Teacher Shi's story, we can see that this motivation primarily comes from the practical functionality of the curriculum. This functionality is demonstrated by whether the curriculum can solve work-related difficulties, improve the issues students face in their development, bring educational outcomes, and of course, whether it satisfies the principal. Teacher Shi reflects on her failure to implement the new curriculum, feeling "sorry for the principal." Once teachers understand and acknowledge the practical functionality of the curriculum, they autonomously use it, refine it, and even reach a stage of "refinement, integration, and innovation." This autonomy in curriculum implementation, driven by the practical functionality of the curriculum, is also discussed in relevant theoretical frameworks.

---

① Hallge, Hord SM. Change in schools: facilitating the process [R]. New York: State University of New York Press,1987:60.

3. Discussion on Key Points of Teacher's Curriculum Action Transformation

3.1 Teacher Perception of the Cost of Curriculum Change is the Core of Teacher Recognition of the New Curriculum

Cost refers to the price paid to obtain benefits. A teacher's perception of the costs and benefits of curriculum change forms their understanding of the curriculum's cost. This cost perception is closely related to the teacher's attitude toward and recognition of the new curriculum. In 1993, Australian scholars Waugh and Godfrey conducted a study on "Teachers' Recognition of Unit Curriculum" using seven related variables for investigation: a. non-monetary costs and benefits of the curriculum; b.the practicality of the curriculum; c. reducing teachers' fear and uncertainty when implementing the curriculum (school support); d. focus on issues related to unit curriculum; e. support for unit curriculum from others; f. teacher participation in school curriculum decision-making; g. feelings after comparing the old and new curriculum. After conducting surveys and quantitative analysis, Waugh and Godfrey concluded that the most important variable affecting teachers' recognition of the curriculum is the cost-benefit balance, followed by the degree of participation in the reform, factors supporting the reform, and previous experiences with reforms. In a comparative study of teachers' recognition of the "local curriculum" and "general knowledge curriculum" in Hong Kong, Li(1998) similarly ranked "teachers' assessment of non-monetary costs and benefits of the curriculum reform" as the most important variable among five factors. Cost perception influences teachers' recognition of the new curriculum, and a teacher's recognition of the curriculum, in turn, affects whether they will substantively adopt and implement the new curriculum. So, what exactly are the costs and benefits perceived by teachers? Some scholars have also summarized them[①] (see Table 4-1):

Table 4-1: Costs and Benefits Perceived by Teachers

Costs	Benefits
Additional learning time and preparation required for innovation Giving up existing skills, learning unfamiliar skills and new knowledge Time required to cover the new curriculum Preparing new teaching materials and resources Time required to implement the new curriculum Changes in teacher-student and teacher-teacher relationships Threat to teachers' subject authority Teacher's perceived professional development	Improvement in teacher-student relationships (e.g., more classroom interaction) Students may not achieve good results in public exams Changes in relationships between the principal and teachers, and among teachers Reduction in teacher autonomy Increased teacher stimulation and satisfaction Improvement in classroom atmosphere and discipline Opportunities for promotion Increased status of teachers participating in the innovation More opportunities for decision-making Salary increases Increased resources More opportunities for professional development and support activities

① Morris. P. Curriculum innovation and implementation: a cautionary note [J]. Educational Research Journal,1987(2):49-54.

In this table, among the ten perceived benefits, nine are non-monetary costs, and six are related to teachers' sense of educational effectiveness. Some scholars even define the cost-benefit expectations of teachers directly as "students' positive responses and improvements in their learning quality."①

In the case of Teacher Shi, she initially resorted to writing Chinese characters in the Morality and Life class, which, in fact, reflects her understanding of the educational cost-benefit principle—improvement in student performance. The factor that subsequently led to her change in curriculum recognition was her discovery of the students' educational needs. After she tried using the new curriculum, she saw a change in student behavior, and her attempts brought new rewards. She realized the new, hidden benefits of the curriculum, which led to a shift in her perception of the costs associated with the Morality and Life course. As she continued to "extend" the course, she continuously received positive feedback, which ultimately helped her develop a strong curriculum recognition. Therefore, in this case, we observe that the core factor influencing teachers' recognition and implementation of the new curriculum is whether they can achieve work-related benefits.

3.2 The Mutual Verification Between Teachers' Attitudes Toward the Curriculum and Their Trial Behaviors

Feng (1995) ②proposed an innovation process model called the "6A process model" based on school reform. The characteristic of this model is that the achievement of reform is non-linear, composed of several repeating cycles. It consists of six stages: awareness, formation of attitude, adoption, adaptation, action, and application. While the process generally follows a

---

① Li, Zijian. *Curriculum, Teaching, and School Reform* [M]. Hong Kong: The Chinese University Press, 2002:100.

② Fung A. Management of educational innovations: the six-a process model in Wong KC and Cheng KM educational leadership and change-an internal perspective [M].Hong Kong: Hong Kong University Press,1995:69-85.

certain sequence, in practice, each trial may lead to a restart of the cycle. In other words, each adoption and trial forms a re-awareness of the reform, and this new attitude will determine whether the actor acknowledges the reform and continues to adopt and reattempt it.

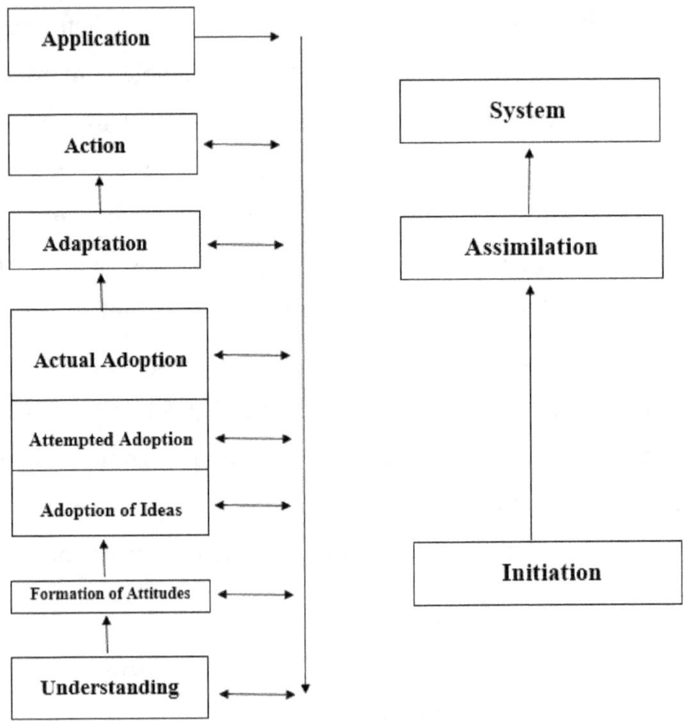

Figure 4-2: Feng Zhihua's Innovation Process Model

Guskey's research also reached a similar conclusion. He found that significant changes in teachers' beliefs and attitudes generally occur after they have engaged in successful practices and seen actual changes in students. He proposed that the model for teachers' professional development starts with changes in teaching practices, which lead to changes in student achievements, and only afterward do teachers' beliefs and attitudes change.[①]

① Guskey TR. Professional development and teacher change [J]. Teacher and Teacher Education, 2002:8.

In the case of Teacher Shi, when she noticed that the illustrations in the Morality and Life textbook "resembled situations in my class," she had already formed an attitude toward the new curriculum. After successfully adopting and trying the curriculum, her recognition and attitude were further confirmed. This led her to invest more enthusiasm and energy into designing more effective thematic unit activities. However, if Teacher Shi's attempt had failed, as shown in the cycle process above, the result of the attempt would have influenced her attitude and recognition, affecting her decision to re-adopt and re-try. In this way, the teacher's attitude toward the curriculum and the actions toward curriculum change are continuously refined and developed. Therefore, when teachers initially adopt and implement a new curriculum with a trial attitude, timely assistance, guidance, collaboration, or providing them with techniques and skills can help them succeed. This, in turn, influences the teachers' attitude toward the change and affects the continued effectiveness of the reform behavior.

3.3 The Role of Autonomy, Practice, and Interaction in Teacher Professional Development

Teacher professional development is intrinsically linked to autonomous learning, which shares similarities with other professions that emphasize independence and practical engagement. European scholars Feo and Bohmensen introduced a "Learning Cube Model"[①] to describe this process (see Figure 4-3). In this model, the X-axis represents the practical dimension of the learning content, the Y-axis represents the communicative aspect of the learning process, and the Z-axis stands for the autonomy of learning. Together, these three axes form the core foundation of professional learning.

① Yu, Kaicheng. Human Resource Management [M]. Dalian: Dalian University of Technology Press, 2001:205.

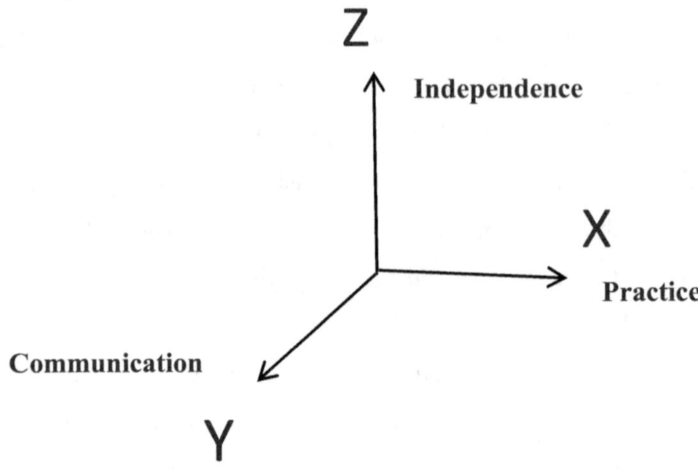

Figure 4-3: The Learning Cube Model

This model provides a useful framework for understanding the key elements and patterns in teacher professional development. These include the desire for self - improvement, the practice of skills, and interaction and collaboration with colleagues and experts. These three elements are interrelated. Specifically, the autonomy and desire for self - development guide how teachers practice, how much they incorporate self - observation and reflection, and their ability to absorb and apply new theories and others' experiences. Teaching, as an inherently practical activity, requires a blend of autonomy, learning, support, and collaboration, resulting in intelligent practice that continually improves teaching quality. Such practice, in turn, reinforces the teacher's desire for autonomous growth and determines the effectiveness of communication and collaboration. Effective interaction, driven by a willingness to cooperate, naturally emerges from this practice. Thus, a teacher's desire for self - development is a crucial factor in fostering meaningful communication. In Teacher Shi's case, her initial attempts at practice were based on trial and error. As she experienced success, her desire to independently develop the curriculum was reinforced. The positive outcomes of her practice supported a collaborative, friendly, and complementary relationship with her colleagues. Throughout this process, whether driven by a sense of responsibility towards her students or a personal motivation for professional development, her pursuit of educational effectiveness remained rooted in her autonomous actions as an educator.

[The original article was published in *Global Education Outlook 2007*, Issue 3 (Lyu Lijie)]

Chapter 17 Surveying Principal Competencies in Curriculum Leadership Using Contextual Judgment Tests

Schools are the fundamental units in the implementation and advancement of curriculum reform. The degree of fidelity in curriculum implementation and the level of innovation in curriculum development directly determine the success or failure of reform efforts. More importantly, these elements influence the overall quality of education a school can offer.

However, assessing the actual state of curriculum development within schools presents a complex challenge. Comprehensive evaluation requires detailed observation of a school's curriculum design, implementation processes, resource allocation, and the broader curricular environment. Given this complexity, large-scale quantitative studies often fall short in capturing the nuanced realities of school-level curriculum development.

To address this challenge, we propose using the principal's competency in curriculum leadership as a proxy indicator for school curriculum development. By evaluating the professional capacity of principals in curriculum leadership, we aim to infer the necessary conditions or potential for school-based curriculum development. In other words, we argue that effective school curriculum development must rely on the principal's curriculum leadership competency—a necessary, though not sufficient, precondition for meaningful and sustainable curriculum reform at the school level.

1. Principal's Curriculum Leadership Competency and Its Theoretical Foundations

1.1 The Connotation of Principal's Curriculum Leadership Competency

Since the 1980s, curriculum leadership has emerged as a central concept in curriculum studies. Scholars such as Bradley, Glatthorn, and Brubaker were among the pioneers who systematically elaborated on this notion. From the late 1990s onwards, researchers across Taiwan, Hong Kong, and Mainland China have also increasingly focused on this area.

Across both international and Chinese contexts, a shared understanding of curriculum leadership has developed. Most definitions situate curriculum leadership within the broader context of curriculum reform, emphasizing the leader's professional role and functional responsibilities. For instance, Bradley conceptualizes curriculum leadership as encompassing tasks such as curriculum development, the provision of necessary resources, the articulation of a philosophical vision, and ensuring continuity in curriculum advancement. His view underscores curriculum leadership as a bridge between theory and practice in curriculum work.①

This perspective highlights that curriculum leadership goes beyond general administrative responsibilities (e.g., managing personnel, budgets, and facilities). Instead, it is a form of professional leadership—focused on planning, guiding, optimizing, and innovating curricular systems in schools. Principals, as curriculum leaders, are thus expected not only to inspire, manage, and motivate staff but also to lead professional efforts related to curriculum construction and reform.

In terms of competency, scholars offer different definitions. Some view competence as a latent personal characteristic that influences one's

① Bradleyl. H. Curriculum leadership and development handbook [M]. New Jersey: Prentice-Hall,1985,23-24.

performance in complex professional contexts, shaping decision-making behaviors and guiding internal criteria. ①Others adopt a more applied view, defining competence as the practical integration of knowledge, skills, motivation, attitudes, and values in specific contexts that lead to effective performance. ② Under either view, competence is multidimensional—encompassing both intrinsic attributes and externalized behaviors.

In this framework, the principal's curriculum leadership competency can be understood as the set of personal attributes—including knowledge, skills, cognitive approaches, and behavioral patterns—that are exhibited in the course of promoting, planning, developing, and supervising curriculum development in the school.

1.2 Theoretical Assumptions of Principal's Curriculum Leadership Competency

As curriculum leaders, principals must leverage both their professional authority and positional influence to guide the development and innovation of school curricula. Professionally, they provide direction and expertise in curriculum design; administratively, they facilitate the organizational and interpersonal conditions necessary for effective implementation. We posit that the principal's curriculum leadership is primarily task-oriented, while interpersonal leadership skills play a significant but secondary role in supporting these tasks.

What specific tasks does curriculum leadership at the school level entail? From a decision-making perspective, Glatthorn categorizes curriculum leadership into four hierarchical levels: national, local, school, and classroom.

---

① Spencer, Lyle M., et al. The Assessment of Talent: Building an Outstanding Performance Model. Translated by Wei Meijin, Shantou: Shantou University Press, 2003: 17-19.
② Woodruffe. C. Competent by any other name [J]. *Personnel Management,*1991(9):30-33.

Each level assumes distinct responsibilities depending on the scope of authority. At the school level, the principal's responsibilities include:

Developing a curriculum vision aligned with local and national goals

Designing school-based learning programs and curricular frameworks

Establishing learning-centered curriculum schedules

Deciding the nature and extent of curriculum integration

Aligning suggested, written, taught, assessed, and learned curricula

Supervising, supporting, and improving curriculum implementation

In the Chinese context, the Ministry of Education's 2013 Professional Standards for Principals of Compulsory Education Schools explicitly includes curriculum leadership as a core competency. These standards require principals to coordinate national, local, and school-based curricula, implement curriculum standards, lead the development of school-based curricula, provide appropriate resources, and engage actively in teaching research and educational reform. Accordingly, we define the key functions of school-level curriculum leadership as follows:

a. Articulating the school's educational philosophy

b. Planning curricula based on educational policy and the school's unique context

c. Adapting national curricula to meet local and school-specific needs

d. Developing school-based curricula that reflect institutional priorities

e. Mobilizing curriculum resources and ensuring their effective use

Establishing curriculum management systems to oversee development and delivery

f. Supervising and refining curriculum implementation processes

Based on these functional tasks and informed by competency-based assessment frameworks, we propose a model for measuring principal curriculum leadership competency (see Figure 4-4). This model emphasizes role-specific professional tasks, underpinned by: mastery of curriculum theory, possession of advanced curriculum concepts, deep understanding of national and local curriculum policies. These forms of professional knowledge are often implicit, manifesting as routine behaviors and decision-making strategies. They collectively shape the effectiveness of curriculum development and signal a principal's capacity to bridge educational ideals with practice.

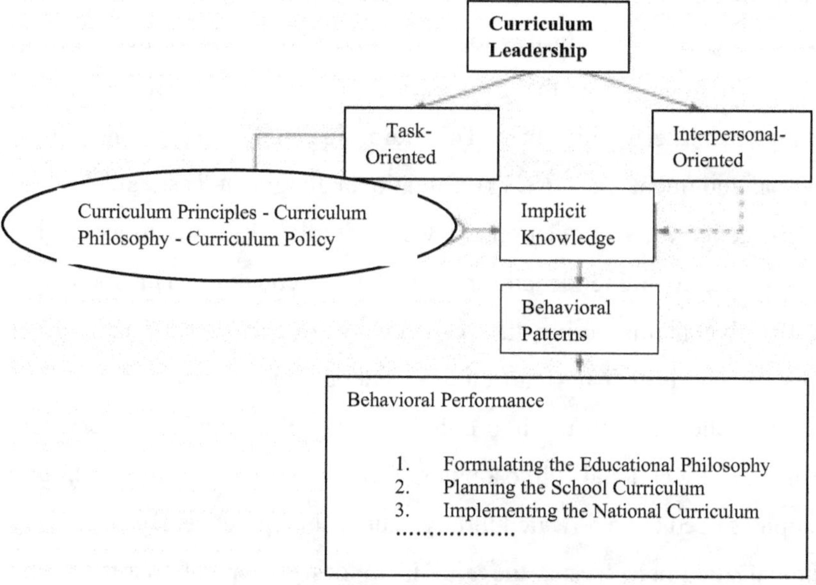

Figure 4-4 Theoretical Framework of Principal's Curriculum Leadership Competency

2. Measurement Design of Principal's Curriculum Leadership Competency

2.1 Selection of Measurement Tools: Situational Judgment Tests

In traditional teacher effectiveness and principal competency measurements, the target content to be measured is directly stated, and the respondents make their own judgments. For example, "I can master knowledge related to curriculum design" or "I can reasonably utilize curriculum resources." Such items are too vague and broad, and directly use the conceptual terms to be measured. Unless the respondents have an in-depth understanding of concepts like curriculum design and curriculum resources, they will struggle to make professional judgments. On the other hand, giving the full right to judge to the respondents will inevitably raise concerns regarding social desirability bias. Therefore, this study uses the method of Situational Judgment Tests (SJTs). Situational Judgment Tests are low- to medium-fidelity work simulations or work samples designed to assess the appropriate behavioral tendencies in a given work context. ①This method is more effective in measuring the respondents' true attitudes and implicit knowledge. The principal's curriculum leadership competency stems from their understanding of curriculum policies, grasp of curriculum theory, and handling of educational philosophies. These cognitions, theories, and philosophies need to be reflected through curriculum practice. By employing Situational Judgment Tests, the aim is to design typical, realistic, and multidimensional practical situations to collect and measure the real behavioral responses of principals in curriculum practice, thereby assessing the actual state of their cognitions and attitudes.

2.2 Development of Situational Judgment Test Tools

Step 1: Curriculum Event Interviews and Situational Setting

Based on the seven competency dimensions identified from the analysis of the principal's curriculum leadership work, interview outlines were prepared for both principals and curriculum experts. Interviews were conducted with ten principals and four curriculum experts as instrumental cases. The ten principals were all active leaders in attempting school curriculum reform, and the four experts had participated in or hosted collaborative projects with educational institutions and had experience helping schools develop curricula. These fourteen experts, as subject matter experts, were asked to share the most effective or most principle-defying curriculum events from their experiences in relation to the interview questions. From over thirty curriculum stories and phenomena collected in the interviews, a value selection was made, based on two main principles: 1) whether the situational stories reflected the key points to be measured, and 2) whether the situational stories had practical generalizability to ensure the construct validity of the questionnaire. Ultimately, nine curriculum phenomena or stories were selected, refined, and retained that reflected the key points being measured, and that also demonstrated complexity and typicality.

Step 2: Collecting Corresponding Situational Responses

As only about a dozen principals or experts were interviewed for the problem situations, the curriculum stories they shared were independent of each other, and thus the responses to each situation were not tested and had saturation issues. Therefore, the nine retained situational problems were compiled into fully open-ended questionnaires. A total of 54 rural principals, excellent principals from Beijing, and principals from Changchun were selected to provide qualitative responses. Then, three doctoral students read and coded each returned questionnaire, organizing the corresponding situational responses for each scenario. Responses that were irrelevant or showed a clear bias were excluded, and similar responses were merged. In the end, 4 to 8 possible situational responses were listed under each situation, and each response was scored using a 0–5-point scale.

Step 3: Determining Scoring Methods and Best Options

Once the situational problems and all response options were determined, two senior curriculum experts and three outstanding provincial-level principals were organized to give the best response for each item. For items where disagreements occurred, a collective consultation process was used to reach a consensus. The best response was assigned 5 points, and other options were assigned scores from 1 to 4 according to their deviation from the best answer. Finally, the difference between the scores given by the principals and the expert panel was calculated. A smaller difference indicates that the principals' responses were closer to the experts' standards, implying a higher level of the principal's curriculum leadership competency. Conversely, a larger difference suggests that the principals' responses were farther from the experts' standards, indicating a lower level of curriculum leadership competency.

3. Results and Analysis of the Measurement of Principal's Curriculum Leadership Competency

A total of 482 questionnaires were distributed in this survey, with 461 valid responses, covering 24 provinces, municipalities, and autonomous regions in China. The specific situation is shown in Table 4-2.

Table 4-2 Basic Information of Sample Principals

Basic Information	Category	Number	Percentage
Gender	Male	305	66.16%
	Female	156	33.84%

Basic Information	Category	Number	Percentage
Age	40 years or younger	56	12.15%
	41-50 years	314	68.11%
	51 years or older	91	19.74%
First Degree	Teacher Training School	202	43.82%
	Normal College	137	29.72%
	Bachelor of Education	93	20.17%
	Non-education Bachelor	11	2.39%
	Others	18	3.90%
Highest Degree	Associate Degree	33	7.16%
	Bachelor's Degree	386	83.73%
	Master's Degree	41	8.89%
	Doctoral Degree	1	0.22%
Level of Schooling	Nine-Year Compulsory Education	73	15.84%
	Junior High School	247	53.58%
	Primary School	141	30.59%

For the reliability test, validity test, correlation analysis, and significance difference analysis, the IBM SPSS Statistics 21.0 software was used to perform statistical analysis on the collected data. The reliability test primarily focused on the homogeneity reliability and split-half reliability of the scale. The homogeneity reliability was measured using Cronbach's Alpha coefficient (α coefficient), while the split-half reliability was calculated using the Spearman-Brown split-half correlation method. The α coefficient of this scale was 0.784, and the split-half coefficient was 0.756. Both values are greater than 0.7, [①]which indicates that the principal curriculum leadership competency scale developed by this research team has good reliability. For the validity analysis, both content validity and discriminant validity were examined. Content validity was judged based on the reasonableness of the item distribution. Based on theoretical and policy analysis, the principal curriculum leadership competency scale in this study is composed of nine key assessment points: "Exploring School Philosophy," "Planning School Curriculum," "Understanding National Curriculum Policies," "Localization of National Curriculum," "Designing School-Based Curriculum," "Implementing School-Based Curriculum," "Utilizing Curriculum Resources," "Establishing Curriculum Management Mechanism," and "Supervising Curriculum Implementation." The five experts in this study analyzed the consistency between the measurement items and the purpose of the evaluation. All five experts agreed that the nine key points of the scale comprehensively and accurately assess the curriculum leadership competency of principals. The situations for measurement were realistic and rich. The Kendall's coefficient of concordance for the consistency of evaluation purposes was 0.317, and the p-value was 0.027 ($P<0.05$), which indicates significant agreement among the experts, proving that the scale has good content validity. In the discriminant validity test, it can be seen from Table 4-3 that the correlation coefficients between the dimensions of the scale range from -0.125 to 0.466, indicating a moderate to low degree of correlation. This suggests that the dimensions of the scale are highly

① Henson R K. Understanding internal consistency reliability estimates: a conceptual primer on coefficient alpha [J]. Measurement &Evaluation in Counseling & Development,2001(3):177-189.

independent and do not influence each other. The correlation coefficients between the dimensions and the total score range from 0.503 to 0.779, indicating a moderate to high degree of correlation. This demonstrates that the dimensions reflect the content that the overall scale aims to measure, indicating that the scale has good discriminant validity.

Table 4-3 Correlation Coefficients Matrix Between Each Dimension and the Total Score

	Exploring School Philosophy	Planning School Curriculum	Understanding National Curriculum Policies	Localization of National Curriculum	Designing School-Based Curriculum	Implementing School-Based Curriculum	Utilizing Curriculum Resources	Establishing Curriculum Management Mechanism	Supervising Curriculum Implementation	Total Score
Exploring School Philosophy	1									
Planning School Curriculum	0.026	1								
Understanding National Curriculum Policies	0.001	0.183**	1							
Localization of National Curriculum	-0.125**	0.173**	0.236**	1						
Designing School-Based Curriculum	-0.045	0.205**	0.233**	0.343**	1					
Implementing School-Based Curriculum	-0.090	0.312**	0.202**	0.223**	0.194**	1				
Utilizing Curriculum Resources	-0.005	0.067	0.076	0.053	-0.060	0.094*	1			
Establishing Curriculum Management	-0.064	0.257**	0.291**	0.445**	0.466**	0.225**	-0.037			
Supervising Curriculum	0.086	0.134**	0.069	0.109*	0.226**	0.108*	-0.003	0.244**	1	
Total Score	0.590**	0.503**	0.660**	0.665**	0.751**	0.642**	0.630**	0.779**	0.669**	1

Note: **indicates P < 0.01.

* indicates P < 0.05.

3.1 Overall Situation of Principals' Curriculum Leadership Competence

1. Overall Situation of Principals' Curriculum Leadership Competence

The score for each assessment point in the principals' curriculum leadership competence is uniformly set at 20 points. Therefore, the total score for the principals' curriculum leadership competence scale is 180 points. Among the 461 principals, the highest score is 160.2 points, and the lowest score is 86.9 points. Only one principal scored above 160 points, 159 principals scored between 140 and 159 points, 263 principals scored between 120 and 139 points, 35 principals scored between 100 and 119 points, and the remaining 3 principals scored between 80 and 99 points.

The average and standard deviation for each assessment point of the principals' curriculum leadership competence were statistically analyzed (specific details are shown in Table 4-4). The highest overall score is for "School-Based Curriculum Implementation," with an average score of 16.53 points. The degree of dispersion (standard deviation) for this dimension is also the smallest among all dimensions, only 1.44. The second highest is "Understanding National Curriculum Policies," with an average score of 16.37 points. However, there is considerable variation among individuals in this dimension, as indicated by a standard deviation of 2.77, which is the second-largest standard deviation among the nine dimensions. The dimension with the lowest score in the principals' curriculum leadership competence in China is "Localization of National Curriculum," with an average score of 13.97. The dimension with the most noticeable individual differences among the nine dimensions is "School-Based Curriculum Design," with a standard deviation of 3.07.

Table 4-4: Overall Mean and Standard Deviation for Each Assessment Point of Principals' Curriculum Leadership Competence and the Total Score

Statistic	Excavating Educational	Planning School Curriculum	Understanding National	Localization of National	School-Based Curriculum Design	School-Based Curriculum	Utilization of Curriculum	Establishing Curriculum	Supervising and Managing	Total Score
Mean	14.21	15.93	16.37	13.97	13.18	16.53	15.04	15.59	14.39	135.23
Standard Deviati	2.39	2.00	2.77	2.20	3.07	1.44	2.05	2.53	2.43	10.22

In order to more intuitively and concretely observe the distribution of principals' scores in each dimension and to analyze whether individual differences are due to the bimodal distribution of the data or a more layered dispersion, we have created a "rose diagram" (specific details shown in Figure 4-5) based on the distribution of scores by intervals. The diagram uses varying shades of color to represent score intervals and the size of each sector to indicate the distribution of the number of individuals in each interval. From the overall observation of this diagram, it is evident that most principals' scores are concentrated in the 10–18 range, indicating generally good scores across all dimensions. From the distribution of individuals across intervals, it is found that the dimension "School-Based Curriculum Implementation" has the most favorable score distribution, as most principals' scores fall within the 14–18 range, which is consistent with its highest average score and smallest standard deviation. In contrast, the "School-Based Curriculum Design" dimension shows large differences due to the layered dispersion of the data. Additionally, in the "Understanding National Curriculum Policies" dimension, the high standard deviation is a result of the polarization of individual scores among principals.

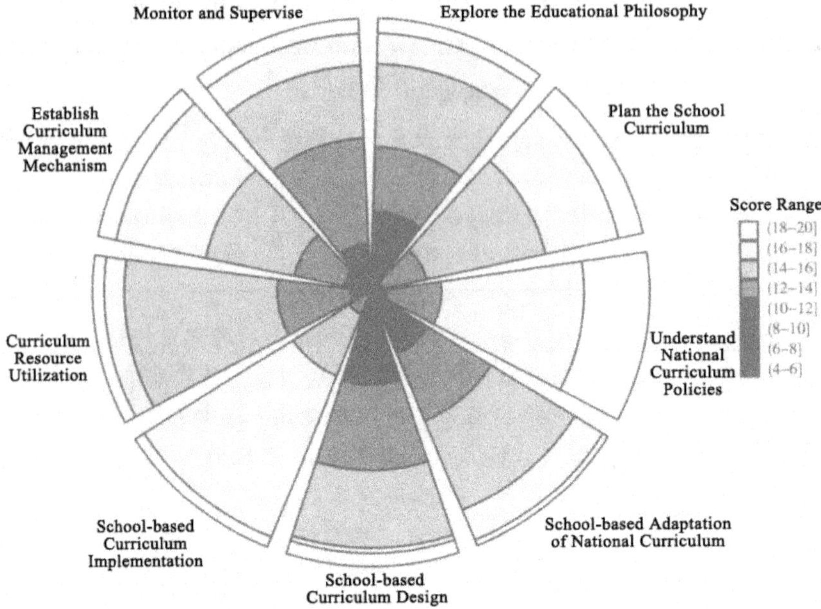

Figure 4-5: Distribution Chart of Score Intervals for Each Dimension of Principals' Curriculum Leadership Competence

2. Cluster Analysis of Principals' Curriculum Leadership Competence

Cluster analysis was performed on the scores of all principals across the nine assessment points based on their mean distance, with the results presented in Figure 4-6. The clustering in this heatmap uses the K-means algorithm based on average distance. Each small square indicates a principal's score in comparison to the average score for that dimension; darker colors represent higher scores, while lighter colors represent lower scores. Each row corresponds to the scores of an individual principal across different dimensions, and the dendrogram on the left shows the clustering results for the principals.

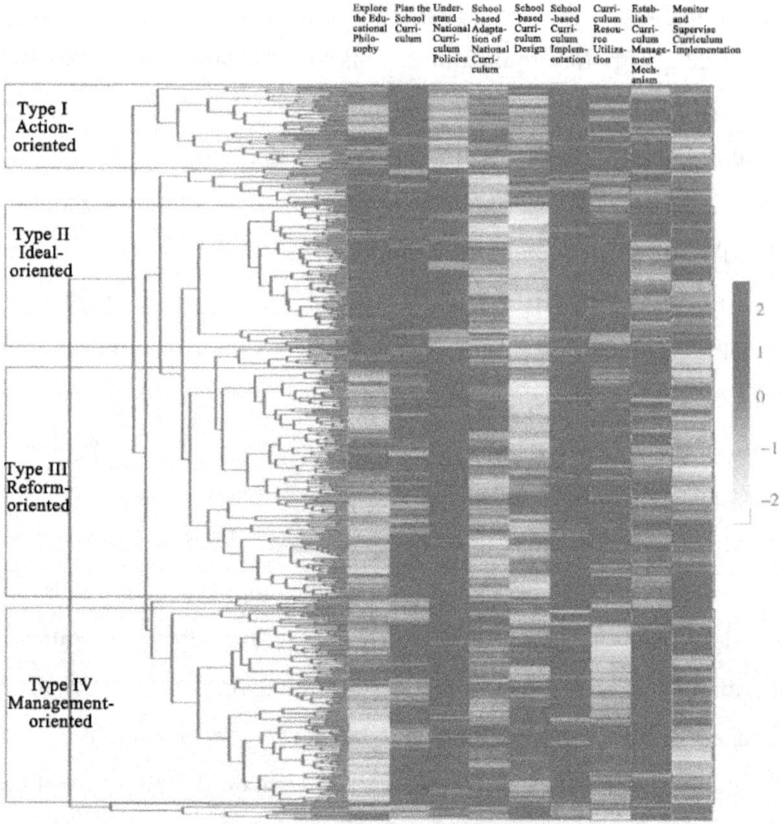

Figure 4-6: Heatmap of Cluster Analysis for Principals' Curriculum Leadership Competence

This study divides the principals into Category I, Category II, Category III, and Category IV, and finds that they exhibit some similar characteristics in specific dimensions, thereby forming four distinct types of principals. Among the 461 principals surveyed, they can roughly be classified into four different types based on their curriculum leadership competencies. Category I principals are action-oriented principals. They perform poorly in "understanding national curriculum policies," but excel in "planning school curricula" and "implementing school-based curricula." This type of principal has experience in leading curriculum reforms, but most of their reform ideas come from direct learning from other schools, with insufficient understanding of policy foundations. This type accounts for approximately 18% of the total number of principals. Category II principals are concept-oriented principals. These principals perform extremely well in "developing school philosophies," but their performance in "designing school-based curricula" and "adapting national curricula to the school context" is relatively poor. This type accounts for about 15% of the total. In practice, these principals are good at macro-managing the direction of school development but lack experience in dealing with curriculum affairs. Category III principals are transformation-oriented principals. They score very high in "understanding national curriculum policies" and also perform well in "planning school curricula" and "adapting national curricula to the school context." However, they perform poorly in "developing school philosophies" and "designing school-based curricula." This type accounts for approximately 30% of the total number of principals. These principals have experience in curriculum reform and have practiced curriculum changes within their schools, but their knowledge of curriculum development theory and professional techniques is somewhat lacking. Category IV principals are management-oriented principals. They perform excellently in "establishing curriculum management mechanisms," but their performance in "utilizing curriculum resources" and "developing school philosophies" is somewhat insufficient. This type of principal is also good at planning the operational mechanisms and structures of the school, but has limited experience in dealing with curriculum-related professional matters. This type accounts for about 20% to 25% of the total number of principals surveyed in this study.

3.2 Differences in Principals' Curriculum Leadership Competencies

1. Gender Differences in Curriculum Leadership Competencies of Principals

The study surveyed a total of 305 male principals and 156 female principals. Using SPSS for significance difference analysis, significant differences were found between male and female principals in both their overall scores and scores across several dimensions. The average total score for male principals was 134.15, with a standard deviation of 10.80, while female principals had an average total score of 137.33, with a standard deviation of 8.66. The difference in total scores was highly significant at the P<0.01 level, indicating that female principals possess significantly higher curriculum leadership competencies compared to their male counterparts. From the data distribution shown in the violin plots (see Figures 4-7), it is evident that female principals outperform male principals. This is primarily because there are no female principals with lower scores, whereas the male principals exhibit a greater degree of score variation.

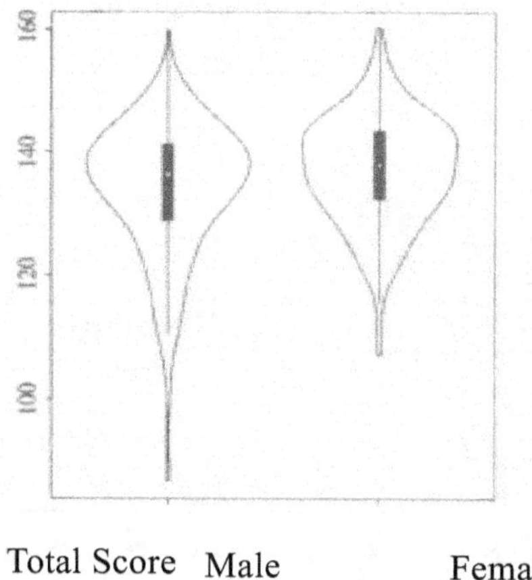

Figure 4-7 Violin Plot of Total Curriculum Leadership Competency Scores of Male and Female Principals

Furthermore, a significance analysis was conducted on gender differences across each individual dimension using SPSS, with dimensions showing significant differences at the P<0.05 level being illustrated in the violin plots (see Figures 4-8). The analysis revealed that male principals scored higher than female principals in the "developing school philosophy" dimension, with the upper quartile and median for male principals being higher than those for female principals. Conversely, female principals showed significantly higher curriculum leadership competencies in the dimensions of "planning school curricula," "understanding national curriculum policies," "adapting national curriculum to the school context," and "establishing curriculum management mechanisms." This difference was most pronounced in the "understanding national curriculum policies" dimension, where the lower quartile of female principals exceeded the upper quartile of male principals. In summary, male principals tend to focus more on macro-level management of the school's direction and philosophy, while female principals are generally more experienced in directly leading curriculum practices.

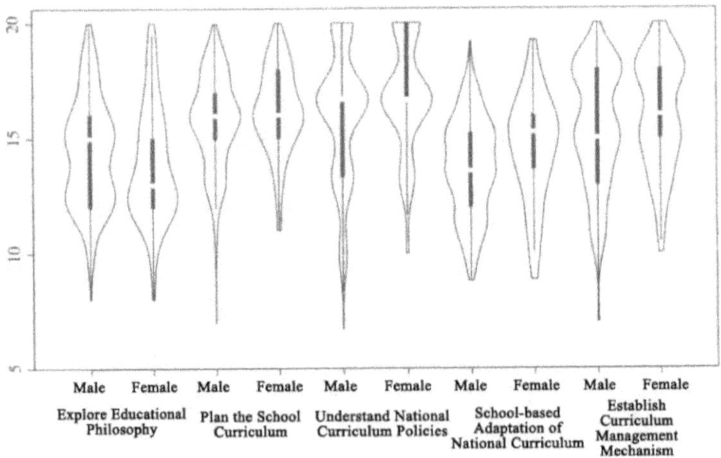

Figures 4-8: Violin Plots of the Dimensions with Significant Gender Differences in Principals' Curriculum Leadership Competencies

2. Differences Between Different Educational Backgrounds

The principals surveyed in this study have the following first-level educational backgrounds: normal school, teacher's college, undergraduate in teacher education, undergraduate in non-teacher education, and others, with numbers of 202, 137, 93, 11, and 18 respectively. Their highest educational qualifications are as follows: associate degree, bachelor's degree, master's degree, and doctoral degree, with numbers of 33, 386, 41, and 1 respectively. There were no significant differences in the total scores of principals with different educational backgrounds. An exception is the only doctoral principal in this survey, whose total score was the highest at 160.2. However, due to the extremely small sample size, this score does not hold statistical significance. In the analysis of significant differences in each dimension, it was found that only in the dimension of "planning school curricula," master's degree holders scored significantly higher than those with bachelor's degrees and associate degrees. The average score differences were 1.45 points ($P = 0.008$) and 0.86 points ($P = 0.031$), respectively. Overall, the educational background had little impact on principals' curriculum leadership competencies.

3. Differences Between Different Educational Stages

The principals surveyed were from three educational stages: nine-year integrated schools, junior high schools, and elementary schools, with numbers of 73, 247, and 141, respectively. From the perspective of total scores, elementary school principals clearly demonstrated superior curriculum leadership competencies compared to principals from nine-year integrated schools and junior high schools, with average score differences of 4.34 points ($P = 0.011$) and 4.773 points ($P < 0.001$), respectively. From the data structure graph (as shown in Figure 4-9), it can be observed that the higher scores of elementary school principals are also due to the absence of lower-scoring individuals, while junior high school principals show considerable representation in the lower score range, with a larger degree of dispersion. However, the highest score also appeared among junior high school principals. In terms of specific dimensions (as shown in Table 4-5), elementary school principals performed significantly better than junior high school principals in the areas of "understanding national curriculum policies," "adapting national curriculum to the school context," "utilizing curriculum resources," and "establishing curriculum management mechanisms." Furthermore, elementary school principals significantly outperformed nine-year integrated school principals in "understanding national curriculum policies" and "establishing curriculum management mechanisms." These findings suggest that elementary school principals have more opportunities to practice curriculum reform and more experience in leading curriculum development, which in turn improves their curriculum leadership competencies.

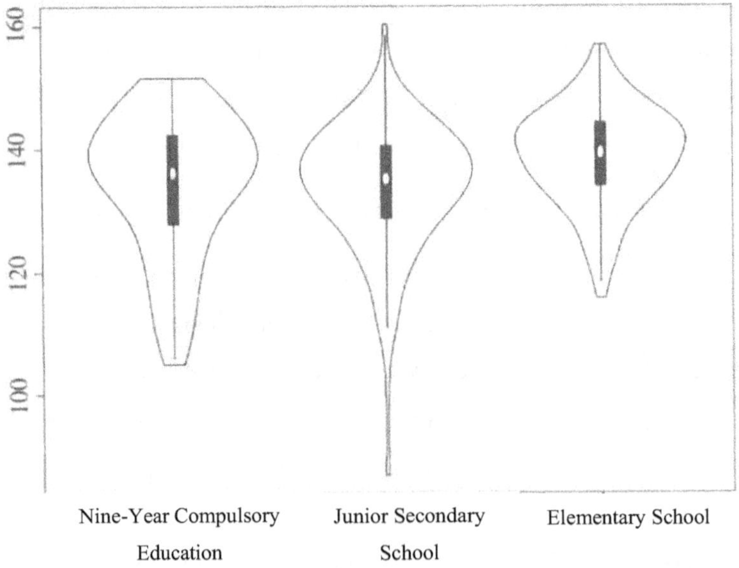

Figure 4-9: Violin Plot of Overall Curriculum Leadership Competency of Principals from Different Educational Levels

Table 4-5: Significance Analysis of Curriculum Leadership Competency Dimensions Among Principals at Different Educational Levels

Dimension	Nine-Year Compulsory Education (M/SD)	Junior Secondary School (M/SD)	Elementary School (M/SD)	F-value	Post-hoc Multiple Comparisons
Developing School Philosophy	14.08/2.14	14.40/2.52	13.96/2.25	1.608	No significant difference
Planning School Curriculum	15.89/2.16	15.85/2.04	16.09/1.84	0.694	No significant difference
Understanding National Curriculum Policies	15.84/3.03	16.03/2.93	17.23/2.11	10.358**	Elementary School > Nine-Year Compulsory Education**; Elementary School > Junior Secondary School**
Adapting National Curriculum to the School Context	14.05/2.37	13.51/2.04	14.74/2.17	14.993**	Elementary School > Junior Secondary School**
School-Based Curriculum Design	13.27/3.27	12.93/3.14	13.58/2.81	2.060	No significant difference
School-Based Curriculum Implementation	16.29/1.44	16.52/1.50	16.68/1.32	1.820	No significant difference
Utilizing Curriculum Resources	15.05/1.89	14.81/2.21	15.43/1.80	4.128*	Elementary School > Junior Secondary School*
Establishing Curriculum	15.37/2.74	15.23/2.54	16.33/2.25	8.991**	Elementary School > Nine-Year Compulsory Education*;

Dimension	Nine-Year Compulsory Education (M/SD)	Junior Secondary School (M/SD)	Elementary School (M/SD)	F-value	Post-hoc Multiple Comparisons
Management Mechanisms					Elementary School > Junior Secondary School**
Supervising Curriculum Implementation	14.27/2.49	14.42/2.48	14.42/2.33	0.106	No significant difference

Note: **indicates P<0.01, * indicates P<0.05.

4. Analysis of Differences in Training Factors

This study investigated whether principals had received more than one month of training in their roles as principals and whether they had received more than one month of training in curriculum development. Among the respondents, 344 principals had received more than one month of principal training, while 117 had not, and 244 principals had received more than one month of curriculum development training, while 217 had not. According to Table 4-6, there is no significant relationship between principal training and the total score of principals' curriculum leadership competencies. However, principal training has a significant impact on the dimension of "developing school philosophy." On the other hand, whether principals had received more than one month of curriculum development training is significantly related to their total curriculum leadership competency score, with a particularly significant correlation found in the dimension of "school-based curriculum design." Clearly, different types of training had different impacts on principals. More than one month of specialized curriculum training had a notable effect on principals' curriculum leadership competencies, particularly in curriculum design, which is a highly specialized and technical area. General management experience alone is insufficient for competence in this area, and specialized training plays a significant role.

Table 4-6: Significance Difference Analysis of Curriculum Leadership Competency Dimensions and Total Scores Under Different Types of Training

	Excavating Educational Philosophy	Planning School Curriculum	Understanding National Curriculum Policies	Localization of National Curriculum	School-Based Curriculum Design	School-Based Curriculum Implementation	Utilization of Curriculum Resources	Establishing Curriculum Management Mechanisms	Supervising and Managing Curriculum Implementation	Total Score
Principal Training	2.123*	1.968	1.089	1.183	-0.085	1.289	0.590	1.537	-1.437	0.737
Curriculum Development Training	—0.023	-0.162	1.042	1.889	2.635**	0.576	—0.359	1.861	1.827	2.342*

Note: * indicates P<0.05, ** indicates P<0.01.

4. Reflections on the Development and Application of the Measurement Tool

1. The Measurement Tool Balances Fidelity and Limitations

Situational testing provides a measurement with a certain degree of fidelity, but it cannot fully replicate the authenticity of real-life situations. Similarly, the measurement tool developed in this study shares this feature. The test assesses whether the subjects can identify the theoretical logic and action principles underlying the scenarios, but its ability to describe and reflect the situation is inherently limited. It cannot completely recreate the complexity of educational practice, and a truly accurate assessment of educational behavior can only occur in real-life contexts. This test primarily focuses on task-oriented competencies, while underestimating factors such as motivation, traits, self-concept, attitudes, and other "below-the-surface" elements of competency.

2. The Typical Nature of the Situational Test Items Limits Their Longevity in Use

The situational test items developed for this study were based on the current curriculum reform and selected typical issues encountered in school curriculum development. These issues reflect the common misconceptions, confusions, and challenges during the curriculum reform process. However, as the reform progresses and as principals gain more practical experience with curriculum leadership, the prevalent problems will gradually improve. New challenges will arise, and new typical problems will emerge in school curricula. Thus, the situational test items developed here have a time-bound applicability and need to be updated continuously to keep pace with ongoing reforms.

3. An Attempt at Multi-Level Data Analysis

This study initially utilized various R language programs from artificial intelligence for graphical representations. For example, violin plots and rose ring plots visualized the multidimensional data distribution patterns. This method not only clarifies basic statistics like principals' competencies' mean and standard deviation but also intuitively explains the direct causes of numerical differences. It enables educational researchers to analyze causes or summarize patterns concretely,[①] making data more comprehensible and describing reality more accurately.

[Original published in *Curriculum · Teaching Materials · Teaching Methods*, Issue 9, 2019 (Lyu Lijie, Ding Yiran, Yang Man)]

---

① Chapmanc, Feitmd. An overview of the R Language [M]. R for Marketing Research and Analytics, Springer International Publishing,2015.

Chapter 18 Curriculum Action Research: Exploring Methodological Approaches

Fuller emphasized that educational change is a process, not an event.[①] Curriculum reform exemplifies this notion, representing not only a pedagogical evolution but also a cultural shift—one that must be inherently research-driven. As the latest round of curriculum reform enters its implementation phase, the promotion of the "teacher-as-researcher" strategy has brought teacher-led curriculum research to the forefront. This research is now recognized as a critical driver of reform and a vital means to enhance teachers' professional development. Among the various forms of teacher research, curriculum action research has emerged as a particularly significant and indispensable approach. It is thus necessary to undertake a theoretical review and reflection on the concept and development of curriculum action research.

1. "Curriculum Action Research": Understanding Its Meaning

1.1 The Emergence of Curriculum Action Research

Action research, understood intuitively as the use of evaluation to inform practical improvements, may be as old as the act of teaching itself. However, as a formal research methodology, it gained recognition in the 20th century, particularly through the efforts of progressive educators. These reformers sought systematic ways to analyze the practices of exemplary teachers, extracting insights that could be generalized and implemented more broadly.

---

① Fullan M. The Meaning of Education Change [M]. New York: Teachers College Press,1982:41.

In the 1940s, John Collier and Kurt Lewin made foundational contributions to action research. Collier applied it within applied anthropology, emphasizing democratic participation, especially in research involving Indigenous communities. He advocated for actions guided by community needs and emphasized that the communities themselves should directly benefit from the research. Lewin, operating in the field of social psychology, articulated a structured model of action research in his 1946 article *"Action Research and Minority Problems."* He proposed a cyclical process involving problem planning, implementation, and continuous evaluation, emphasizing the necessity of engaging practitioners throughout every stage of research. Their work, situated within the broader contexts of the Great Depression, World War II, and the emergence of minority issues, aligned with the goals of the progressive movement.

Following a decline in interest during the 1950s, action research re-emerged in the mid-1970s as a response to new demands for educational reform, especially in the UK, the US, and Australia. Landmark initiatives such as Stenhouse's Humanities Curriculum Project, Elliott's Ford Teaching Project, and Kemmis's work at Deakin University significantly advanced the use of action research in education.

In the late 1980s, James McKernan formally introduced the term curriculum action research. His 1991 book Curriculum Action Research provided a comprehensive account of the movement's historical and philosophical foundations. McKernan discussed ethical standards for teacher-researchers, qualitative methodologies, and strategies for addressing teaching and learning problems through collaborative problem-solving and critical reflection. His work helped to establish a supportive network and community for action researchers and offered practical case studies of action research in education.

1.2 The Concept of Curriculum Action Research: Commonalities Amid Complexity

Concepts, by nature, represent interpretations of reality. Different scholars emphasize distinct aspects of action research: Elliott defines action research as practitioner-led inquiry aimed at improving work-related activities[①]. Its primary purpose is not academic publication but enhancing understanding and effectiveness in real-world settings. Kolb[②], extending the concept, views action research as a cyclical learning process. Individuals critically reflect on their experiences, generate new knowledge, develop abstract concepts, and test them in evolving contexts. Wilfred Carr[③], from a critical-liberation perspective, regards action research as a self-reflective inquiry. It enables practitioners to improve both their practices and their understanding of those practices, while also questioning the fairness and ethical dimensions of educational decisions.

Action research goes by many other names—*cooperative inquiry*, *participatory action research*, *appreciative inquiry*, among others—underscoring its diversity. It is not a rigid method but rather a research approach that blends reflection with action. Despite varied definitions, curriculum action research shares common foundational beliefs. Four central elements unify its diverse forms: power sharing, collaborative participation, knowledge generation, and commitment to social change. The goal is to address real-world curriculum challenges faced by teachers through collaborative inquiry that:

A. Emerges from the school's unique curriculum context;

---

① Elliot J. Action research for educational change [M]. Bristol, Pennsylvania: Open University Press,1991.
② Kolb D. Experiential learning: experience as the source of learning and development [M]. Englewood Cliffs, New Jersey: Prentice-Hall,1984.
③ Carr W, Kemmis S. Becoming critical: education, knowledge, and action research [M]. Philadelphia, PA: The Falmer Press, Taylor&-Francis Inc,1986.

B. Focuses on solving practical problems rather than producing generalized theory;

C. Integrates curriculum implementation with curriculum research;

D. Ensures teachers participate equitably with researchers;

E. Involves iterative evaluation and continuous improvement.

McKernan summarized the guiding principles of curriculum action research as[①]:

A. Teachers as Researchers: Those engaged in real-world practice are best positioned to conduct meaningful inquiry.

B. Naturalism and Practicality: Human behavior is deeply contextual, requiring situational understanding rather than decontextualized theorizing.

C. Field-based and Qualitative Orientation: Emphasizing narrative, subjective interpretation, and thick description over quantification.

1.3 Types of Curriculum Action Research

Curriculum action research can be categorized into three types—technical, practical, and emancipatory—based on the philosophical assumptions underpinning the research[②]:

1. Technical Action Research

This type assumes an existing, objective curriculum model and focuses on verifying and improving its implementation. Researchers often lead the process, while practitioners carry out prescribed methods. Communication flows from expert facilitators to practitioners, and the focus is on measurable outcomes and effective implementation strategies.

---

① Mckernan J. Curriculum action research: a handbook ofmethods and resources for the reflective practitioner [M]. New York: St. Martin's Press Inc,1991.
② Grundy S. Three modes of action research [J]. Curriculum Perspectives,1982(3): 23-24.

2. Practical Action Research

Here, research assumptions are open-ended, and questions emerge through the process. Researchers and practitioners collaboratively plan and refine actions. Emphasis is placed on understanding evolving curriculum issues and improving practice through reflective dialogue. Communication is reciprocal and grounded in mutual respect, with the research process itself considered as valuable as its outcomes.

3. Emancipatory Action Research

This approach seeks to foster critical consciousness and transformative change, particularly in political or socially complex contexts. It aims to strengthen the connection between theory and the lived realities of practitioners. The research is entirely participant-driven, requiring long-term collaboration and shared commitment to reform. It is the rarest form due to the high level of critical engagement and coordination it demands.

Curriculum action research reflects a paradigm shift in how curriculum development and teacher professionalism are conceptualized. As both a method and a movement, it empowers teachers to become active agents in educational change through reflective inquiry and collaborative problem-solving. Understanding its theoretical foundations, methodological diversity, and practical implications is essential for effectively integrating action research into the ongoing process of curriculum reform.

2.2 Methodology and Methodological Examination of Curriculum Action Research

1. General Procedure of Curriculum Action Research

There is a general consensus on the procedures of action research, which is one of the key reasons for the widespread acceptance of the concept of curriculum action research. Drawing from Altrichter's perspective, educational action research can be divided into four stages: identifying the starting point, clarifying the context, developing action strategies and implementing them, and publicizing the findings. Carr and Kemmis also view action research as a continuous cycle involving problem identification, action planning, implementation, evaluation, and reflection. These stages evolve from the initial cycle to the planning of the next, with action plans being adjusted and the research process repeated.

Thus, curriculum action research can be defined as a continuous, cyclical process consisting of the following stages: a. Identifying the Problem: Problems arise from the difficulties encountered in practice and serve as the entry point for research. For example, studying the effectiveness of classroom group discussions. This issue originates from a teacher's challenge in implementing the curriculum and represents an urgent teaching problem. b. Collecting and Analyzing Data: In this phase, the research activities include observation, reflection, and communication between researchers and practitioners. For instance, the teacher reflects on the rationale for designing group discussions, the classroom context, observes the students' discussion processes and outcomes, and seeks to understand students' perceptions of the discussions. The data should be detailed and free from excessive value judgments by the researcher. c. Formulating a Specific Action Plan: This stage involves hypothesizing the factors that influence group discussions, such as the appropriateness of the curriculum content, the organization of the activity, or student interests. Action plans and strategies are then devised. c. Implementation, Reflection, and Meaning-making: These three stages occur simultaneously, with continuous monitoring and reflection during implementation. Strategies may be adjusted, or actions and outcomes explained. Conclusions from these observations and reflections are shared through formats such as group discussions, written reports, or papers.

2. Methodological Interpretation of Curriculum Action Research

The resurgence of curriculum action research is tied to the paradigm shift in curriculum studies during the 20th century[①], and is rooted in a broader shift in human thought, offering a methodological alternative to traditional positivism. Reflecting on the methodology of curriculum action research is essential for improving the selection, application, and understanding of different methods in educational practice. Curriculum action research can be seen as a rebellion against rationalist doctrines, particularly instrumental rationality. Since the Enlightenment, Western intellectual currents have centered on liberating humanity from divine authority, with reason as the driving force behind truth and progress. If Galileo's experimental method marks the beginning of the empirical foundation of the natural sciences, Descartes and Bacon further rationalized and intellectualized this approach. The slogans "I think, therefore I am" and "Knowledge is power" reflect the essence of modern rationalist movements. The 16th and 17th centuries were periods of great advances in the natural sciences, whose methodologies set them apart from other knowledge forms.

In the 1820s, French philosopher Comte introduced the empirical spirit to the social sciences, arguing that society could be studied logically and rationally, just like biology or physics. With the Industrial Revolution, the shift toward human power and control led to the emergence of "instrumental rationality," where the opposition between mathematical and experimental traditions merged. In the early 20th century, reason was applied not only to the analysis of social phenomena but also to the management of social activities and the study of education. Thorndike, for instance, argued that everything that exists has a quantity, and anything that can be quantified

① Ma Yunpeng, & Tang Lifang. Current Situation and Countermeasures of Curriculum Implementation: Analysis and Reflection Based on Some Pilot Area Evaluations [J]. *Journal of Northeast Normal University (Philosophy and Social Sciences Edition)*, 2002(5):124–129.

can be measured. This belief in quantification and experimentation led educational research, including curriculum studies, to follow a trajectory separate from practice. There is no doubt that the scientific advancements of the 20th century radically transformed human life, even as they plunged humanity into crises such as environmental pollution, energy shortages, and world wars. The deification of rationality similarly brought humanity to a crisis point, prompting a rebellion and a shift in human thought. The groundbreaking discoveries in physics, particularly quantum mechanics and Einstein's theory of relativity, shattered the foundations of Newtonian mechanics. This scientific revolution prompted philosophers like Popper and Kuhn to challenge rationality itself. In sociology, critiques of Comte's positivism emerged, arguing that the differences, plasticity, and unverifiability of human society set it apart from the natural world, requiring a different approach to research. German philosopher Dilthey represented this view, suggesting that human behavior, shaped by free will, is unpredictable, and historical events are unique and contingent, requiring subjective methods of interpretation. At the beginning of the 20th century, Dewey responded to the widespread belief in rationalism in educational research, suggesting that "educational science cannot be established solely by the experimental and measurement techniques of physics," and instead should seek methods for analyzing the work of great teachers to allow others to learn from them. [①]This shift helps explain why doctrines such as action research gained widespread acceptance after the deconstruction of rationalism in the mid-20th century.

Curriculum Action Research: Key Intellectual Foundations

① Norfolk. International Action Research: A Cases for Educational Reform, edited by Sandra Holingsworth, translated by Huang Yu, Beijing: China Light Industry Press, 2000.

1. Humans as Self-Determining Subjects

Rationalism, having been extensively explored by thinkers like Kant and Hegel, seemed to have completed its mission by the mid-19th century. However, a new wave of philosophical thought emerged, advocating for the liberation of reason and giving rise to a humanist movement that profoundly influenced the 20th century. Nietzsche argued that an overreliance on reason had stifled the "tree of life," causing humanity to lose its essence. Declaring "God is dead," he envisioned the rise of the Übermensch—an ideal of autonomous human existence. Bergson regarded God as a vital force of eternal life—an impulse of freedom and creative action. For him, the universe is not a product of divine creation but a continuous unfolding of life's inner vitality. Similarly, Kierkegaard, from the perspective of the "isolated individual," criticized Hegel's rationalism, asserting that only the emotional experience of the spiritual self reveals authentic existence.

This humanist tradition sought to advocate for individuality and freedom, challenging the new "divinities" of reason and law, and promoting human agency in choosing, creating, and existing. In contrast, rationalist research often objectifies its subjects, stripping them of agency and distancing them from the research process. Research, in such cases, becomes "divinized" itself—appearing objective but failing to capture the subject's wholeness, authenticity, and fluidity. Action research, however, restores agency to individuals by positioning them as authors of their own actions. It recognizes that behavior emerges from personal judgment and choice. Thus, those who shape the research questions, processes, and outcomes—whether as actors or interveners—must be included as part of the research subject.

2. All Human Knowledge is Inherently Value-Laden

The objectivity of human knowledge has long been contested. As Kuhn noted, observation is shaped not only by the object but also by prior conceptual experiences. Einstein claimed that theory determines what can be observed; Hanson described observation as theory-laden; Popper argued that theory precedes observation [①]; and Chalmers emphasized that observation depends on theoretical frameworks.

Phenomenology, beginning with Husserl, addressed these doubts by advocating a return "to the things themselves." Through Heidegger's existential philosophy and Gadamer's hermeneutics, phenomenology evolved into a form of philosophical ontology. These thinkers argued that human beings are "thrown" into the world, inevitably bearing "prejudices"—or pre-understandings—which make our interpretations historically and culturally situated. Understanding is not a subjective interpretation of an objective object but part of a historically conditioned interaction.[②]

In action research, researchers and participants are not value-neutral. They bring to the research their educational beliefs and normative judgments. What matters is not eliminating bias, but fostering mutual understanding and perspective-sharing among collaborators. This requires moving from a singular subjectivity to an intersubjective framework—recognizing the legitimacy of multiple voices. In addressing shared curricular issues, diverse perspectives influence each other—subjectively, but not destructively—allowing for the emergence of shared meaning and collaborative insight.

---

① Popper, Karl R. *Popper's Autobiography of His Thought*. Translated by Zhao Yueshe, Shanghai: Shanghai Translation Publishing House, 1988.

② Gadamer, Hans-Georg. Truth and Method: 2nd Edition. Classics of Hermeneutics, edited by Hong Handing, Beijing: Oriental Publishing House, 2001, p. 182.

3. Human Activities Have Emancipatory Interests

Critical theory, as developed by Frankfurt School scholars such as Horkheimer and Habermas, represents a powerful stream of modern thought. Drawing from Marxism and hermeneutics, these theorists offered a unique lens for analyzing society. Habermas posited that all scientific inquiry is driven by cognitive interests, which fall into three categories: technical (control of the environment), practical (understanding through interaction), and emancipatory (freedom and autonomy of the subject). Emancipatory interest refers to the human pursuit of freedom, independence, and self-determination—liberating individuals from objectifying systems and ideologies.

Habermas argued that only social science driven by emancipatory interests can resolve crises in human relationships. Emancipatory activities are inherently self-reflective and transformative.[①] In action research, this is manifested in the questioning, suspension, critique, and re-examination of dominant theories, conclusions, and norms, with the goal of uncovering the deeper socio-historical and cultural dynamics behind behavior.

Western Marxist critiques have noted that action research sometimes overlooks structural forces—historical, social, political, and cultural—that shape students' silence or defensiveness. To address this, action research is aligned with emancipatory pedagogy, as exemplified by Paulo Freire. Freire's approach emphasizes dialogue between teachers and students, grounding the curriculum in real-life issues, and using questioning and reflection to seek transformative solutions. Even if actions do not lead to immediate success, students gain new knowledge, broaden their

---

① Habermas, Jürgen. Knowledge and Human Interests. Translated by Guo Guanyi and Li Li, Shanghai: Xuelin Publishing House, 1999.

perspectives, and develop critical thinking skills through the process of engagement.

3. Defense of the Rationality of Curriculum Action Research

3.1 Curriculum Action Research as the Pursuit of Goodness

The resurgence of curriculum action research is closely linked to the 20th-century paradigm shift in human thought. Unlike experimental or quantitatively driven empirical research, curriculum action research redirects attention from external curriculum standards to internal human dimensions. It emphasizes the interpretation of experience, the acknowledgment of interaction, and the presentation of wholeness. Rather than seeking laws of the phenomenal world, this research orientation is grounded in ontological inquiry—not in the metaphysical sense of physical being, but in a teleological sense: the pursuit of ideal human purposes rooted in, yet transcending, lived reality.

Such an orientation reflects a commitment to the intrinsic goodness of human action, continually driven by self-reflection and self-transcendence. The ethical justification of curriculum research lies in its continuous search for essence—an ideal, dialectically generated through critical reflection on current curriculum realities. In this process, existing conditions are not merely accepted but are questioned and negated in pursuit of improvement.

Curriculum action research rejects the absolutism and determinism of positivism. Instead, it adopts a practical, open-ended stance that allows for the revision of misinterpretations, the challenging of assumptions, and the deconstruction of dogmatic ideas. It is dynamic, problem-oriented, and methodologically flexible. Within this framework, no method is inherently right or wrong; rather, what matters is the appropriateness and skillfulness with which methods are applied. Researchers are not bound by fixed methodological frameworks, nor are they required to reject any approach a priori. Rationality here lies in the capacity to make informed choices within a framework of complementarity and methodological pluralism.

3.2 The Practical Value of Curriculum Action Research Stemming from the Nature of Curriculum

Curriculum reform is not simply a matter of changing policies, materials, or tools (e.g., textbooks or technology). At its core, it represents a cultural transformation—embedded in every school, every classroom, and every teacher. Many Western curriculum theorists have pointed out that numerous reform efforts fail before they are fully implemented, often because they do not adequately engage teachers. Teachers are the agents who ultimately steer the direction of curriculum reform.

As a strategy for cultural transformation, curriculum action research functions as an effective bridge between national curriculum policy and classroom practice. According to Elliot, action research enables a reconciliation between top-down curriculum development and teacher-centered curriculum enactment. [①]On one hand, national curricula benefit from the iterative feedback that action research provides through localized experimentation and continuous revision. On the other hand, school-level and teacher-led curriculum development gains a stronger theoretical foundation and improved educational efficacy through action research engagement.

Moreover, curriculum action research plays a crucial role in enhancing teachers' professional competence and building collective professional confidence. In traditional educational research, researchers often lead the process, while teachers play a marginal or supportive role. By contrast, action research involves all participants as co-constructors of knowledge.

---

① Huang Guangxiong, & Cai, Qingtian. *Curriculum Design* [M]. Taipei: Wu-Nan Book Publishing Company, 1999:190.

Teachers retain decision-making power, aligning research more closely with their own practices. Through deep engagement with practical problems, teachers experience reflection and transformation, thereby improving their professional capacity.

Furthermore, the articulation of tacit knowledge in collaborative settings fosters critical reflection and professional growth. Teachers begin to develop sustained habits of evaluation, critique, and curricular construction. Typically, teacher-conducted action research leads to three significant outcomes:

A deeper theoretical and practical understanding of teaching;

Greater insight into the meaning of curriculum implementation behaviors;

Enhanced effectiveness in enacting curriculum reforms.

3.3 Justifying the Rationality of Curriculum Action Research Conclusions

Curriculum action research emerges from specific, context-bound educational settings—shaped by particular curricular content, available resources, teacher expertise, and student characteristics. As a result, both the research process and its conclusions are inherently subjective, individual, and holistic. Compared to quantitative research, such findings may lack broad generalizability and predictive power, prompting skepticism about their validity.

However, qualitative researchers argue convincingly that the value of a case study does not lie in its representativeness per se, but in the type or category it exemplifies. When readers with similar experiences resonate with the findings, the research gains relevance and credibility. In this view, curriculum action research does not need to produce universally applicable results to be valid. Rather, it contributes meaningfully to a broader conversation, forming part of the informational ecosystem available to decision-makers. Moreover, not all research is intended to dictate decisions. Action research findings can inform, enrich, and interact with other forms of knowledge within a broader decision-making network. In presenting findings, it is essential to highlight the researcher's learning journey. Chinese scholar Fang Zhihua, drawing from the ethics of care, emphasizes that educational writing should reflect subjective emotion and engagement. By doing so, readers are not only informed of technical solutions but also moved and inspired by the practitioner's commitment and creativity.

Therefore, research reports should do more than document outcomes. They should convey the researcher's reflections, emotional investment, and growth throughout the process. This personal dimension enhances the communicative power of the research and contributes to a deeper, more human understanding of educational inquiry.[①]

[The original article was published in *Foreign Educational Research*, Issue 3 of 2003 (Lyu Lijie, Ma Yunpeng)]

---

① National Institute for Educational Policy Research, Ministry of Education, Culture, Sports, Science and Technology of Japan. Survey on the Implementation Status of School Education Curricula in Primary and Secondary (High) Schools.
[2015-11-01].http://www.Mext.go.jp/b_menu/shingi/chukyo/chukyo3/004siryo/06080913/010/012.htm

Chapter 19 Reflections and Insights on Researching Teachers' Practical Knowledge

Since the 1980s, influenced by scholars such as Elbaz, Connelly, Clandinin, and Schön, the concept of practical knowledge has become a central concern in teacher research. These scholars shifted the focus from assembling a fixed body of knowledge for competent teachers to exploring what teachers actually know and how they generate that knowledge. This advocacy for practical knowledge emphasizes the centrality of classroom practice and clarifies the purpose of knowledge production in teachers' professional lives. However, prioritizing practical knowledge does not imply simply inverting the traditional hierarchy between theory and practice. Doing so would not necessarily lead to meaningful professional development. What, then, defines practical knowledge, and what role does it play in teachers' work?

1. Reflections on the Study of Practical Knowledge

1.1 The Need for Relative Certainty

Educational philosopher Gary D. Fenstermacher (1993) argues that practical knowledge does not automatically arise from practice. To qualify as knowledge, it must exhibit a certain degree of *stability* and *reliability*. While Connelly and Clandinin are well-known proponents of practical knowledge in teacher research, Fenstermacher critiques their work for emphasizing what teachers know without sufficiently addressing whether that knowledge should be epistemologically validated.①

His concern is justified: the risk of misinterpreting practical knowledge lies in treating every practice-derived insight as valid knowledge. While

① Gary D Fenstermacher. The knower and the known: the nature of knowledge in research on teaching [J]. *Review of Research in Education*,1994(20):3-59.

knowledge can certainly *emerge* from practice, it is the product of a *historical and reflective process*. As Fenstermacher cautions, "many studies of teachers' practical knowledge clearly show teachers' beliefs, intuitions, feelings, and reflections, but the epistemological issue here is that these mental activities do not necessarily lead to real knowledge." ①For such inferences to be recognized as knowledge, they must undergo cognitive evaluation and rational scrutiny.

1.2 The Relative Individuality of Practical Knowledge

Although practical knowledge requires validation, it differs from theoretical knowledge in that it is often grounded in *individual experience*. But is practice entirely individualized? Chinese philosopher Wang Nanti suggests, "While the objects of practice may indeed be different individual things, the practice itself cannot adopt a fully individualistic approach to each object." ②He argues that treating each object individually is merely an aesthetic ideal. Even within aesthetic practices, it is difficult to treat each object as entirely unique, and one can only strive towards this ideal. The denial of absolute individuality in practice does not imply the use of abstract universal laws, but instead proposes the creation of a method that lies between universal theoretical methods and absolute individualistic practices. This approach, which he calls "limited individuality," classifies objects into varying categories and applies practice according to these categories. "In extreme terms, treating individual things individually is not a human ability, but a divine one." ③Thus, "the practical world is one constructed through human practice, and it can only be a world that has been to some extent typified—a world made up of quasi-individual things." Practical knowledge,

① Gary D Fenstermacher. The knower and the known: the nature of knowledge in research on teaching [J]. Review of Research in Education,1994(20): 3-59.
② Wang Nanti. Rethinking the Relationship Between Theory and Practice [J]. *Zhejiang Academic Journal*, 2005(6):5–14.
③ Wang Nanti. Rethinking the Relationship Between Theory and Practice [J]. *Zhejiang Academic Journal*, 2005(6):5–14.

therefore, is relatively individualistic. It is knowledge that can be compared, imitated, and also felt and evaluated.

1.3 Deliberation as a Means of Validation

While there may be no definitive method for validating practical knowledge, scholars such as Cochran-Smith,[①] Lytle, and Fenstermacher advocate for deliberation as a viable approach. Cochran-Smith and Lytle, for instance, emphasize collaboration between teachers and university researchers. Their model builds on Schön's concept of reflective practice, combining personal insights with theoretical perspectives to foster informed and shared judgments. Deliberation allows for practical knowledge to be interpreted and validated within its context. It also accommodates the moral and value-laden dimensions of educational practice, recognizing that practical decisions are never entirely neutral or technical.

1.4 Differentiating Types of Knowledge and Modes of Cognition

Fenstermacher further argues that researchers must distinguish between types of knowledge and cognitive approaches. The former refers to the nature of the knowledge itself, while the latter concerns how knowledge is acquired. Two individuals might examine the same phenomenon through different cognitive lenses and arrive at distinct understandings, yet the epistemic nature of the knowledge may remain unchanged.

In education, there are two primary cognitive modes: One common among teachers, which emphasizes intuitive judgment and contextual analysis; The other used by academic researchers, which emphasizes abstract reasoning and theoretical generalization.

---

① Cochran-Smithlytle. Relationships of knowledge and practice: teacher learning in communities [J]. *American Education Research Association*,1999(24):249-296.

While both approaches can yield practical knowledge, their methods, goals, and outputs differ. Academic research seeks consistency and universality, aiming to identify general principles. Teachers' research, on the other hand, is problem-oriented, emphasizing context-specific knowledge, practical reasoning, and informed decision-making. Though it may not aim for universal laws, it supports the application of theoretical models in real-world teaching and provides a foundation for pedagogical judgment.

In short, the unity of knowledge does not imply identical processes or outcomes between practical and theoretical research. Instead, recognizing their differences allows for a more coherent understanding of how both contribute to educational inquiry and teacher development.

2. Characteristics of the Application of Teachers' Practical Knowledge

Teaching is a profession deeply embedded in practice. Within this practice, theoretical and practical knowledge intersect and integrate, shaping the judgments, decisions, and actions of teachers. The application of practical knowledge is not mechanical but situated, dynamic, and responsive.

2.1 Judgments in Teaching Contexts Are Modular and Simulative in Nature

This issue warrants careful examination. Much of the critique of traditional classrooms focuses on their mechanical, rigid, and formulaic operation—where all students are treated as a homogeneous group and classroom situations are reduced to fixed templates. In response, contemporary educational thinking advocates for classrooms that are vibrant, ecological, and generative.

However, as epistemological scholars caution, human practice must avoid excessive reliance on categorization. When teachers confront practical problems, they engage in a process of interpretation and meaning-making. This is a self-constructed understanding grounded in chunking (modular thinking) and simulation. Teachers tend to classify current situations and student behaviors by referencing familiar patterns based on their own or others' past judgments.

It is this very act of categorization and simulation that enables human cognition. While absolute individuality may reflect the actual complexity of teaching situations, such nuanced knowledge is cognitively inaccessible in real-time classroom contexts. As a result, practical knowledge is inherently a subjective and interpretive construction. In addressing specific challenges, teachers map them onto existing categories or models within their knowledge framework, and then attempt to integrate or reconcile them with current circumstances. In this way, new judgments are shaped and constrained by pre-existing knowledge structures.

2.2 Teachers' Decision-making Involves the Negotiation of Multiple Factors

Reflecting on teachers' practical knowledge does not imply a denial of its value. Rather, it affirms the inherently unsystematic, pluralistic, and multilayered nature of teacher knowledge. Unlike formal theoretical reasoning, teachers' thinking is typically non-linear and context-specific. It is situational decision-making based on real-time selection and combination of elements drawn from principles, conventions, cognitive schemas, and experiential understanding.

This process of decision-making is not governed by strict logic but involves intuitive and sometimes ambiguous reasoning. The decisions teachers make are shaped not only by cognitive considerations but also by their beliefs, emotions, needs, life experiences, personalities, and motivations. The strategies they ultimately adopt result from an ongoing negotiation among these diverse and often competing internal and external influences.

2.3 The Validation of Practical Knowledge Depends on Problem-Solving Effectiveness

Teachers' practical knowledge is constantly being shaped and refined through the interaction of theoretical reflection and experiential learning. Whether new insights or conclusions—drawn either from theory or practice—become accepted as valid components of a teacher's practical knowledge depends on their effectiveness in solving real-world educational problems. Validation, in this context, is performance-based and grounded in praxis.

However, challenges arise when teachers either overestimate the authority of theory—assuming it offers universally applicable solutions—or reduce the meaning of "effectiveness" to immediate or short-term outcomes. Both tendencies can distort the process of knowledge validation. Therefore, practical knowledge must be subject to continuous critique, revision, and dialogic engagement. It is through reflective inquiry and collaborative dialogue that practical knowledge gains robustness, adaptability, and relevance.

3. Examining the Pathways to Construct Teacher Practical Knowledge

3.1 Practical Knowledge Begins with Occasional Reflection

This involves engaging in deeper reflection on the issues that teachers contemplate. Some teachers have said: "In recent years, our school has also been promoting teacher reflection. We are required to submit a reflection journal every week, but in reality, we don't really know how to reflect. Honestly, I just think about whether my work is done properly and how I could improve it." Teachers can make two types of judgments based on their observations: normative judgments and descriptive judgments. The value of teacher reflection lies in raising descriptive judgments to the level of normative judgments, or in using relevant normative standards to evaluate and explain descriptive judgments, thereby creating the "value" of reflection. While descriptions of facts can be vivid and engaging, they should not serve as the final point of teacher reflection. Western scholar Clark has pointed out that in the past, the call for teacher reflection only encouraged teachers to reflect more or to carefully consider what they were doing and why. He argued that although this slogan-like advocacy prompts teachers to think, it does not necessarily contribute to their professional development. More profound research, however, encourages teachers to address questions such as: "How does one think critically? What should one focus on? What is the purpose of thinking?" [①]Human actions are always accompanied by thought, but not all activities that qualify as reflection can be foreseen. Reflection is often incidental and thematic. Ainott (1994) also believed that Schön's distinction between "reflection-in-action" and "reflection-on-action" was more theoretical than practical. When examining actual examples, it is difficult to draw a distinct line between the two. [②]Teacher reflection is not simply about time or frequency. When an "incidental" event arises, it requires certain processes, platforms, or activities to deepen or extend the reflection. Teacher reflection is intrinsically tied to actions that validate knowledge and inevitably involves

① Authony Clarke. Born of incidents but thematic in nature: knowledge construction in practicum settings [J]. *Canadian Journal of Education*,1998(1):47-62.
② Amy B. M. Tsui. Understanding Expertise in Teaching: Case Studies of Second Language Teachers. Translated by Chen Jing and Li Zhongru, *Beijing: People's Education Press*, 2003, p. 50.

dialogues with others or with theoretical frameworks. The emergence of incidental events is indeed unforeseen.

3.2 Collaboration Requires Certain Prerequisites

When discussing the critical significance of theory for practice, Shulman mentioned an "intermediary theory," which does not treat theory as an inevitable law that directly predicts or controls educational practice, but instead, theory must play the role of providing elements for teachers' reflection, monitoring, and constraints. "Even with limitations in scope and duration, they can make a critical contribution to reflective thinking on educational practice, enhancing understanding of observed phenomena"[①]. Thus, on the one hand, theory does not have absolute guiding power, and on the other hand, practice cannot move toward absolute relativity without any constraints. In practice, the relationship between theory and practice is sometimes specifically reflected in the relationship between researchers and teachers. A consensus that can currently be reached is that simply applying authoritative knowledge to judge teachers' actions in specific contexts is inappropriate. At the same time, there is another aspect to this issue: some teachers tend to passively wait for researchers to announce the "correct answer," even expecting the correct answer to directly solve the problem rather than explain it. Communication between researchers and teachers is necessary, but the premise is that teachers' subjectivity must be present, accepting theory's adjustment or even "destruction" of their practical knowledge structure. On the other hand, researchers must also dismantle their systematic theoretical knowledge structures, learning to adapt, extract, critique, and create in the changing, complex, and chaotic situations of practice.

---

① Shulman, Lee S. "Theory, Practice, and the Professionalization of Education." Comparative Education Research, no. 3, 1999: 36-40.

3.3 Teachers' Practical Knowledge Does Not Necessarily Have Universality

Teachers are both the possessors and creators of knowledge. The role of teachers as researchers should be affirmed, but such knowledge, creativity, and research should be appropriately defined and understood. Teachers' research is practical research, aimed at solving problems, not constructing theory. Teachers' theoretical knowledge is expressed in the process of explaining and applying knowledge in specific contexts and in solving individual problems. In the process of application, teachers may enrich, develop, limit, or revise their theoretical understanding, but these creative insights do not necessarily have universality. Of course, many teachers have the ability to verify practical knowledge and elevate it to theory, but this only demonstrates that they are playing two roles: as knowledge holders and researchers. For most teachers, this is difficult to achieve. However, the practical knowledge of excellent teachers, if only spread among their peers, is still limited. Moreover, as teachers retire, this practical knowledge naturally disappears. Therefore, more theoretical workers need to make practical knowledge the object of their thinking, enter the teaching context, and use inductive, generalized, and refined cognitive forms to process, organize, elevate, and disseminate it, ultimately completing the cycle of reconstructing practical knowledge into theoretical knowledge.

[Original article published in *Educational Development Research*, 2007, Issue 22 (Lyu Lijie)]

Chapter 20 The Structure and Approaches of Collaborative Teacher Teams

In China, collaboration among primary and secondary school teachers has a long-standing tradition. Since the 1950s, schools have implemented systems such as collective lesson planning and regular meetings within subject groups or grade-level teams. With the implementation of the new curriculum reform, the national educational policy framework has shifted. The government now provides only macro-level curriculum standards, granting teachers increased autonomy and responsibility to redesign curricula. This includes adapting to new course formats such as interdisciplinary programs and integrated practical activities. These innovations rely heavily on effective teacher collaboration. Furthermore, the development of school-based curricula requires teachers to explore and create collaboratively. As such, collaboration has reemerged as a key strategy for promoting curriculum innovation and ensuring the effective implementation of reforms. The role of collaboration in shaping school culture and enhancing educational quality has become widely acknowledged. However, in practice, new collaborative initiatives often clash with long-standing institutional norms and entrenched school cultures, which are resistant to change. As a result, several challenges persist in the implementation of authentic teacher collaboration.

1. The problems that have emerged in current teacher cooperation

1.1 Overly Standardized Collaboration Makes Some Teachers Passive

In the context of curriculum reform, teacher collaboration has become a visible indicator of reform implementation. As a result, routine collaborative activities—such as teacher discussion forums and curriculum seminars—have become institutionalized in many schools. These activities often follow rigid formats, with fixed schedules, locations, and pre-set topics. However, genuine collaboration is not simply about fulfilling procedural requirements; rather, it is about fostering an open, dynamic space where teachers can engage intellectually and emotionally. When collaborative activities become excessively formalized and top-down, they tend to suppress individual autonomy and creativity. Teachers are compelled to participate in discussions on topics they may not find relevant or meaningful. In such cases, collaboration becomes performative—a means of complying with administrative expectations—rather than a substantive form of professional engagement.

1.2 Administrative Overreach Silences Teacher Voices

Observation and feedback are essential components of teacher development, providing opportunities for reflection and professional growth. They also serve as tools for school administrators to assess teacher performance. However, problems arise when administrators or grade-level coordinators—who hold supervisory power—participate in collaborative settings without clearly separating their evaluative and collegial roles. This blurring of research and management functions can create a climate of distrust, where teachers feel that their professional contributions are being judged rather than valued. As a result, many teachers may choose to withhold their thoughts, avoid meaningful participation, and adopt a strategy of compliance—echoing the views of administrators rather than expressing their own perspectives.

1.3 Distorted Performance Evaluation Undermines Teacher Collaboration

The exam-oriented culture in schools intensifies competition and erodes collegial trust. When teachers are held directly accountable for students' test scores—especially when poor performance may lead to penalties or even dismissal—the incentive to collaborate diminishes. In such high-stakes environments, teachers may view collaboration as a risk rather than a benefit. According to management theory, individuals can be described as "eagles" or "pigeons": the former are highly competitive, while the latter are more cooperative. The current evaluation system, which links teacher performance to tangible outcomes such as financial rewards, professional status, and job security, fosters a culture of "eagles." In this environment, sharing effective strategies or instructional resources becomes counterintuitive, as teachers fear that collaboration may compromise their individual competitive advantage. As a result, meaningful peer support and knowledge exchange are significantly hindered.

2. The First Strategy for Enhancing Teacher Collaboration: Creating a Structured Team

How can teachers collaborate in a way that ensures meaningful and effective cooperation? One widely recognized approach is to establish teacher research teams. The effectiveness of such collaborative efforts depends significantly on the structural characteristics of the team itself.

Management theory provides a useful framework for understanding effective teamwork. High-performance teams in the workplace typically share the following characteristics:[①]

A. Small Size: Effective teams are usually composed of a small number of members.

B. Complementary Skills: Members bring a mix of technical expertise, problem-solving and decision-making capabilities, and interpersonal skills.

---

① Katzenbach, J., a& D. Smith. *The Wisdom of Teams. New York: Harper*, 1993. Quoted in Barlow, Mark. Collaborative Classroom, translated by Zeng Shouchui, et al., Shanghai: East China Normal University Press, 2005.

C. Shared Purpose: The team collectively identifies with a meaningful goal, motivated by pride and responsibility.

D. Clear and Compelling Goals: These goals align with the team's overarching purpose.

E. Intentional Collaboration: Members consciously reflect on how to collaborate, build mutual trust, and manage conflict constructively.

F. Commitment and Accountability: A strong sense of trust and commitment underpins the team's ability to assume collective responsibility.

Educational scholars such as MacLean and Mohr have extended these ideas to teacher collaboration in schools. They propose that effective teacher research teams typically consist of 3 to 5 members who support, challenge, and learn from one another as they engage in practice-oriented inquiry. These teams usually meet twice a month during the school year. At each meeting, members share their progress, listen attentively, and engage in joint analysis—often supported by at least one member with prior research experience. Through discussions of research logs and teaching data, team members collectively refine their insights and clarify initial findings. This process can reduce teacher isolation, facilitate experience sharing, and contribute to solving real classroom problems.

To ensure meaningful collaboration, teacher research teams should integrate the following core elements:

2.1 Stable and Appropriately Sized Membership

The number of team members is related to the team's cohesion. In a small-scale team, every individual plays a crucial role, which ensures that each member has their own rights and responsibilities. Of course, the turnover of members can severely impact the team. In addition, there should be someone in the team who plays the role of a leader. This leader need not hold an administrative position, but should be good at communication, possess organizational skills, research experience, and considerable professional judgment. The leader's main responsibilities are: reminding everyone to organize group meetings on time, maintaining public contact information such as email addresses and phone numbers, selecting appropriate meeting locations, coordinating relationships to maintain team vitality, establishing team functions, resolving disagreements by facilitating discussions that connect teaching and research, providing research methodology, and offering guidance to team members.[①]

2.2 Shared and Clear Work Goals

A cohesive team is built on shared willingness and clearly defined goals. A specific and meaningful objective—such as co-developing a curriculum or addressing a pressing classroom challenge—serves as a stable anchor for collaboration. When the team lacks a shared problem or if the goals are overly vague or too long-term, collaboration becomes a burdensome formality rather than a source of professional growth. Clear goals help sustain engagement, motivation, and focus.

2.3 Team Identification

Team identification occurs on two levels: identification with the group as a whole and mutual recognition among team members. Strong identification fosters adherence to team norms and promotes open communication and compromise when conflicts arise. It also contributes to the development of a shared team culture—an important foundation for collaboration.

---

① Maclean Marions, Mohr Marian M. *Teacher-researchers at work* [M]. Berkeley, California: National Writing Project,1999.

2.4 Members' Autonomy

Although it may seem paradoxical, autonomy is a necessary precondition for genuine team identification. True autonomy implies that team members participate as independent thinkers, willing to contribute their perspectives. This form of intellectual engagement involves self-reflection and honest discussion, which may lead to disagreements. Yet it is precisely through these disagreements—when ideas clash and are negotiated—that deeper understanding and meaningful learning occur. Autonomy, in this sense, supports both personal growth and the collective development of the team.

2.5 Practice-Driven Research Problems

Effective teacher research must be rooted in the complex realities of educational practice. Theories emerge from experience through abstraction and categorization, but these abstractions cannot fully account for the nuances of new teaching contexts. Each classroom situation is shaped by multiple, often conflicting forces: subject matter constraints, student characteristics, cultural dynamics, and more. Teachers must navigate this complexity through informed judgment and responsive action.

As such, research problems should arise directly from teaching practice. Bringing real, often messy problems to the table allows teachers to explore their causes, identify patterns, and reflect on possible solutions. Though contexts differ, many challenges share underlying commonalities. By engaging in contextual inquiry, teachers move beyond isolated problem-solving toward a richer understanding of theory-practice relationships. This process does not aim to systematize theory prematurely, but instead encourages teachers to *re-experience* and *re-evaluate* existing knowledge through critical reflection—thus enabling informed decisions and purposeful actions in the classroom.

3. The Second Strategy for Ensuring the Effectiveness of Teacher Collaboration: Focusing on Method

Once the reasonable elements of a teacher collaboration team have been identified, the way in which these elements interact and function, i.e., the mode of operation of these elements, also determines the effectiveness of the collaboration. Clatthorn believes that there are at least five methods for teacher groups to work together: [①] a. professional discussions; b. curriculum development; c. peer observation; d. peer coaching; e. action research. The activities of teacher collaboration groups, as emphasized by Johnson et al., focus on classroom teaching activities. It can be a cyclical process of joint design, separate teaching, and joint analysis. In this cycle, the work can be categorized into six tasks: [②] a. regular collaborative professional discussions; b. joint planning and design, with everyone sharing the responsibility of finding course resources and methods; c. separately or jointly teaching collaborative lessons and analyzing the outcomes; d. jointly evaluating the success of the collaborative lessons; e. jointly planning for the revision, refinement, and improvement of new lessons; f. separately or jointly teaching the new lessons.

In China, the existing forms of collaborative research in school-based teaching research include collective lesson planning, peer classroom observation, salon forums, mentoring systems, and project research. These can be categorized into three major types:

A. Routine collaboration. This involves reflecting on, debating, and inspiring one another over practical problems among teachers in the same grade or subject. It is a relatively loose team, which may appear in regular

---

① Good, Thomas L., and Jere E. Brophy. Looking in the Classroom. Translated by Tao Zhiqiong, Wang Feng, and Deng Xiaofang, Beijing: China Light Industry Press, 2002, p. 1.
② Johnson, David W. Leading the Collaborative School. Translated by Tang Zongqing, et al., Shanghai: Shanghai Education Publishing House, 2003, p. 198.

teaching research group activities, collective lesson planning, or teacher discussion meetings. This type of collaboration is characterized by the spontaneous generation of problems, the unpredictability of conclusions, and often involves continuous re-engagement and further discussions.

B. Task-oriented collaboration. School-based curricula in the new curriculum reform in China can be either entirely new courses independently developed by teachers or modifications and adaptations of the national curriculum. To develop school-based curricula, teachers from the same grade or subject, or even from different subjects within the same theme, come together with

specific goals and time constraints. They engage in collaborative course design, implementation, reflection, and exchange of experiences. The collaborative outcome is not only the newly developed curriculum, but also the self-development arising from mutual inspiration.

C. Developmental collaboration. When collaborating with universities on project research, there may be a clear research goal. If the project itself originates from real issues in the classroom or curriculum context, teachers will be motivated to continue researching based on the gains from the research. Teachers need to engage in research within a team, drawing strength, motivation, and encouragement from mutual support, and gaining new information and perspectives. Ultimately, teachers need to establish teams and conduct research independently, without administrative management, supervision, or guidance from theoretical researchers, in order to achieve development.

[The original text was published in *Teaching and Management*, Issue 15, 2007 (Lyu Lijie, Yu Cong)]

Chapter 21 Reflecting on the Effectiveness of Classroom Assessment and Shifting Toward a Research-Oriented Role— Discussing the Impact of Classroom Learning Research on Teacher Professional Growth

Classroom evaluation refers to the process of making value judgments about classroom activities through methods such as classroom observation. It may involve teachers' assessments of students' academic performance or classroom behavior, or it may refer to evaluations of the quality and effectiveness of teachers' instruction. This paper specifically focuses on the latter. In China, classroom teaching evaluation has undergone a process of transformation—from initial disorder to greater structure, and from a focus on administrative control to an emphasis on promoting teacher development.

1. Changes in Classroom Evaluation and the Paradox of Effectiveness

Promoting teacher development has now become the central function of classroom evaluation. As a result, many studies have focused on improving evaluation methods—such as by updating evaluation criteria, employing diverse evaluation tools, and incorporating multiple evaluators. However, in practice, these schemes are often underutilized or even become obstacles that constrain teachers' classroom performance.

1.1 The Evolution of the Focus of Contemporary Classroom Evaluation

Prior to the mid-1980s, classroom evaluation in China mainly relied on lesson observations and subjective judgments based on personal experience. During this period, teaching quality was evaluated largely through personal impressions, and feedback was given to help guide improvement. This method had several issues, including excessive reliance on authority, subjectivity, and arbitrariness. With the introduction of Western measurement and evaluation theories, more quantitative methods began to be applied. These included structured evaluation frameworks, rating scales, and data analysis techniques. However, such approaches did not entirely replace subjective observation; instead, they provided a more objective and persuasive foundation for judgment.

What changed during this phase was that classroom evaluation began to focus on clarifying the expected objectives of instruction, using those objectives as the basis for both quantitative and subjective assessment. Since the 1990s, as pedagogical theories have continued to evolve, the image of the "ideal" classroom has become more complex and diversified. Consequently, evaluation practices have also expanded in scope. Nevertheless, a critical issue has emerged: despite increasingly detailed scoring rubrics and broader evaluative perspectives, a significant gap has appeared between the types of lessons being evaluated and everyday teaching. This has given rise to a distinct phenomenon known as the "performance lesson"—a stylized lesson crafted to meet evaluation criteria rather than reflect regular classroom reality.

This phenomenon can be attributed to the fact that classroom evaluation standards are often constructed around idealized visions of teaching. While these reflect progressive educational philosophies, for many schools they have become little more than formalized evaluative exercises, such as end-of-term assessments.

1.2 The Theoretical Limitations of Improving Classroom Evaluation Techniques

Contemporary educational theory emphasizes student-centered learning, respect for learners' subjectivity, attention to classroom experiences, and recognition of the diverse value outcomes that education can provide. These principles should form the basis of classroom evaluation. However, these ideals function as aspirational standards within specific educational stages. They are logically structured and easy to quantify, compare, and manage—but they are also generalized from a broad set of common features found across many classrooms.

The challenge arises when these generalized standards are applied to individual, real-life classrooms, each of which operates within a unique context. These differences can stem from the lesson type (e.g., new instruction, review, or practice), the nature of the content (e.g., requiring teacher explanation versus student exploration), the subject being taught, student age, teaching style, students' prior knowledge and learning habits, and the relational dynamics between teachers and students.

While evaluation frameworks reflect an idealized version of classroom structure, it is nearly impossible for any single lesson to fully align with all such criteria. The practical classroom often cannot—and need not—replicate the idealized structure that the evaluation system prescribes. When this idealized system is broken down into technical indicators and used in a rigid, one-size-fits-all manner, it essentially attempts to assess a dynamic, developmental process using a static, simultaneous snapshot.

Recognizing the ontological nature of these evaluation indicators helps us understand how they are applied. Unsurprisingly, schools often use them to judge teachers' effectiveness and attitudes. Because these indicators are clear, quantifiable, and seemingly objective, they are appealing to administrators and are often tied to decisions about promotions, bonuses, or honors. In this way, the evaluation system becomes a managerial tool used to minimize disputes and enforce standardization.

However, such evaluations are often limited to formal occasions like lesson observations, public demonstration classes, or teaching competitions—situations that expect teachers to compress the results of an entire teaching sequence into a single class. This paradox suggests that improving classroom evaluation is not merely about aligning content with modern teaching concepts; it also requires rethinking how evaluations are designed and implemented.

1.3 The Functional Limitations of Improving Classroom Evaluation Techniques

The ultimate goal of classroom evaluation is to improve the quality of instruction and promote student learning by influencing teachers' behavior. However, focusing too narrowly on specific aspects of teaching can produce unintended side effects.

First, from a management perspective, such evaluations often fail to result in meaningful changes in teachers' attitudes or behaviors. Since these evaluations are sporadic and detached from the ongoing teaching process, they lack continuity and fail to provide diagnostic value.

Second, evaluations can significantly impact teachers' psychological states. A survey on teachers' psychological reactions during teaching evaluations [①] show that teachers often experience fear, anxiety, and a sense of being monitored prior to evaluation. During the evaluation, they may respond with compliance, resistance, or mere formality. Afterward, they may feel sensitive, defensive, or compelled to justify themselves. This psychological dynamic stems from the adversarial relationship between evaluators and those being evaluated. In such conditions, sincere reflection and meaningful improvement are difficult to achieve.

---

① Cai Min, & Feng Ying. Survey on Teachers' Psychological Responses in Teaching Evaluation [J]. *Chinese Journal of Education*, 2006(1):65–68.

Even when teachers genuinely hope to use evaluations to examine and enhance their teaching, the information such assessments provide is often incomplete or superficial. Typically, they consist of broad judgments—such as labeling a lesson as "good" or "bad"—but these are based on isolated observations that may lack statistical significance. Furthermore, such evaluations rarely explore the underlying reasons, contextual factors, or processes behind the observed outcomes. As a result, teachers often struggle to identify what exactly was effective, what was not, and to what degree.

In reality, the limitations of evaluation mean that "these standards and indicators are rarely used in actual classroom evaluations. Research that applies them to real classroom teaching is almost nonexistent. Originally, these systems were considered highly applicable, but in practice they have become theoretical constructs, lacking practical relevance. Consequently, despite continuous development of new evaluation systems by researchers, these tools are often short-lived. In actual school settings, educational administrators and teachers continue to rely on their personal experiences to conduct evaluations."①

2. The Proposal of Developmental Classroom Evaluation and the Concept of Its Research Function

In recent years, more and more scholars have emphasized that the primary function of classroom evaluation is not to manage or oversee teachers' work, but rather to foster teachers' professional development through evaluation, with the ultimate aim of enhancing the overall quality of education and teaching. Professor Ye Lan, while summarizing the evaluation reforms in the New Basic Education Experiment, described developmental teacher evaluation as follows:

---

① Ding, Chaopeng. Overview, Problems, and Proposals of Research on Classroom Teaching Evaluation in China [J]. *Educational Science Research*, 2006(12):10.

"Our goal is not merely to assess outcomes (whether they are interim or final), nor is it simply to recognize and explain facts. Instead, the aim is to uncover problems, experiences, and the varying levels of achievement reached by teachers throughout the reform process, and to create an abstract structure for the new classroom teaching process. Our goal goes beyond merely improving our understanding of the process; we also aim to use evaluation to promote teachers' self-reflection and to reflect on our own research. This is an evaluation that integrates the roles of researchers, practitioners, and evaluators, offering a comprehensive and complex approach to the practice of reform. It requires not just an evaluation tool but a comprehensive system of evaluation that supports the achievement of these goals, which can only be gradually developed through the ongoing process of reform."[①] Whether this evaluation system can truly promote teachers' professional development depends not only on the rationalization of its content and structure but also on how this function is implemented—whether through identifying issues or through research. Given the nature of teachers' professional development, the evaluation process should be both process-oriented and human-centered. Classroom evaluation must integrate with research-based models that guide teacher development, which is the only way to ensure it contributes meaningfully to professional growth. The integration of research, teaching, and evaluation should thus be at the heart of developmental teacher evaluation. In such a model, teachers can expect the following:

2.1 Research-Oriented Thinking and Approaches

In a system where research, teaching, and evaluation are integrated, both the evaluator and the teacher being evaluated take on the role of researcher. Collaborative research activities can begin in the classroom

① Ye Lan, & Wu Yaping. Reform of Classroom Teaching and Reform of Classroom Teaching Evaluation [J]. *Educational Research*, 2003(8).

preparation stage, where both parties work together to study the students, the course content, and the teaching plans. Through this process, teachers are provided with new ways of thinking about research and an expanded perspective, while evaluators also gain a true understanding of the classroom environment, the teacher's background, capabilities, strengths, and areas for growth.

2.2 Contextualized Feedback and Reflection

The main issue with traditional technical evaluations lies not in the evaluation technique itself, but in how it is applied—often with an over-reliance on its objectivity and scientific nature, using a generalized standard to assess each individual classroom. In integrated evaluation, evaluators do not simply judge whether a teacher's performance is "right" or "wrong" based on a standard. Instead, they aim to collect as much relevant information from the classroom as possible, which forms the basis for collaborative discussions and reflective practices with the teacher. The decisions teachers make in the classroom are influenced by a negotiation of contextual factors, and the rationality behind their choices is unique and cannot be fully captured by universal standards. Only through the interaction of the evaluator's feedback and the teacher's reflection can deep insights and shifts in understanding occur.

2.3 Personalized and Ongoing Information for Teacher Development

In the process of integrating evaluation with research and teaching, long-term cooperation between the evaluator and the evaluated teacher is essential. The evaluator gains insight into the teacher's professional growth over time, and the evaluation process becomes both formative and individualized. Such an evaluation, which is not driven by managerial objectives, can lead to meaningful and practical outcomes for both the teacher and the institution.

3. The Evaluation Aimed at Research in the Classroom Learning Research Model: Functions and Insights

3.1 Classroom Learning Research: A Model of Teacher Professional Development Integrating Research, Teaching, and Evaluation

Classroom learning research refers to the process of collective lesson preparation, classroom observation, collaborative work, and systematic reflection on the teaching content of a specific class, with the aim of achieving more effective teaching and learning and facilitating the professional development of teachers. Its ultimate goal is to enable students to engage in more effective learning. It is a form of action research, where teachers act both as educators and researchers, engaging in reflection through their actions and refining their teaching through this reflection. It also serves as a form of collaborative learning, in which teachers engage in joint lesson planning, pre- and post-lesson meetings, classroom observation, and peer evaluation to improve collectively. Classroom learning research takes different forms in various countries and regions. Japan has a history of over fifty years of classroom learning research. This activity in Japan is called "lesson study"[①], which is "collaborative research occurring within the scope of classroom activities." In Japan, teachers regard professional development and the improvement of teaching skills as lifelong pursuits. They believe that personal experience, self-research, peer critique, and self-reflection are essential components of the professionalization process. Teachers are grouped by subject and grade to prepare a "research lesson"; each group holds regular meetings to discuss the lesson content, identify its key points, and analyze whether these points can address students' learning difficulties. Teaching is then designed to address these challenges, and one teacher is designated to deliver the lesson. The entire process lasts from one

---

① Matoba M. Lesson study: international perspective on policy and practice [M]. Beijing: Educational Science Publishing House, 2006: 1-2.

month to a year. At the end, teachers share the results of their seminar with other educators through workshops or publications. Many educational practices in Japan have attracted attention from Western educators, who have attempted to apply these practices in the United States and other countries. Scholars in the U.S. have analyzed teaching videos of teachers from Japan, Germany, and the U.S. ①to systematically introduce the impact of Japanese classroom learning research on teacher professional development and explore the potential of applying this model in the U.S. In recent years, many educational scholars in the U.S. have joined action research programs similar to classroom learning research. In Hong Kong, classroom learning research emerged over the past decade, stemming from reflections on the reform of basic education at the turn of the century. This approach was inspired by Japan's lesson study model, while also incorporating mainland China's teaching research practices. It uses the theory of "change" as a theoretical framework for implementing classroom learning research. After multiple research lessons, this model has gradually evolved into a systematic approach for conducting classroom learning research.②

In classroom learning research, identifying the research question is the starting point that guides the entire research process. These questions can be broad in nature—such as how to engage students in learning mathematics—or more specific, such as how to improve students' understanding of adding fractions with different denominators. These questions typically arise from issues encountered in the teacher's instructional practice and the challenges faced by students in their learning. After determining the learning objectives, teachers engage in collective

① James w. Stigler, James Hiebert. The teaching gap [M]. The Free Press, 1999:112-115.
② Lu, Minling, Pang Yongxin, and Zhi Peimin. Classroom Learning Research: How to Address Individual Differences in Students. Translated by Li Shuying and Guo Yongxian, Beijing: Education Science Press, 2006, p. VIII.

lesson planning. Based on reviewing relevant materials, teachers aim to validate certain perspectives within the specific classroom context. The objective of the research lesson is not only to design an effective lesson but also to understand how classroom practices can foster student comprehension of the content. Once the initial lesson plan is finalized, feedback is sought during faculty meetings, and necessary revisions are made in preparation for the lesson's implementation. During the lesson, aside from the teacher delivering the content, other members of the research group set aside their own teaching duties and attend the lesson as observers. When students are asked to engage in independent thinking, discussion, and learning, the observing teachers move around the classroom to observe student engagement and take detailed notes, sometimes even recording the session. After the lesson, the research group convenes for a meeting, where the teacher who delivered the lesson first summarizes their experience and the challenges faced. Other teachers then provide feedback on various aspects of the lesson, offering evaluations on the issues within each segment. The focus of this evaluation is on the teaching process rather than on the individual teacher. Since the lesson represents a collective effort, the evaluation process is essentially an assessment of the group's work, serving as a means of self-improvement in teaching practices. Based on the observations and reflections during the lesson, the research group revises the lesson plan, addressing any misconceptions that students demonstrated regarding specific concepts. Revisions may include changes to the learning materials, adjustments to activities, or reworking of the questions posed during the lesson.

Once the revised lesson plan is confirmed, it will be taught in a different class. This could be the same teacher from the original lesson, but more typically, a different teacher from the research group will teach the revised lesson. The distinction is that, on this occasion, all teachers in the school are invited to observe the lesson. After the lesson, all the school's teachers are invited to join a discussion to reflect on the lesson's implementation. External experts may also be invited to participate. As with the initial process, the teacher delivering the lesson will first explain the goals the research group intended to achieve, evaluate the successful aspects of the lesson, and identify areas for reconsideration. Observing teachers then analyze the lesson and provide suggestions for improvement. However, evaluations and analyses of the research lesson must respect both the students' learning outcomes and the underlying value assumptions that shaped the lesson's design. The sharing of the final results can take various forms: one common method is for the research group to write a report that outlines the story of their work process, sometimes published as a book, for school teachers, principals, and even educational policymakers to read. Another approach is to invite teachers from other schools to observe the revised lesson when it is taught.

The ultimate function of evaluation is to promote the professional development of teachers, but this function can only be effectively realized if it is grounded in practical experience and addresses specific problems. This is because each teacher faces different issues in their practice. The initiation of classroom learning research can help answer these questions.

Classroom learning research, as a collaborative model for teacher development, generally consists of several steps: exploring problems, designing courses, teaching in the classroom, evaluating outcomes, rewriting lesson plans, retesting, reflection, and finally sharing results. Throughout this process, teachers are always involved. From an evaluation perspective, this ongoing process, which lasts for a certain period, offers the following insights:

1. Maintain a Calm Attitude and Take a Long-Term View of Evaluation

All participants, whether researchers, practitioners, or evaluators, approach the entire process with a calm attitude. Each evaluation is indicative rather than conclusive. The purpose of every evaluation is to guide further development, not to provide a final judgment. Every classroom learning research process adheres to the assumption that the improvement of teaching quality is a continuous, gradual process. Research on a single lesson will involve several rounds of discussion, design, and reimplementation. Therefore, the significance of evaluation lies in its ongoing correction of each component, guiding the development of the classroom learning research towards an ideal state.

2. Return Evaluation Goals to Student Development

A key dimension of evaluation in classroom learning research is the improvement of student learning outcomes. Evaluation is not about assigning teachers a score (good, average, or poor); rather, the focus is on students' academic achievements and classroom performance. The teacher's role is seen as a process and means to foster student development. This approach to evaluation can minimize the emphasis on superficial details or formalities.

3. Focus Evaluation on Teaching Rather Than the Teacher

Classroom learning research is a collaborative process, and its success ultimately depends on the continuous efforts of all the teachers in the group. Although each research lesson is delivered by one teacher, and the teacher's individual abilities are important, the continuous improvement of classroom learning research depends on the sustained effort and reflective design of the research team, not on the personal abilities of any one outstanding teacher. Teachers should analyze the teaching work and potential factors involved, avoiding turning the evaluation process into an assessment of a teacher's personal competence.

4. Context-Specific Evaluation

Each research lesson takes place in a specific classroom context, with particular students, teachers, and courses. Therefore, evaluation should avoid the pitfall of "borrowed standards"—applying external standards to measure one's own work. Abstract standards are often cold and detached, while the concrete classroom environment is rich and multifaceted. In the context of a specific classroom learning environment, evaluation should provide detailed, context-sensitive value judgments based on the issues that arise during the lesson.

5. Teachers as Key Participants in Evaluation

Many factors contribute to the development of classroom learning research—students, parents, administrators, and so on—but teachers are the primary driving force. Teachers jointly identify problems, design courses, implement lessons, observe each other, and reflect together. As firsthand participants and experiencers of classroom teaching, they have the clearest understanding of student needs and the real problems in practice. Their evaluation of the issues at hand is an important perspective.

3.3 The Guiding Value of Classroom Learning Research for Teacher Professional Development

Classroom learning research, as a form of team-based work, has the dual goals of student development and teacher professional growth. Over a set period, through collective effort, team members define the research question, design the curriculum, conduct teaching, reflect and evaluate, and redesign the lessons, continuously improving the design and implementation of each research lesson. As a form and part of teacher professional development, classroom learning research enables participating teachers to experience various degrees of professional growth.

1. Aspirations for the Future

Every teacher has a deep-seated aspiration to become an outstanding educator. This desire is especially strong at the beginning of their career, motivating teachers to seek out various training opportunities to advance their professional development. The initiation of classroom learning research effectively preserves and extends this aspiration. It formalizes teacher professional development into a structured process, becoming a strong motivating force for teachers to engage in research.

2. The Power of Collaboration

Classroom learning research is a collaborative, team-based effort. Each member of the team, driven by shared goals, works together, dividing responsibilities, brainstorming, and collectively improving the quality of the research. For example, in Hong Kong, the research lesson cycle lasts 3 to 4 months and involves significant tasks, such as selecting content from various resources, conducting pre-tests, applying theories of change to identify key attributes, designing curriculum, observing lessons, collecting and analyzing data. These tasks cannot be completed by a single person. Therefore, classroom learning research is an effective way for teachers to develop professionally through collective effort.

3. The Wisdom of Reflection

Classroom learning research encourages teachers to move beyond simply repeating familiar teaching methods. They begin reflecting on their own teaching practices and student outcomes. Feedback from peers and observations of teaching behaviors often lead teachers to re-examine their approaches. This process helps teachers shift from external control to self-regulation, consciously adjusting their teaching strategies. Reflection fosters a strong sense of professional development by helping teachers reevaluate their habitual practices, building more effective problem-solving strategies through thought and discussion.

4. Communication and Collaboration

Classroom learning research provides teachers with an opportunity to step out of their individual silos and reflect on the collective results of their efforts. During the exchange of ideas, differing perspectives on the same issue significantly broaden teachers' viewpoints. Diverse understandings of the same problem can offer new insights. Through dialogue in a shared context, teachers discuss, reflect on, and revise their teaching practices, continually enhancing their professional growth.

4. Classroom Evaluation: From Management to Research

The introduction of developmental evaluation redirects the focus of evaluation back to teacher development. However, under this concept, different approaches can be taken to create an evaluation system. These may include expanding the evaluation participants to include teachers, peers, principals, and students, increasing the frequency of evaluations, or focusing on emergent classroom factors. In this reform, evaluation still serves management purposes, such as determining professional titles, salaries, and bonuses, thus remaining caught in the paradox of technical classroom evaluation. The workflow of planning, organizing, implementing, and evaluating, typical of early 20th-century management models, aimed at maximizing efficiency through control, based on the assumption that human behavior can be changed through supervision or incentives. However, since the mid-20th century, various social movements have critiqued and adjusted this managerial approach. Teaching requires wisdom and passion, and every teacher's work is a vital link in the chain of student growth. Yet, each teacher's work is performed independently. Therefore, significant changes in teachers' attitudes and abilities require more democratic, personal, and professional leadership. Teachers need an environment where they are respected and encouraged to strive for greater achievements. Evaluating teachers based solely on one lesson or categorizing their work into rankings like good, average, or poor only fosters heightened sensitivity and unhealthy competition. Since the purpose of classroom evaluation is to improve teacher professionalism and achieve high-quality teaching, evaluations must function within a new system. This system should focus on research, not management. The classroom learning research model provides an effective framework for this. Evaluation thus serves as part of a broader process aimed at improving both teaching quality and teacher professional development. While school management is necessary for smooth operation, a research-based evaluation framework will naturally allow differences in teacher abilities to emerge through research, discussion, and teaching, but in a supportive, collaborative way. This leads to genuine professional growth for teachers and fulfills the true purpose of classroom evaluation.

[Original Article Published in *Journal of Northeast Normal University* (Philosophy and Social Sciences Edition), Issue 2, 2007 (Lyu Lijie, Zhao Tongyou)]

www.ingramcontent.com/pod-product-compliance
Lightning Source LLC
LaVergne TN
LVHW010559100826
845148LV00014B/2770

* 9 7 9 8 9 0 1 8 6 0 0 3 8 *